ASP.NET Data Presentation Controls Essentials

Master the standard ASP.NET server controls for displaying and managing data

Joydip Kanjilal

PACKT PUBLISHING

BIRMINGHAM - MUMBAI

ASP.NET Data Presentation Controls Essentials

First published: December 2007

Production Reference: 1141207

Published by Packt Publishing Ltd.
32 Lincoln Road
Olton
Birmingham, B27 6PA, UK.

ISBN 978-1-847193-95-7

`www.packtpub.com`

Cover Image by Karl Moore (`karl.moore@ukonline.co.uk`)

Credits

Author
Joydip Kanjilal

Reviewers
Steven M. Swafford
Anand Narayanaswamy

Senior Acquisition Editor
Douglas Patterson

Development Editor
Rashmi Phadnis

Technical Editor
Bhupali Khule

Code Testing
Mithun Sehgal

Editorial Team Leader
Mithil Kulkarni

Project Manager
Abhijeet Deobhakta

Indexer
Hemangini Bari

Proofreader
Harminder Singh
Chris Smith
Cathy Cumberlidge
Angie Butcher

Production Coordinator
Shantanu Zagade

Cover Designer
Shantanu Zagade

About the Author

Joydip Kanjilal is a Microsoft MVP in ASP.NET. He has over 12 years of industry experience in IT with more than 6 years in Microsoft .NET and its related technologies. He has authored a lot of articles for some of the most reputable sites like, www.asptoday.com, www.devx.com, www.aspalliance.com, www.aspnetpro.com, www.sswug.com, www.sql-server-performance.com, etc. A lot of these articles have been selected at www.asp.net—Microsoft's Official Site on ASP.NET. Joydip was also a community credit winner at www.community-credit.com a number of times.

He is currently working as a Senior Consultant in a reputable company in Hyderabad, INDIA. He has years of experience in designing and architecting solutions for various domains. His technical strengths include, C, C++, VC++, Java, C#, Microsoft .NET, Ajax, Design Patterns, SQL Server, Operating Systems and Computer Architecture. Joydip blogs at http://aspadvice.com/blogs/joydip and spends most of his time reading books, blogs and writing books and articles. His hobbies include watching cricket and soccer and playing chess.

Mail: joydipkanjilal@yahoo.com

Acknowledgements

I am grateful to my parents for their love, support, and inspiration throughout my life and would like to express my deepest respects to them. I am thankful to Piku, Indronil, and little Jini in particular for their co-operation, patience, and support. I am also thankful to the other members of my family for their continued encouragement and support.

I am thankful to Douglas Paterson and the entire PacktPub team for providing me the opportunity to author my first book. I am also thankful to Steve Smith and the entire AspAlliance team for providing me the opportunity to author my first ever article at AspAlliance. I would also like to thank the reviewers of this book for their invaluable feedback. I am thankful to Anand Narayanaswamy, Douglas Paterson, and Steven M. Swafford for their excellent suggestions, which I hope have helped a lot in improving the quality of the book. I am also thankful to Russell Jones of DevX and Jude Kelly of Sql-Server-Performance for their valuable technical advices. I am also thankful to Stephen Wynkoop of SSWUG and David Riggs of AspNetPro for giving me the opportunity to author articles there. I would also like to thank Abhishek Kant of Microsoft for the MVP award that I received in 2007.

I am thankful to my friends Sriram Putrevu, Rakesh Gujjar, and Tilak Tarafder and the readers of my articles for their invaluable feedback and suggestions. My special thanks to Balaji Desari, Ashish Agarwal, and Sanjay Golani for their inspiration and support.

Writing my first ever book has been a challenging, learning and a rewarding experience. It was really a nice time and I enjoyed it.

About the Reviewers

Steven M. Swafford began developing software in 1995 while serving in the United States Air Force (USAF). Upon leaving the USAF he continued developing leading-edge solutions in support of the America's war fighters as part of the original USAF enterprise portal development team. His roots are now in Auburn, Alabama where he works for Northrop Grumman Information Technology. Steven's credits his wife Su Ok and daughter Sarah for supporting and inspiring his ongoing passion for software development and the resultant challenges of life near the bleeding edge as well as his mother Pat Harris and father Cliff Swafford for believing in him. Steven would like to thank Tim Stewart and Edward Habal who were his professional mentors and to this day remain close friends as well as Frankie Elston, Joe Chaplin, and Glenn Regan all of whom are colleagues that Steven worked closely with for years.

This is Steven's second technical review. Steven previously worked as a technical editor on ODP.NET Developers Guide.

Mail: `steven.swafford@radicaldevelopment.net`

Website: `http://www.radicaldevelopment.net`

Blog: `http://www.blog.radicaldevelopment.net`

Anand Narayanaswamy works as an independent consultant and runs NetAns Hosting Services (www.netans.com), which provides web hosting services based in Trivandrum, Kerala State, India. Anand is a Microsoft Most Valuable Professional (MVP) in Visual C# (`https://mvp.support.microsoft.com/profile/Anand`) and is the author of *Community Server Quickly* (`http://www.packtpub.com/community-server/book`) published by Packt Publishing.

He works as the chief technical editor for ASPAlliance.com (`http://aspalliance.com/author.aspx?uId=384030`) and is also a member of ASPAlliance.com Advisory Board. He regularly contributes articles, and book and product reviews to ASPAlliance.com, C-Sharpcorner.com, Developer.com, Codeguru.com, Microsoft Academic Alliance and asp.netPRO magazine.

Anand has worked as a technical editor for several popular publishers such as Sams, Addison-Wesley Professional, Wrox, Deitel, and Manning. His technical editing skills helped the authors of Sams *Teach Yourself the C# Language in 21 Days, Core C# and .NET, Professional ADO.NET 2, ASP.NET 2.0 Web Parts in Action and Internet and World Wide Web* (4th Edition) to fine-tune the content. He has also contributed articles for Microsoft Knowledge Base and delivered podcast shows for Aspnetpodcast.com. He is a moderator for Windows MarketPlace Newsgroups.

Anand also runs LearnXpress.com (`www.learnxpress.com`), Dotnetalbum.com (`www.dotnetalbum.com`), CsharpFAQ.com (`www.csharpfaq.com`) and Devreviews.com (`www.devreviews.com`). LearnXpress.com is a featured site at MSDN's Visual C# .NET communities section. Anand has won several prizes at Community-Credit.com and has been featured as "All Time" contributor at the site. He is one of the founders of Trivandrum Microsoft Usergroup. He regularly blogs under the banner "I type what I feel" at `http://msmvps.com/blogs/anandn`.

Website: `http://www.visualanand.net`

Blog: `http://weblogs.asp.net/anandn`

Table of Contents

Preface

When you design and implement an ASP.NET web application, you need to manage and display data to the end user in more than one way. Data Presentation Controls in ASP.NET are server controls to which you can bind data to organize and display it in different ways. This book covers the major data controls in ASP.NET (from ASP.NET 1.x to ASP.NET 3.5/Orcas). Packed with plenty of real-life code examples, tips, and notes, this book is a good resource for readers who want to display and manage complex data in web applications using ASP.NET by fully leveraging the awesome features that these data controls provide.

What This Book Covers

Chapter 1 discusses the ASP.NET data binding model and how we can work with the data source controls in ASP.NET.

Chapter 2 discusses how we can work with the various list controls in ASP.NET and illustrates how we can implement a custom control that extends the CheckBoxList control to provide added functionalities.

Chapter 3 discusses how we can display tables of data with the Repeater control. It also discusses how we can perform other operations, like paging and sorting data using this control.

Chapter 4 discusses how we can use the DataList control in ASP.NET. It also illustrates how we can bind images to the DataList control dynamically.

Chapter 5 discusses how we can display, edit, delete, and format data for customized display using the DataGrid control. It discusses how we can use this control for paging and sorting data. It also illustrates the implementation of a sample application using this control and how we can use this control to display data in a customized format.

Chapter 6 presents a discussion on the GridView control and performing various operation with it, like paging, sorting, inserting data, updating data, deleting data, and displaying data in customized format. It also discusses how one can implement a custom GridView control to display hierarchical data. It also discusses how one can export a GridView control to MS Excel and MS Word.

Chapter 7 explores the other view controls in ASP.NET, like DetailsView, FormView, and the TreeView control, and how we can use them to perform various operations.

Chapter 8 discusses LINQ, its features and benefits, and how it can be used to bind data to the new data controls in Orcas.

What You Need for This Book

This book is for ASP.NET developers who want to display or manage data in ASP.NET applications. To use this book, you need to have access to ASP.NET and SQL Server.

The following is the list of software required for this book:

- ASP.NET 2.0 (For Chapters 1 - 7)
- ASP.NET 3.5 (Orcas) (For Chapter 8)
- SQL Server 2005

Who is This Book for

This book is for ASP.NET developers who want to display or manage data in ASP.NET applications. The code examples are in C#.

Conventions

In this book, you will find a number of styles of text that distinguish between different kinds of information. Here are some examples of these styles, and an explanation of their meaning.

There are two styles for code. Code words in text are shown as follows: "You can also use the static method `Eval()` of the `DataBinder` class for binding data to your controls."

A block of code will be set as follows:

```
<asp:ListBox ID="ListBox1" runat="server" Height="125px"
     Width="214px">
    <asp:ListItem Value="1">Joydip</asp:ListItem>
    <asp:ListItem Value="2">Douglas</asp:ListItem>
    <asp:ListItem Value="3">Jini</asp:ListItem>
    <asp:ListItem Value="4">Piku</asp:ListItem>
    <asp:ListItem Value="5">Rama</asp:ListItem>
    <asp:ListItem Value="6">Amal</asp:ListItem>
    <asp:ListItem Value="7">Indronil</asp:ListItem>
</asp:ListBox>
```

New terms and **important words** are introduced in a bold-type font. Words that you see on the screen, in menus or dialog boxes for example, appear in our text like this: "The second record is set to editable mode on clicking the **Edit** command button ".

> Important notes appear in a box like this.

> Tips and tricks appear like this.

Reader Feedback

Feedback from our readers is always welcome. Let us know what you think about this book, what you liked or may have disliked. Reader feedback is important for us to develop titles that you really get the most out of.

To send us general feedback, simply drop an email to `feedback@packtpub.com`, making sure to mention the book title in the subject of your message.

If there is a book that you need and would like to see us publish, please send us a note in the **SUGGEST A TITLE** form on `www.packtpub.com` or email `suggest@packtpub.com`.

If there is a topic that you have expertise in and you are interested in either writing or contributing to a book, see our author guide on `www.packtpub.com/authors`.

Customer Support

Now that you are the proud owner of a Packt book, we have a number of things to help you to get the most from your purchase.

Downloading the Example Code for the Book

Visit `http://www.packtpub.com/support`, and select this book from the list of titles to download any example code or extra resources for this book. The files available for download will then be displayed.

The downloadable files contain instructions on how to use them.

Errata

Although we have taken every care to ensure the accuracy of our contents, mistakes do happen. If you find a mistake in one of our books—maybe a mistake in text or code—we would be grateful if you would report this to us. By doing this you can save other readers from frustration, and help to improve subsequent versions of this book. If you find any errata, report them by visiting `http://www.packtpub.com/support`, selecting your book, clicking on the **Submit Errata** link, and entering the details of your errata. Once your errata are verified, your submission will be accepted and the errata added to the list of existing errata. The existing errata can be viewed by selecting your title from `http://www.packtpub.com/support`.

Questions

You can contact us at `questions@packtpub.com` if you are having a problem with some aspect of the book, and we will do our best to address it.

1
Introduction to Data Binding in ASP.NET

In ASP.NET, the term **Data Binding** implies binding the controls to data that is retrieved from the data source and hence providing a read or write connectivity between these controls and the data, that they are bound to. These data sources can be one of databases, xml files or even, flat files. We would use the word **data controls** often in this book to imply controls that can be bound to data from external data sources. In ASP.NET 1.x, you were introduced to a powerful data binding technique where you could eliminate the need of writing lengthy code that was used in earlier for binding data to data controls. With ASP.NET 2.0, you have a lot of new controls and features added in this context. You now have simplified paging, filtering, sorting, automatic updates, data source controls, and a host of other powerful features.

In this chapter, we will cover the following points:

- The ASP.NET Data Binding Model
- Data Binding Expressions
- The ASP.NET Data Source Controls
    - Object Data Source Control
    - SQL Data Source Control
    - Access Data Source Control
    - XML Data Source Control

The ASP.NET Data Binding Model

In data binding, as we have discussed in the beginning, the controls are bound to data from the data source resulting in read or write connectivity between the controls and the data they are bound to. The controls are actually bound to the columns of the result set that contains the data. This result set can be a data set, a data table, a data reader, or any other instance of a collection type.

> We need not write any code to display the control values after they are bound to these data sources. This kind of data binding allows you to bind data to the user interface controls without the need to write code.

In its simplest form, the syntax for using data binding in your ASPX pages is as follows:

```
<%# Data Source Name %>
```

Depending on whether you require binding single value data or a multiple or repeated value data to a control, you can have the following types of binding mechanisms in ASP.NET data controls:

- Single Value Data Binding
- Repeated Value Data Binding

Single value data binding, as the name suggests implies, binding of a single value or a single record, say, an employee's record. In contrast, repeated value data binding implies binding a set or a table of employee records.

You can use any of the following for single value data binding:

```
<%# Name of the Property %>
<%# Expression %>
<%# Method Name, Parameter List %>
```

For repeated value data binding, you can use the following syntax:

```
<%# Name of the Data Source %>
```

The following sections presents a discussion on how you can use the data binding expressions in ASP.NET to bind data to the controls and a discussion on the newly added data source controls in ASP.NET 2.0 and their usage.

Using the Data Binding Expressions

What are data binding expressions? Well, they are the code snippets that you use between the `<%#` and `%>` blocks in your ASP.NET web page. According to MSDN, "Data-binding expressions create bindings between any property on an ASP.NET page, including a server control property, and a data source when the `DataBind()` method is called on the page. You can include data-binding expressions on the value side of an attribute or value pair in the opening tag of a server control or anywhere in the page".

The following are the advantages of using Data Binding expressions in ASP.NET controls in the presentation layer:

- Flexibility to use any data binding expressions provided that the value it resolves to is one that the data control can use.
- You can use these expressions to bind any property to its corresponding data.
- Flexibility to bind one property to one data source and another property to another data source.

You should use data binding in the ASP.NET web pages in the presentation layer of your application. The syntax used for data binding in ASP.NET 1.x is as follows:

```
<%# Container.DataItem("expression") %>
```

The following code snippet illustrates how you can bind data to a label control using the syntax shown above:

```
<asp:Label id="lblUserName" runat="server"
  Text='<%# Container.DataItem("UserName") %>'>
</asp:Label>
```

You can also use the static method `Eval()` of the `DataBinder` class for binding data to your controls. This method has an overloaded version that accepts the format expression as an additional parameter that relates to the type of formatting that you would require on the data to be displayed. The syntax for using the `Eval()` method is shown as follows:

```
<%# DataBinder.Eval(Container.DataItem, "expression"[, "format"]) %>
```

As shown in the code snippet the `Eval()` method accepts two parameters:

- The first of these parameters is the data container, that is, a data table, a data set or a data view.
- The second parameter is a reference to the value that needs to be assigned to the control.

Refer to the following code snippet that illustrates, how you can use the `DataBinder.Eval()` method to bind data:

```
<asp:Label id="lblUserName" runat="server"
  Text='<%# DataBinder.Eval(Container.DataItem, "UserName") %>'>
</asp:Label>
```

You can use the overloaded version of the `Eval()` method to specify the format expression (as an additional optional parameter) to display the data in your required format. Refer to the following code snippet:

```
<asp:Label id="lblLoginDate" runat="server"
  Text='<%# DataBinder.Eval(Container.DataItem, "LoginDate", "{0:dddd
   d MMMM"]) %>'>
</asp:Label>
```

This code would display the `LoginDate` in the label control named `lblLoginDate` as Sunday 15, April.

With ASP.NET 2.0, you have a much simpler syntax as the `DataBinder` instance is now the default context for all data binding expressions that are used for displaying non-hierarchical data in your presentation layer. You can now use any of the following overloaded versions of the `Eval()` method for binding data.

```
<%# Eval("expression") %>
<%# Eval("expression"[, "format"]) %>
```

The Employee and the Data Manager Classes

Before we dig into a discussion on the data source controls in ASP.NET that follows this section, I would present here two classes that we would frequently be using here and after in the book; I would use these classes throughout this book. In order to reduce code duplication or redundancy, I am providing here the source code for both these classes; we would refer them elsewhere.

The `Employee` class in this example is the **Business Entity** class. It contains a set of public properties that expose the data members of the class. The source code for this class is as follows:

```
public class Employee
{
    private string empCode = String.Empty;
    private string empName = String.Empty;
    private double basic = 0.0;
    private string deptCode = String.Empty;
    private DateTime joiningDate;
```

```
public string EmpCode
{
    get
    {
        return empCode;
    }
    set
    {
        empCode = value;
    }
}
public string EmpName
{
    get
    {
        return empName;
    }
    set
    {
        empName = value;
    }
}
public double Basic
{
    get
    {
        return basic;
    }
    set
    {
        basic = value;
    }
}
public string DeptCode
{
    get
    {
        return deptCode;
    }
    set
    {
        deptCode = value;
    }
```

```
    }
    public DateTime JoiningDate
    {
        get
        {
            return joiningDate;
        }
        set
        {
            joiningDate = value;
        }
    }
}
```

We will use the fields `basic` and `Salary` interchangeably throughout this book. You will find some code examples that refer to the former and some that refer to the later. In either case, you can use the same Employee class as the BusinessEntity with a minor change, that is, replace the name of the public property called `basic` with `Salary` depending on whether you need to use `basic` or `Salary` as the column for displaying data. So, if you would like to use `Salary` as the name of the column data bound to a data control, just change the public property called `basic` shown as follows:

```
public double Salary
    {
        get
        {
            return basic;
        }
        set
        {
            basic = value;
        }
    }
```

To execute the programs listed in this book, ensure that the field names used in the DataManager is the same as the field names that you have used in the database table. We will revisit the Employee class in Chapter 5 of this book to incorporate some more variable and properties.

The `DataManager` class contains a set of methods that return data that would be used in the presentation layer of the application. The source code for the `DataManager` class is as follows:

```
public class DataManager
{
    ArrayList data = new ArrayList();
    String connectionString = String.Empty;
    public DataManager()
    {
        connectionString = ConfigurationManager.ConnectionStrings
              ["joydipConnectionString"].
               ConnectionString.Trim();
    }
    public ArrayList GetAllEmployees()
    {
        SqlConnection conn = null;
        ArrayList employeeList = null;
        try
        {
            conn = new SqlConnection(connectionString);
            conn.Open();
            string sql = "select EmpCode, EmpName, Basic,
              JoiningDate, DeptCode from employee e, Department
              d where e.DeptID = d.DeptID";
            SqlCommand cmd = new SqlCommand(sql, conn);
            SqlDataReader dr = cmd.ExecuteReader();
            employeeList = new ArrayList();
            while (dr.Read())
            {
                Employee emp = new Employee();
                if (dr["EmpCode"] != DBNull.Value)
                    emp.EmpCode = dr["EmpCode"].ToString();
                if (dr["EmpName"] != DBNull.Value)
                    emp.EmpName = dr["EmpName"].ToString();
                if (dr["Basic"] != DBNull.Value)
                    emp.Basic = Convert.ToDouble(dr["Basic"].
                    ToString());
                if (dr["JoiningDate"] != DBNull.Value)
                    emp.JoiningDate =
                    Convert.ToDateTime(dr["JoiningDate"].
                    ToString());
                if (dr["DeptCode"] != DBNull.Value)
                    emp.DeptCode = dr["DeptCode"].ToString();
```

```
                employeeList.Add(emp);
                emp = null;
            }
        }
        catch
        {
            throw;
        }
        finally
        {
            conn.Close();
        }
        return employeeList;
    }
    public ArrayList GetEmployeeByDept(string deptCode)
    {
         SqlConnection conn = null;
         ArrayList employeeList = null;
         try
         {
             conn = new SqlConnection(connectionString); conn.Open();
             string sql = «select EmpCode, EmpName, Basic,
             JoiningDate, DeptCode from employee e, Department
             d where e.DeptID = d.DeptID and
             d.DeptCode = '» + deptCode + «'»;
             SqlCommand cmd = new SqlCommand(sql, conn);
             SqlDataReader dr = cmd.ExecuteReader();
             employeeList = new ArrayList();
             while (dr.Read())
             {
                 Employee emp = new Employee();
                 if (dr[«EmpCode»] != DBNull.Value)
                     emp.EmpCode = dr[«EmpCode»].ToString();
                 if (dr[«EmpName»] != DBNull.Value)
                     emp.EmpName = dr[«EmpName»].ToString();
                 if (dr[«Basic»] != DBNull.Value)
                     emp.Basic = Convert.ToDouble(dr[«Basic»].
                     ToString());
                 if (dr[«JoiningDate»] != DBNull.Value)
                     emp.JoiningDate =
                      Convert.ToDateTime(dr[«JoiningDate»].
                      ToString());
                 if (dr[«DeptCode»] != DBNull.Value)
```

```
                    emp.DeptCode = dr["DeptCode"].ToString();
                employeeList.Add(emp);
                emp = null;
            }
        }
        catch
        {
            throw;
        }
        finally
        {
            conn.Close();
        }
        return employeeList;
    }

}
```

In this code, the `GetAllEmployees()` method returns all records from the Employee table, whereas, the `GetEmployeeByDept()` method returns the records of all employees of a specific department.

New Data Source Controls in ASP.NET 2.0

With ASP.NET 2.0, data binding has been simplified a lot with the introduction of a number of data source controls. These data source controls are server controls that can be used to bind data to a number of data sources. You now have a more simplified, powerful, consistent, and extensible approach towards binding data between your presentation layer controls and a number of data source controls. You can use these controls to bind data between the data bound controls in your presentation layer to a variety of data sources seamlessly. You only need to choose the appropriate data source control that fits your requirement.

These data source controls facilitate a "Declarative programming model and an automatic data binding behavior". You can use them declaratively in your presentation layer or programmatically in your source code. The data store that contains the data and the operations that are performed on this data are abstracted, and you need not worry about how the data access and data binding logic works underneath. In essence, the entire ADO.NET Object Model is abstracted using these data source controls. Further, you can use these data source controls to display both tabular data as well as hierarchical data in your presentation layer.

In ASP.NET 2.0, you have the following data source controls that are of utmost importance; these would be discussed in detail later in this chapter:

- **Object data source control**: This control can be used to bind data to middle-tier objects to the presentation layer components in an N-tier design.
- **SQL data source control:** This control enables you to connect to and bind data to a number of underlying data sources, that is, Microsoft SQL Server, OLEDB, ODBC or Oracle databases.
- **Access data source control:** This control can be used to bind data to Microsoft Access databases.
- **Xml data source control:** This control can be used to bind data to XML data sources, that is, external XML data files, dataset instances, etc.

With these data source controls, you can easily implement data driven ASP.NET applications without the need to write the data access code. The only thing you have to do is, add and configure a data source control in your web page and then associate the DataSourceID property of any web control in your web page to the ID property of the data source control in use. The web control would now display the data using the data source control that you have used in your web page. You are done!

In the sections that follow, we would explore how you can use each of these controls to bind data to your controls seamlessly.

The Object Data Source Control

The Object data source control, one of the new data source controls added in ASP.NET 2.0, can be used to de-couple the User Interface or the Presentation Layer of the application from the Business Logic and the Data Access Layers. It is a non-visual control and is typically used to bind data to the data-bound controls in a consistent way and can be used for seamless CRUD (Create, Update, Read and Delete) operations in your applications.

Object Data Source Control Methods

The following are the four main methods of the Object data source control aligned to the CRUD operations that you need in your applications:

- **Update Method:** This method is used for updating data using the Object data source control.

- **Insert Method:** This method is used for inserting data using the Object data source control.
- **Select Method:** This method is used for reading data using the Object data source control.
- **Delete Method:** This method is used for deleting data using the Object data source control.

We would use the Object data source control to bind data to data bound controls with components that represent data collections, that is, those which return a set of data. We would use the Object data source control to bind data to a data bound component with a `DataSet` instance, a `DataReader` instance, a `WebService` instance that returns `Data` and a `Collection` instance. Hence, we would create a polymorphic method called `GetData()` that would accept a parameter that would indicate the source of the data that we need to retrieve the data from. The term **polymorphic** used here implies that we can have multiple methods of name `GetData()`, differing in their signatures. Hence, we may also say that the `GetData()` method is overloaded. We would use these methods throughout this book for all the subsequent chapters that would require data retrieval.

Using the Object Data Source Control

To use the Object data source control:

1. Create a new web application in Visual Studio, open the `default.aspx` file and then switch to design view mode.
2. Now, add the **ObjectDataSource** control by dragging it from the toolbox. An **ObjectDataSource** control with the default name of **ObjectDataSource1** is added to the web page.
3. We now require a data bound control to which we would bind the data using this control. We will choose the **GridView** control for this and drag one from the toolbox onto the web page. The default name of the control is **GridView1**.
4. The next step is to configure the **ObjectDataSource** control.

5. We associate the Object data source control to the **GridView** Control and set its **DataSource** property to the **ObjectDataSource** Control that we have added in our web page. The following screenshot illustrates how we associate the data source for the **GridView** control to our **ObjectDataSource** control.

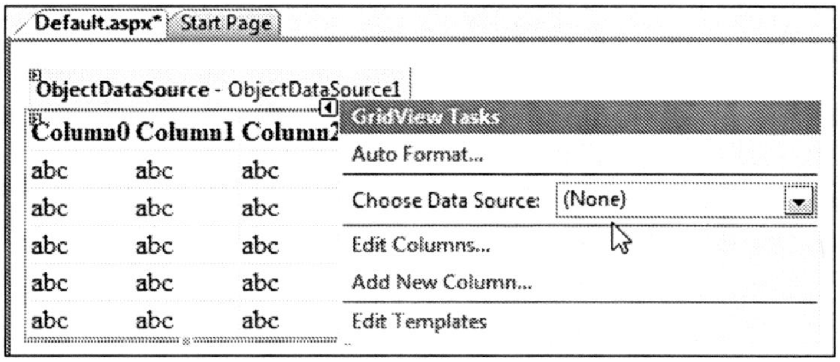

Note how the data source for the **GridView** Control is associated with the **ObjectDataSource** control using the **Choose Data Source** option.

To configure, click on the **Configure Data Source** option and then select the business object that would be used for the CRUD operations. Then click on **Next**. The **Configure Data Source** window pops up. Refer to the following screenshot:

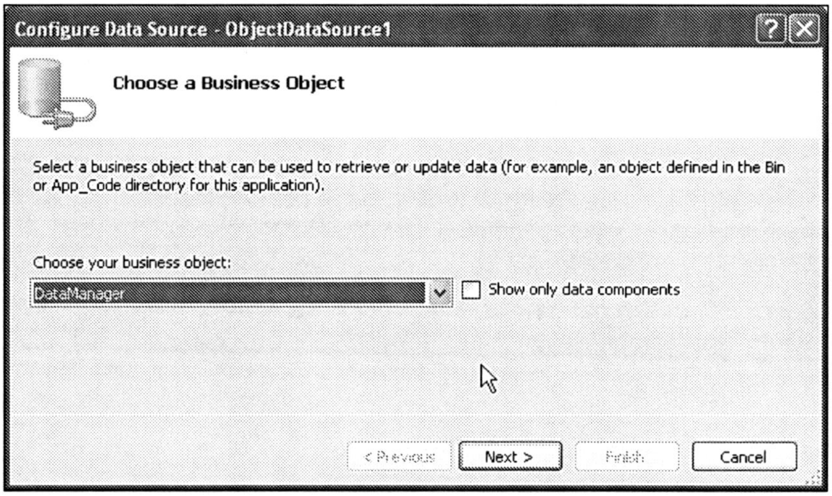

In our example, the business object class is `DataManager` and the business entity class is `Employee`. Hence, we would now select **DataManager** as the business object from the **Choose your business object** option of the **Configure Data Source** window.

Then, click **Next** and select the **GetAllEmployees(), returns ArrayList** as our business method (that would be used to retrieve data) from the **Choose a method** option. Refer to the following screenshot:

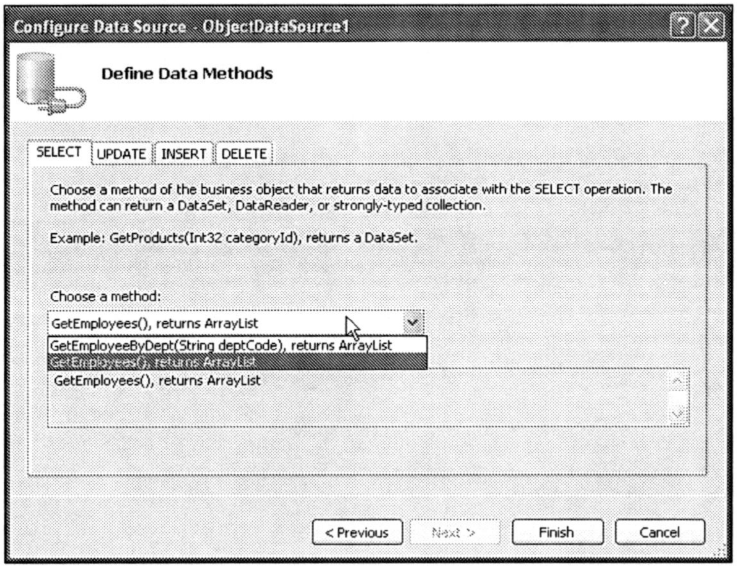

Then click on **Finish**. You are done!

When you execute the application, the output will be something like the following screenshot:

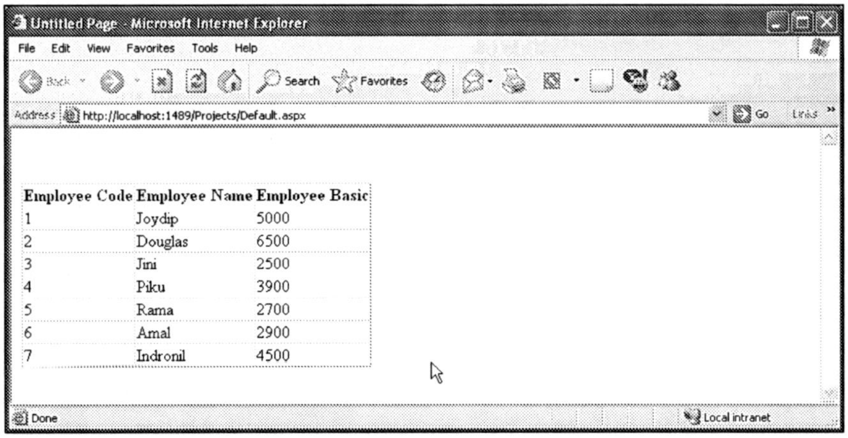

The SQL Data Source Control

Built on top of ADO.NET, the SQL data source control is a non-visual control and uses the built in ADO.NET objects for its operation. The SQL data source control is used to access data from any relational database, SQL Server database in particular. You can follow some simple steps described below that can be used to connect to your database and perform your CRUD operations in your applications with minimal or no coding at all!

Using the SQL Data Source Control

To use the SQL data source control, drag-and-drop it from the toolbox into your web page. The default name of the control would be **SqlDataSource1**. Next, you need to configure the data source as shown in the following screenshot:

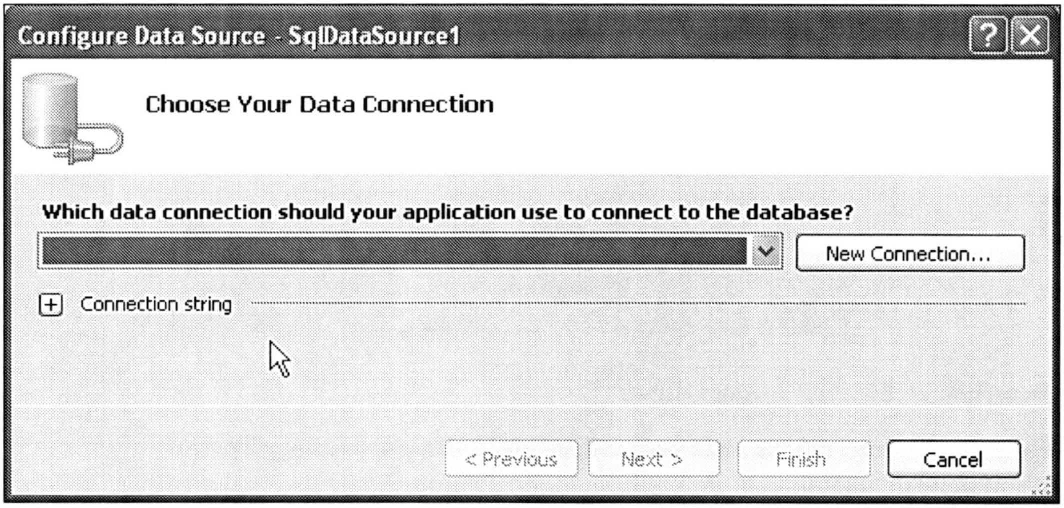

Click on the **New Connection** button to create a new connection with the database. A window as shown in the following screenshot pops up.

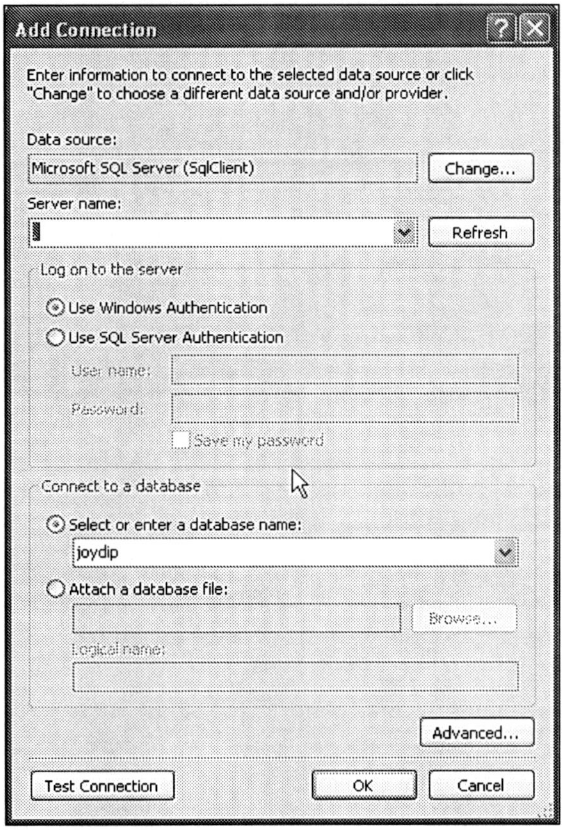

We would select the data source as **Microsoft SQL Server** and we would specify the **Server Name** as **.** (a dot) to indicate that the database to be connected to, is a local database. Select **SQL Server Authentication** mode and the database as shown in the screenshot above. Test your connection to check whether the connection was successful by clicking on the **Test Connection** button.

Once you click on **OK**, the next window that is displayed is as shown in the following screenshot:

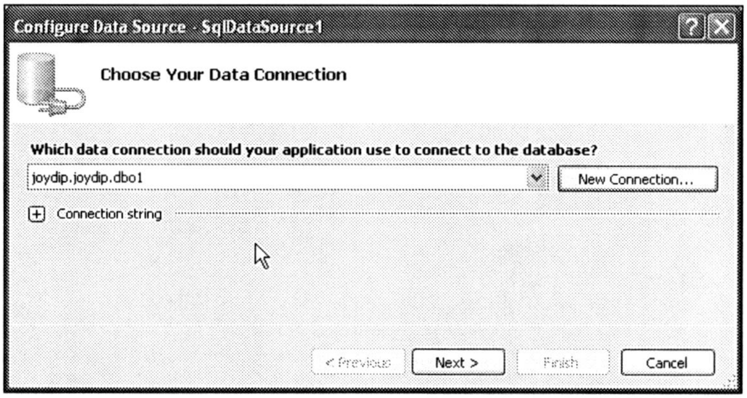

You now need to configure the data source. Check to see whether the connection string is as desired and then click on the **Next** button. The next window that is displayed is as shown in the following screenshot:

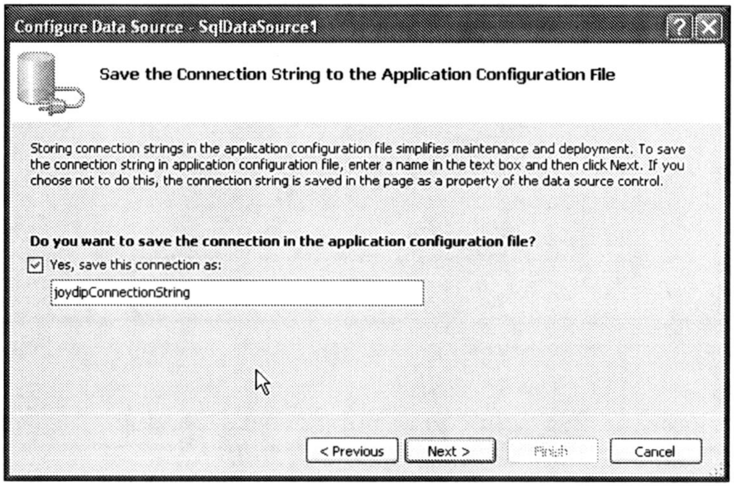

You can save the connection string generated earlier in the configuration file of your application by selecting the **check box** as shown in this screenshot. The saved connection string in the application's configuration file would resemble the following:

```
<connectionStrings>
  <add name="joydipConnectionString" connectionString="Data
   Source=.;Initial Catalog=joydip;User ID=sa;Password=sa"
   providerName="System.Data.SqlClient" />
</connectionStrings>
```

Click on the **Next** button to proceed further. The next window that gets displayed allows you to configure your **Select** statement. You can specify the fields, the conditions, etc, that you require in the output. Once you are done, click on the **Next** button.

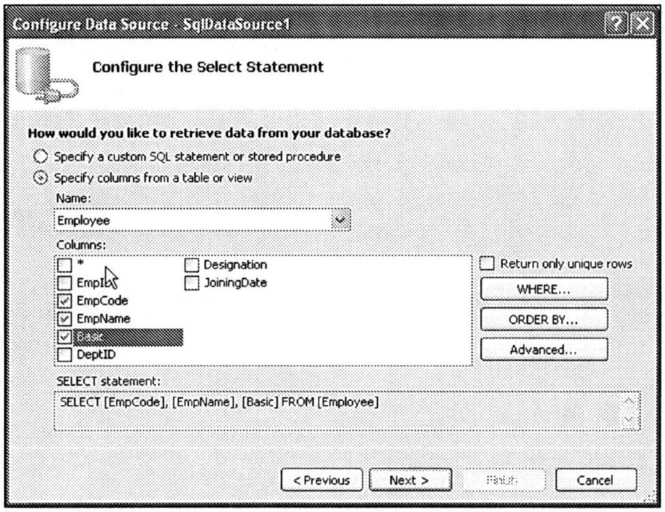

The final window that gets displayed would allow you to test the query prior to using it in the presentation layer of your application. Note that we have used the **Employee** table in our example and it contains the same set of data as we used when working with the Object data source control earlier in this chapter. Refer to the following screenshot:

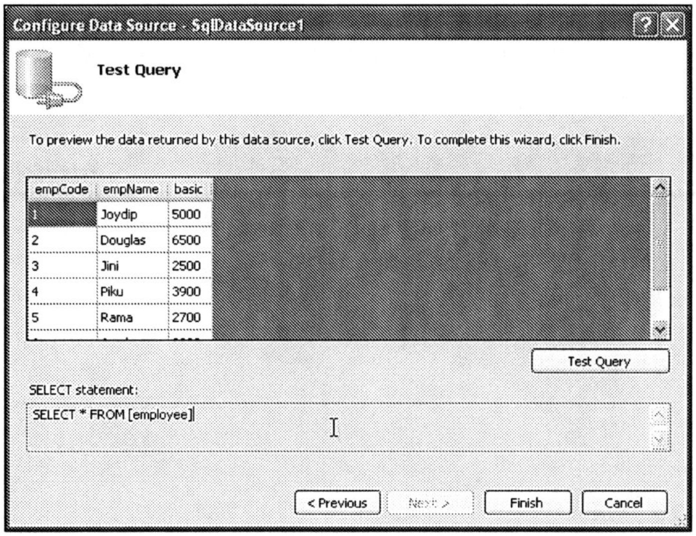

Notice the output of the query once the **Test Query** button is clicked. This is the final step in this process of configuring the SQL data source control. Click on **Finish** button to complete the process. The code that is generated for the SQL data source control in the `.aspx` file is as follows:

```
<asp:SqlDataSource ID="SqlDataSource1" runat="server"
   ConnectionString="<%$ ConnectionStrings:joydipConnectionString %>"
   SelectCommand="SELECT * FROM [employee]"></asp:SqlDataSource>
```

Now we need to drag and drop a **GridView** control from the toolbox and configure it with the SQL data source control, using the same process that we followed earlier, for configuring it with the Object data source Control. Once we are done, we can execute the web page; the output on execution of the web page is shown as follows:

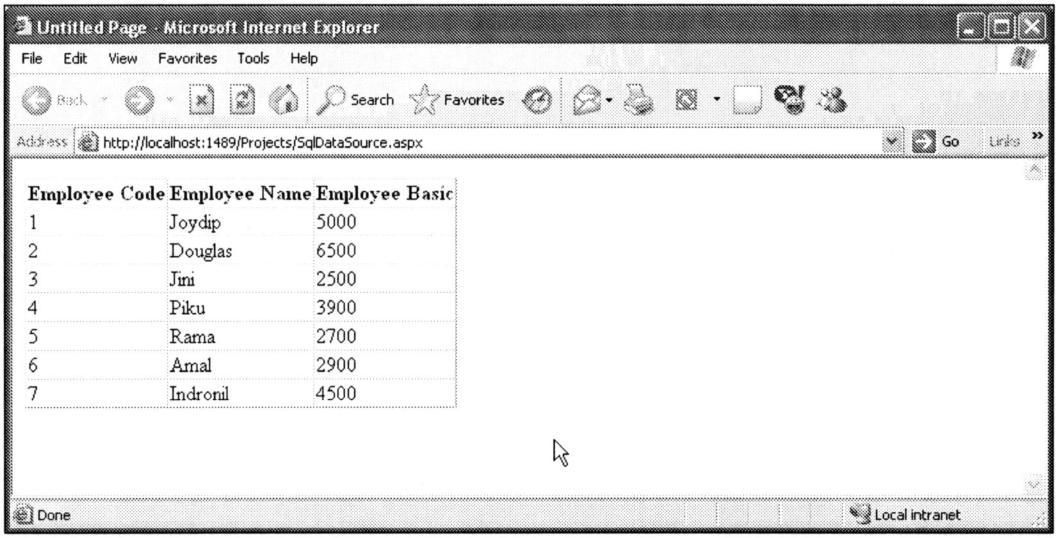

The Access Data Source Control

The Access data source control can be used to connect to **Microsoft Access databases** and perform CRUD operations in your applications. The following section discusses how we can use this control in our applications.

Using the Access Data Source Control

To start with, drag and drop the **Access Data Source** Control from the toolbox onto your web page. Then configure the control by selecting the **Configure Data Source** option. Refer to the following screenshot:

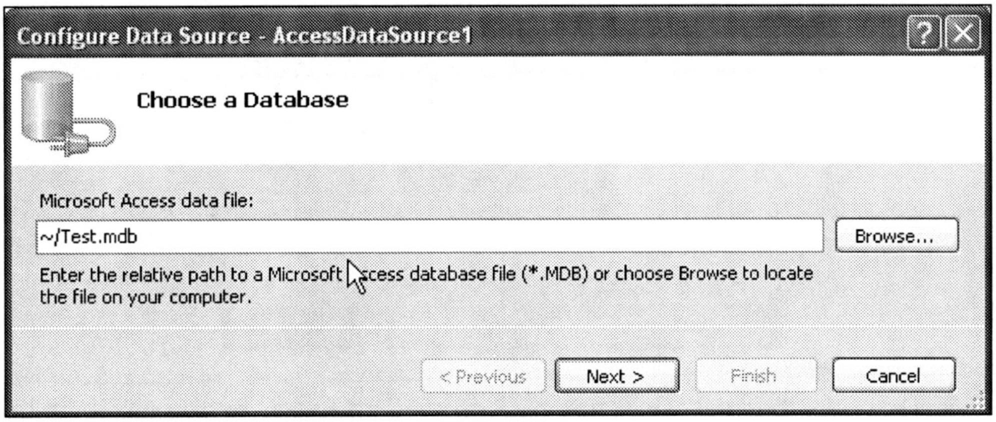

Specify the name and the path to the **MS Access database** as shown in the screenshot above and click on the **Next** button. Now, configure the select statement as you did earlier when working with SQL data source control. Refer to the following screenshot:

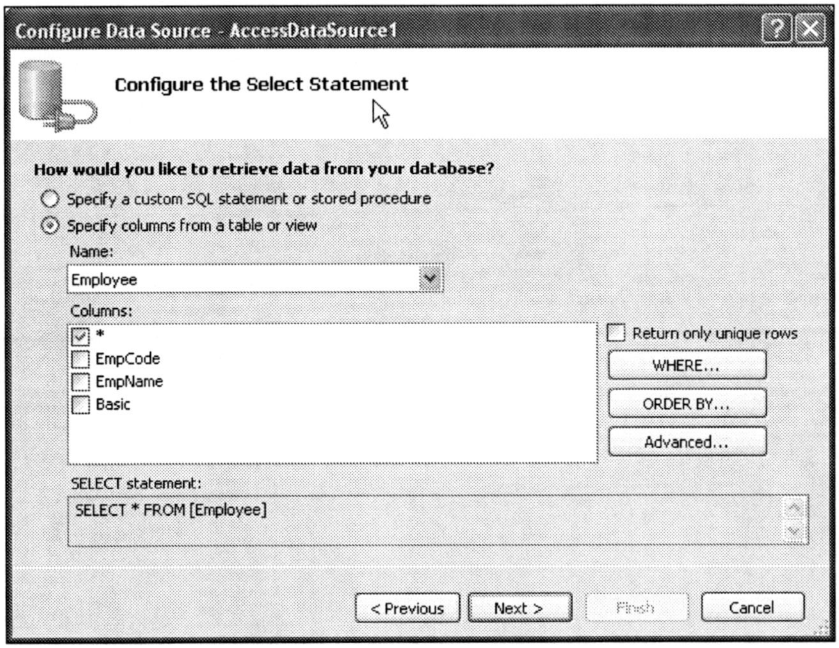

Click on the **Next** button to invoke a window where you can test your query. Refer to the following screenshot:

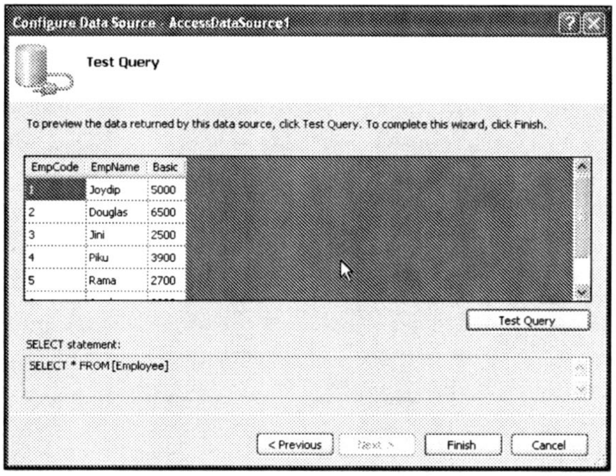

Note the output of the query once you click on the **Test Query** button as shown in the screenshot above. Click on the **Finish** button when done.

Next, drag-and-drop a **GridView** Control to display the data retrieved from the **Access Data Source** Control. Now, bind the **GridView** control to the **Access Data Source** control created earlier using the **Choose Data Source** option, as shown in the following screenshot.

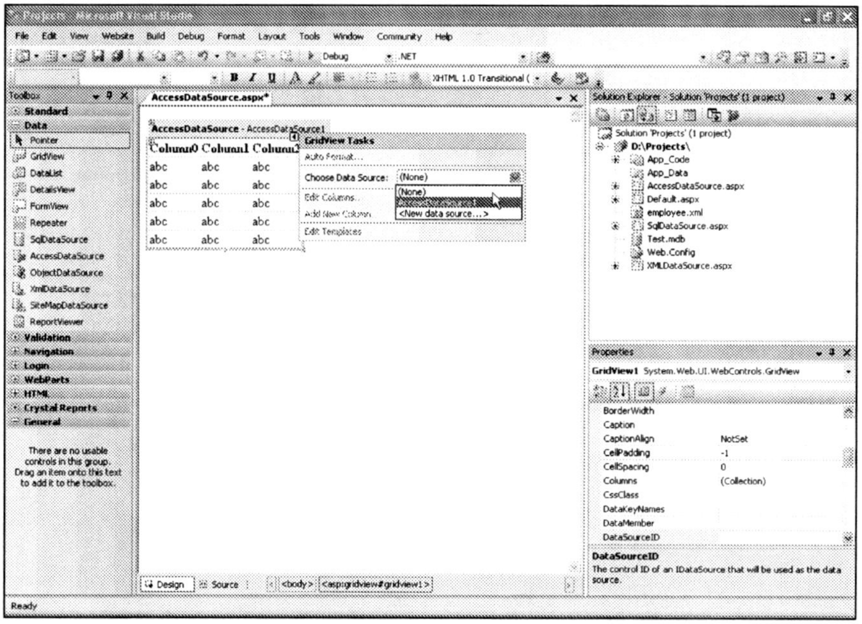

You are done! Execute the web page as the last step; the output on execution is shown in the following screenshot:

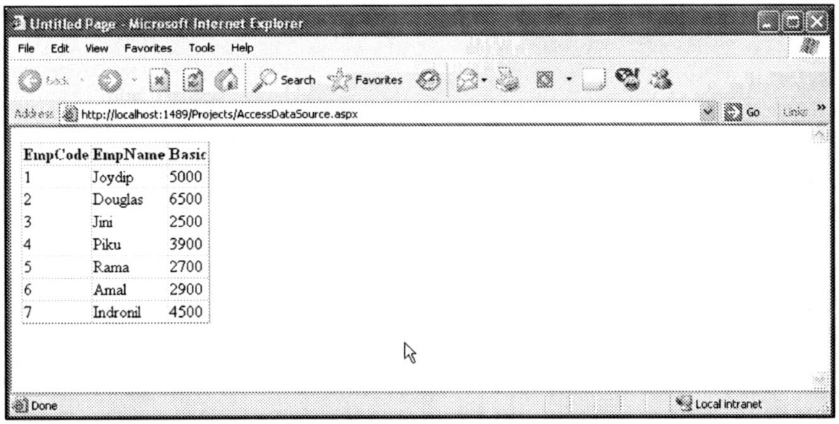

The XML Data Source Control

The **XML data source** control introduced in ASP.NET 2.0 can be used to bind to an XML Document seamlessly. It can also be used to bind hierarchical data with data controls that supports it.

Using the XML Data Source Control

To use this control, drag-and-drop the control from the toolbox onto your web form. The default name of this control would be **XmlDataSource1**. Now, configure the control by clicking on the **Configure Data Source** option as shown in the following screenshot:

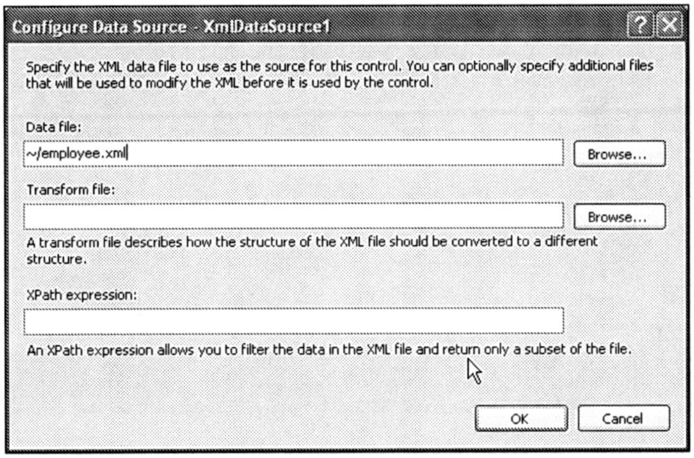

Specify the name and the path to the XML **Data file** as shown above. Then click on the **OK** button. In our example, the XML data file is **employee.xml**, present in the application's root directory. The following is the schema for the **employee.xml** file:

```
<?xml version="1.0" encoding="utf-8" ?>
<Employees>
  <Employee Code ="1" Name = "Joydip" Basic ="5000"/>
  <Employee Code ="2" Name = "Douglas" Basic ="6500"/>
  <Employee Code ="2" Name = "Jini" Basic ="2500"/>
  <Employee Code ="2" Name = "Piku" Basic ="3900"/>
  <Employee Code ="2" Name = "Rama" Basic ="2700"/>
  <Employee Code ="2" Name = "Amal" Basic="2900"/>
  <Employee Code ="2" Name = "Indronil" Basic="4500"/>
</Employees>
```

We now need a data control for displaying the data that would be retrieved by the **XML data source** control. For this, drag and drop a **GridView** control from the toolbox and associate the data source of this control with the **XMLDataSource** control created and configured earlier. Refer to the following screenshot:

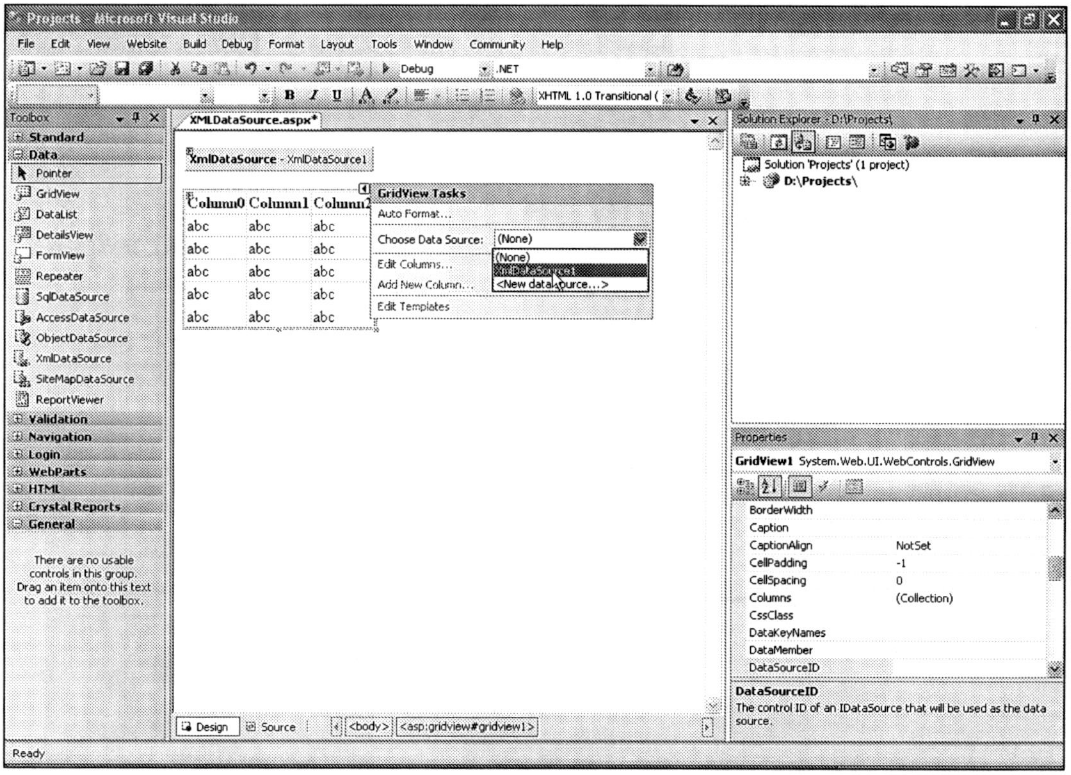

You are done! On execution of the web page, the output is as follows:

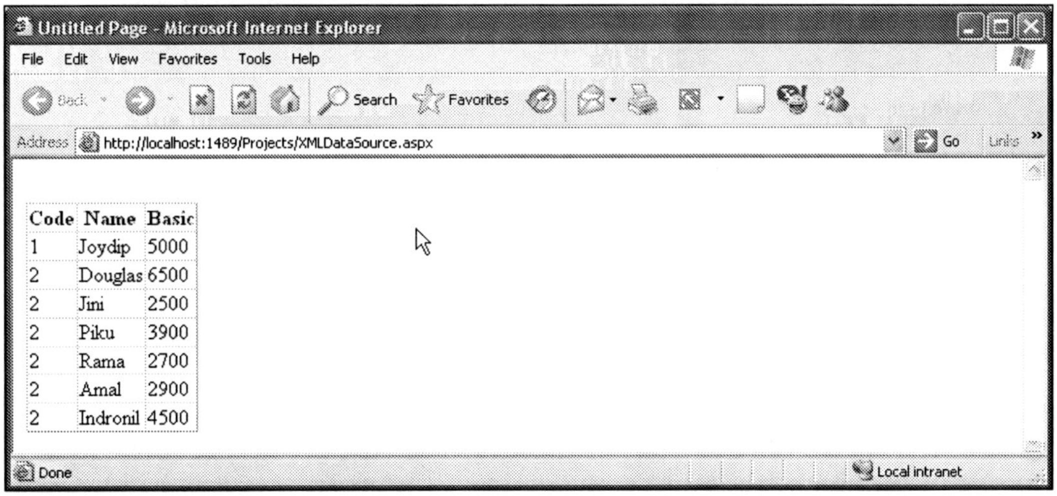

User Interface and Data Source Paging

Paging, **Sorting**, and **Filtering** of data is much more simplified using these Data Source Controls. You have two options for data paging and data sorting when using Object data source control. These are:

- User Interface Paging or Sorting
- Server Side Paging or Sorting

While the former is much simpler to use, the later can offer you much improved performance. Let us now see how we can implement **User Interface Paging** using Object data source control.

Refer to our discussion on Object data source control earlier. For the sake of simplicity, we would consider the same Object data source control data binding and the **GridView** control to present data to the User Interface. For working with **User Interface Paging**, simply set the `Allow Paging` property of the `GridView` to `true`. Further, set the `Page Size` property to the number of records that you would like to be displayed for each page. We would set the page size to a value of **5** for this example. On execution of the web page, the output is as follows:

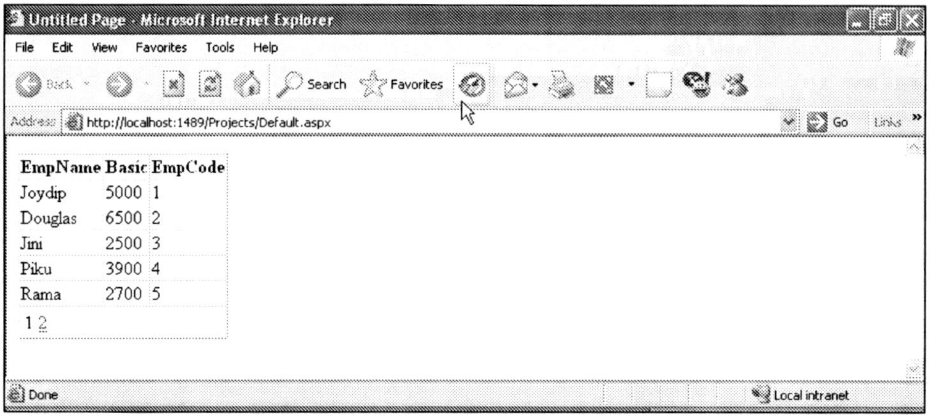

Though User Interface Paging is very easy to use, the major drawback of using this approach is that it would load all the records in the server's memory even though only a specified number of records would actually be displayed. These drawbacks can be overcome using the other option of paging, that is, Data Source Paging.

For implementing Data Source Paging, you would require a method that returns `paged data` and one that returns the `count` of the data from the database table. The following two methods return a page of **Employee** records and the count of the Employee records respectively, from the database table `Employee`.

```
public SqlDataReader GetDataFromDataReader(int StartRowIndex,int
MaximumRows)
    {
        String connectionString = "Data Source=.;Initial
        Catalog=joydip;User ID=sa;Password=sa";
        String procedureName = "GetPagedEmployeeRecords";
        SqlConnection sqlConnection = new
        SqlConnection(connectionString);
        SqlCommand sqlCommand = new SqlCommand(procedureName,
        sqlConnection);
        sqlCommand.CommandType = CommandType.StoredProcedure;
        sqlCommand.Parameters.AddWithValue("@StartRowIndex",
        StartRowIndex);
        sqlCommand.Parameters.AddWithValue("@MaximumRows",
        MaximumRows);
        sqlConnection.Open();
        return sqlCommand.ExecuteReader
        (CommandBehavior.CloseConnection);
    }
    public int GetDataCountFromDataReader()
    {
        String connectionString = "Data Source=.;Initial
        Catalog=joydip;User ID=sa;Password=sa";
```

```
        String sqlString = "Select count(*) from employee";
        SqlConnection sqlConnection = new
        SqlConnection(connectionString);
        SqlCommand sqlCommand = new SqlCommand(sqlString,
        sqlConnection);
        sqlCommand.CommandType = CommandType.Text;
        sqlConnection.Open();
        return int.Parse(sqlCommand.ExecuteScalar().ToString());
    }
```

The following is the stored procedure called `GetPagedEmployeeRecords` that returns a page of **Employee** records from the `Employee` table:

```
Create Procedure GetPagedEmployeeRecords
(
  @StartRowIndex int, @MaximumRows int
)
as
select a.empCode,a.empName,a.basic from employee a inner join employee
b on a.empcode = b.empCode where b.empCode >=@StartRowIndex and
b.empCode <( @StartRowIndex + @MaximumRows)
```

Set the `SelectMethod` property of the Object data source control to the `GetDataFromDataReader()` method and the `SelectCountMethod` property to the `GetDataCountFromDataReader()` method. Ensure that the `AllowPaging` property for the `GridView` Control is set to `true`. Next, you need to set the `EnablePaging` property of the Object data source control to `true`. On doing so, this control would pass the parameters `StartRowIndex` and `MaximumRows` when calling the method represented by the `SelectMethod` property. Refer to the following source code snippet that gets generated for the `.aspx` file:

```
<asp:ObjectDataSource ID="ObjectDataSource1" runat="server"
         EnablePaging="True"
         SelectCountMethod="GetDataCountFromDataReader"
         SelectMethod="GetDataFromDataReader" TypeName="DataManager"
>
</asp:ObjectDataSource>
<asp:GridView ID="GridView1" runat="server" AllowPaging="True"
     DataSourceID="ObjectDataSource1" PageSize="5">
</asp:GridView>
```

The following is the output on execution:

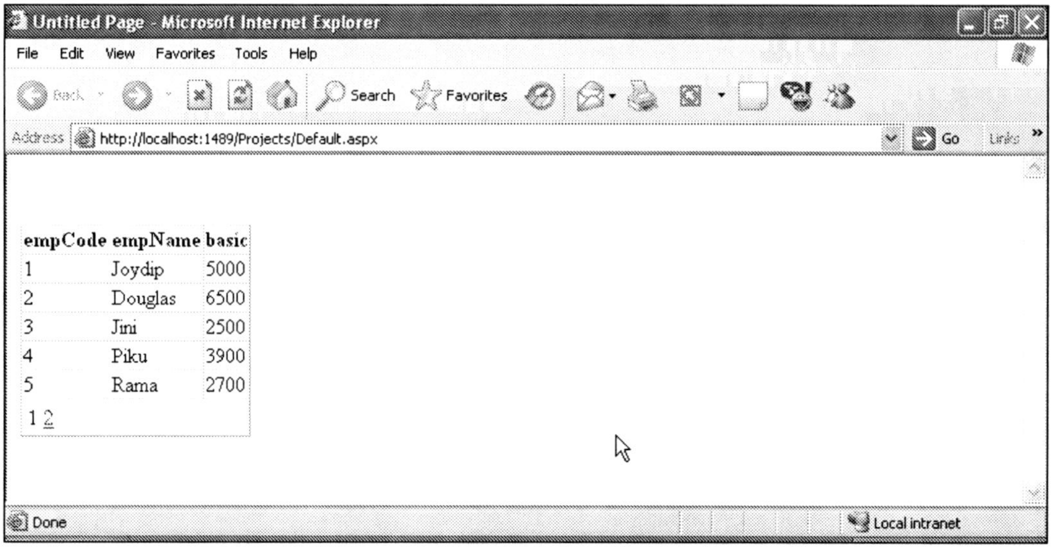

User Interface and Data Source Sorting

The previous section discussed how we can implement paging seamlessly using the Object data source Control. This section will discuss how we can implement User Interface and Data Source sorting of data.

For User Interface Sorting, set the `AllowSorting` property of the `GridView` Control to `true`. Note that automatic data sorting with Object data source Control is supported with `DataView`, `DataTable` or a `DataSet` only. The following method illustrates how we can retrieve data from the Employee table, populate a `DataSet` with it and then return it.

```
public DataSet GetDataFromDataSet()
    {
        String connectionString = "Data Source=.;Initial
        Catalog=joydip;User ID=sa;Password=sa";
        String procedureName = "GetEmployeeRecords";
        SqlConnection sqlConnection = new
        SqlConnection(connectionString);
        sqlConnection.Open();
        SqlDataAdapter sqlDataAdapter = new
        SqlDataAdapter(procedureName, sqlConnection);
        DataSet dataSet = new DataSet();
        sqlDataAdapter.Fill(dataSet);
        return dataSet;
    }
```

Now, set the Object data source Control's `SelectMethod` property to refer to the `GetDataFromDataSet()` method shown above. The code generated in the `.aspx` file is as follows.

```
<asp:ObjectDataSource ID="ObjectDataSource1" runat="server"
           SelectMethod="GetDataFromDataSet"
           TypeName="DataManager">
</asp:ObjectDataSource>
<asp:GridView ID="GridView1" runat="server" AllowSorting="True"
     DataSourceID="ObjectDataSource1">
 </asp:GridView>
```

On execution, the following is the output:

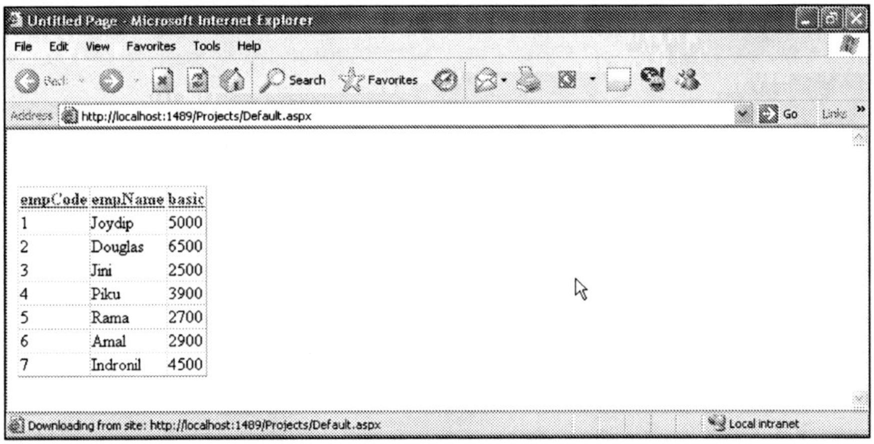

On clicking in the **empName** column, the output is sorted by employee name and the resultant output is as shown in the following screenshot:

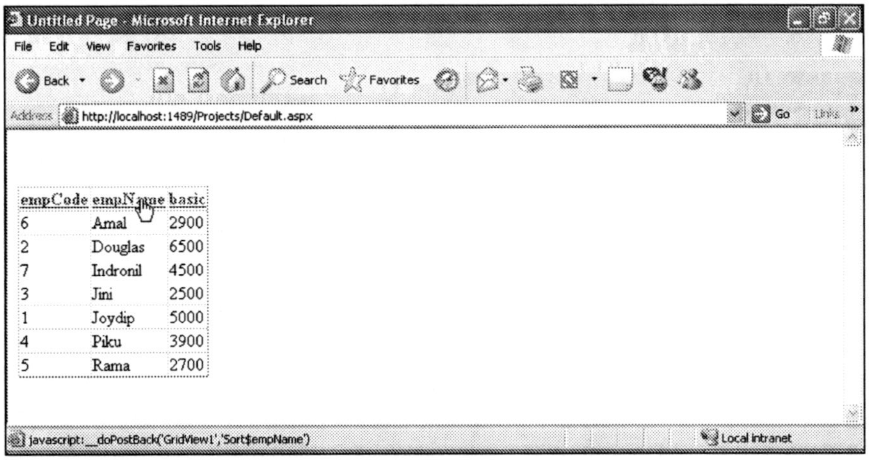

For data source sorting, you have to set the **SortParameterName** property of the Object data source Control to the desired sort expression. If this property is set, **Data Source Sorting** would be used in place of **User Interface Sorting**. Note that the default sorting mode for this control, that is, if this property is not specified, is **User Interface Sorting**.

The following is the stored procedure that fetches sorted `Employee Records` from the `Employee` table:

```
create procedure GetSortedEmployeeRecords
(
  @sortColumn int
)
as
select empCode,empName,basic from employee
order by
case when @sortColumn = 1 then empCode end asc,
case when @sortColumn = 2 then empName end asc,
case when @sortColumn = 3 then basic end
```

The following is the `GetSortedEmployeeData()` method that returns a list of sorted **Employee** records using the `GetSortedEmployeeRecords()` stored procedure.

```
public SqlDataReader GetSortedEmployeeData(int sortColumn)
{
    String connectionString = "Data Source=.;Initial
    Catalog=joydip;User ID=sa;Password=sa";
    String procedureName = "GetSortedEmployeeRecords";
    SqlConnection sqlConnection = new
    SqlConnection(connectionString);
    SqlCommand sqlCommand = new SqlCommand(procedureName,
    sqlConnection);
    sqlCommand.Parameters.AddWithValue("@sortColumn",
    sortColumn);
    sqlConnection.Open();
    return sqlCommand.ExecuteReader
    (CommandBehavior.CloseConnection);
}
```

Filtering Data Using the Object Data Source Control

The Object data source control supports filtering data provided the Select method property returns a **DataSet, DataTable** or a **DataView** instance. The **FilterExpression** property of the Object data source control can be used to specify the expression that should be used to filter the data. Note that you can retrieve data using the method that is specified by the `SelectMethod` property of the Object data source control.

To apply a filter on the data, specify `basic > 3500` in the **FilterExpression** property of the Object data source control. Refer to the following screenshot:

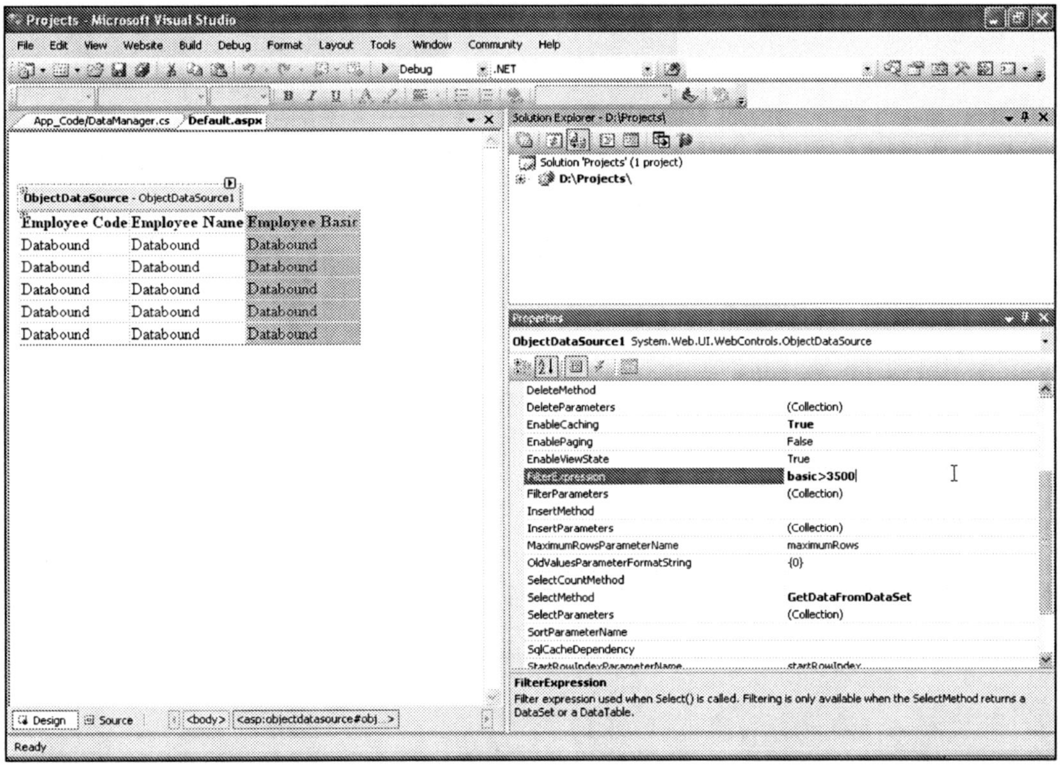

Note the resultant code that gets generated in the `.aspx` file as a result of the above screenshot:

```
<asp:ObjectDataSource ID="ObjectDataSource1" runat="server" SelectMeth
od="GetDataFromDataSet" TypeName="DataManager" EnableCaching="True"
FilterExpression=" basic>3500"></asp:ObjectDataSource>
```

The output on execution is shown in the following screenshot:

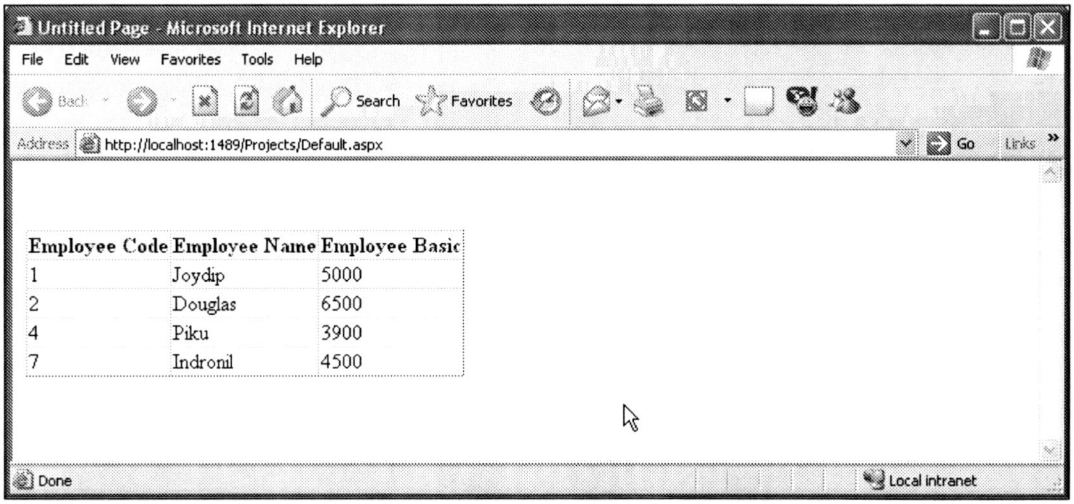

Summary

This chapter gave a bird's eye view at ASP.NET's Data Binding Model and the Data Source Controls. We have discussed how we can work with the Data Source Controls like, Object data source, SQL data source, Xml data source and the Access data source control. We also had a look at how we can implement Paging, Sorting, and Filtering data using these controls. The next chapter, will discuss how we can bind data to the List Controls in ASP.NET and use them in our ASP.NET applications.

2

Working with List Controls in ASP.NET

In chapter 1, we saw the basics of Data Binding in ASP.NET and how we can bind and retrieve data to and from the newly added Data Source controls in our applications. In this chapter, we will explore ASP.NET List controls, which controls those display lists of data items bound to them from where the user can select one or more such list items.

We will discuss how we can Add, Display, Select, and Delete the items of each of these controls and handle events of each of these controls. We will see how we can associate event handlers to a dynamic DropDownList control and design. We will also learn how to design and implement a custom CheckBoxList control that will allow you to select one or more items at one go.

The ASP.NET List Controls

The List controls display a list of data items from where the user can select one or more data items. These are all derived from the ListControl base class due to which they have a common set of properties and methods. You can bind data to any of the above controls using the DataSource property. In binding data to these controls, you can have two approaches, the declarative data binding approach and the programmatic data binding approach.

> Note that while you use the declarative approach from your HTML source code mode or in the design view mode and you hardly require any code to bind data to the controls, you use the programmatic approach to accomplish the same task from your code behind file. The declarative approach comes in handy in situations where you need not, or want to avoid writing code to bind data to the controls of your web form. However, you can have more control and provide more flexibility or customization when you do the same programmatically.

You have a variety of List Controls in ASP.NET to choose from. These are as follows:

- ListBox Control
- DropDownList Control
- CheckBoxList Control
- BulletedList Control
- RadioButtonList Control

Each of these controls will be discussed in the sections that follow. You would learn how to bind static data to all of these controls through your .aspx page and also dynamic data at runtime programmatically. We will discuss how we can add, remove, and select list items for these controls.

Working with the ListBox Control

The ListBox control, a container of list items, can be used to create and display a list of items and select one or multiple items from such list of items. However, you can control the number of list items displayed in the control, and adjust the size of the control, that is, height and width.

In order to work with a ListBox control, simply drag-and-drop an instance of the control from the toolbox into your web form.

Appending List Items to the ListBox Control

You populate data in a `ListBox` control using the list items. You can add the list items through the `.aspx` page as shown in the following code snippet:

```
<asp:ListBox ID="ListBox1" runat="server" Height="125px"
     Width="214px">
    <asp:ListItem Value="1">Joydip</asp:ListItem>
    <asp:ListItem Value="2">Douglas</asp:ListItem>
    <asp:ListItem Value="3">Jini</asp:ListItem>
    <asp:ListItem Value="4">Piku</asp:ListItem>
    <asp:ListItem Value="5">Rama</asp:ListItem>
    <asp:ListItem Value="6">Amal</asp:ListItem>
    <asp:ListItem Value="7">Indronil</asp:ListItem>
</asp:ListBox>
```

You can also add list items to the `ListBox` control programmatically using the overloaded `Add()` method of the Items property of this control as shown in the following code snippet:

```
protected void Page_Load(object sender, EventArgs e)
{
          if (!IsPostBack)
          {
              PopulateListItems();
          }

   private void PopulateListItems()
   {
       ListBox1.Items.Add("Joydip");
        ListBox1.Items.Add("Douglas");
        ListBox1.Items.Add("Jini");
        ListBox1.Items.Add("Piku");
        ListBox1.Items.Add("Rama");
        ListBox1.Items.Add("Amal");
        ListBox1.Items.Add("Indronil");
   }
   }
```

Now, the ListBox control is populated with data. The following figure displays the ListBox control populated with data at runtime.

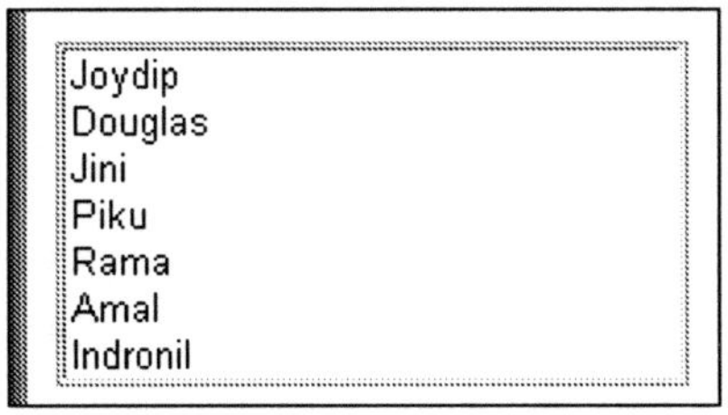

Selecting One or More List Items

Now, let us see how to select one or more list items from the ListBox control. The following figure displays the list items that have been selected from a ListBox control in a Label control on click of a **Button**.

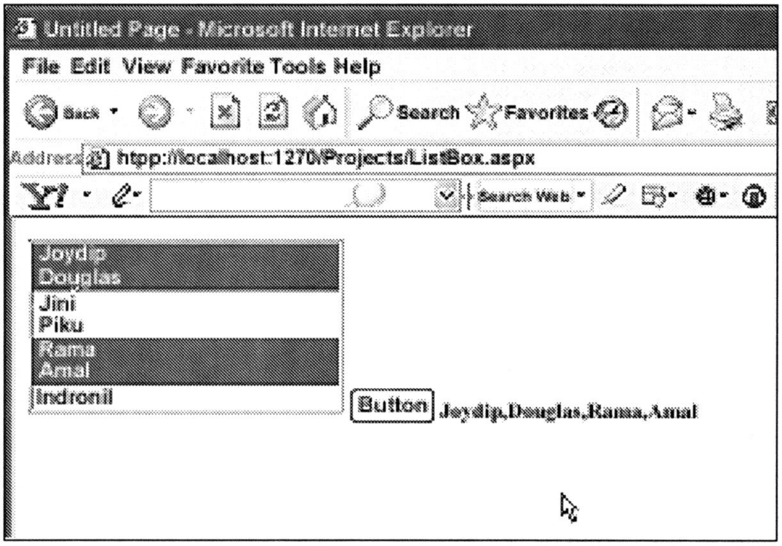

This section discusses how to accomplish the above. You can select one of more list items from a ListBox. Drag-and-drop a Button control and a Label control onto your web form. In the `Click` event of the `Button`, write the following code to retrieve the selected text from the ListBox control in a single selection mode and display it in the `Label` control once the Button control is clicked.

```
protected void Button1_Click(object sender, EventArgs e)
    {
        Label1.Text = ListBox1.SelectedItem.Text;
    }
```

As you can see in the above code snippet, the SelectionMode property or a ListBox control having an ID of `ListBox1`, is set to "Single", implying that we can select only one List Item from the control at any point in time. The text of the selected item from the ListBox control is being displayed in a Label control in the `Click` event of a `Button`.

Now, you need to change the selection mode of the ListBox control from the default "Single" to "Multiple" so as to enable multiple list item selection from the control. You can do this by changing the SelectionMode property in the design view or in your `.aspx` file.

[Irrespective of whether the ListBox control's selection mode is set to "Single" or "Multiple", the `Count` property of the Items collection of the control would always return you the total number of list items in the control.]

Now, refer to the following code snippet that shows how you can retrieve the selected text for multiple selected list items from the ListBox control:

```
protected void Button1_Click(object sender, EventArgs e)
    {
        string str = String.Empty;
        for (int i = 0; i < ListBox1.Items.Count - 1; i++)
        {
            if (ListBox1.Items[i].Selected)
                str += ListBox1.Items[i].Text+",";
        }
        str = str.Substring(0,str.LastIndexOf(','));
        Label1.Text = str;
    }
```

[You can select any ListItem in the ListBox control by its Text or by its Value properties. The following code snippets illustrate how you can do this.]

```
ListBox1.Items.FindByText("Joydip").Selected = true;
```

or

```
ListBox1.Items.FindByValue("Record 1").Selected = true;
```

Removing List Items from the ListBox Control

You can remove a list item from the ListBox control using the `RemoveAt()` method that accepts the index number of the list item that you need to remove from the collection of list items.

```
ListBox1.Items.RemoveAt(0);
```

To remove all the list items from the ListBox control, use the following code:

```
ListBox1.Items.Clear();
```

Binding Data to the ListBox Control

We have already discussed how we can bind static data to this control declaratively. For programmatic data binding we can use the `DataManager` class that we designed in Chapter 1. Note that we would use this class for programmatic data binding for this and the other list controls that we would cover in this chapter.

To bind data to the ListBox control programmatically, we need to set the `DataTextField` and the `DataValueField` properties appropriately and then make a call to the `DataBind()` method shown as follows:

```
protected void Page_Load(object sender, EventArgs e)
    {
        if (!IsPostBack)
        {
            DataManager dataManager = new DataManager();
            listBox.DataSource = dataManager.GetDataFromArrayList();
            listBox.DataValueField = "EmpCode";
            listBox.DataTextField = "EmpName";
            listBox.DataBind();
        }
    }
```

The `DataTextField` property is used to retrieve the contents of the Text property of the control, whereas the `DataValueField` property is used to retrieve the contents of the Value property of the control. Note that the Text property contains text which is what is displayed in the web page and a Value property which is in the HTML.

> Value is a unique value of an item in any list control. Text is the value which is actually displayed in an item of the control. Moreover, you can have duplicate Text values.

Handling ListBox Control Events

The `SelectedIndexChanged` event in the ListBox class is fired whenever the `SelectedIndex` in the ListBox changes as and when your web page postbacks to the Web Server. The following code snippet shows how this event can be used:

```
private void lstBox_SelectedIndexChanged(object sender,
 System.EventArgs e)
{
   //Usual Code
}
```

Working with the DropDown List Control

The DropDownList control in ASP.NET consists of a list of options or data items that allows the user to choose a data item. Hence, unlike the ListBox control, the DropDownList control allows you to select one data item only, at a time. These selectable data items are actually referred to as a List Item.

> Note that, like the ListBox control, you can bind data to this control either manually or by writing code.

Similar to the ListBox control, you can use the Add(), Insert(), RemoveAt(), and Clear() methods of the Items collection of the DropDownList control to programmatically Add, Insert, Edit or Remove the list items. You can get the number of items in the items collection, that is, the count of the list items in the control using the count property.

The list items in a DropDownList control, as in a ListBox control, are indexed with index 0 as the starting index. You can get the index of the selected item from the DropDownList control using the SelectedIndex property of this control. The SelectedValue or SelectedItem.Value properties can be used to retrieve the value of the selected List Item. The text of the selected list item can be retrieved using the SelectedItem.Text property of the control. Note that once a web page is posted back, the first index of this control is selected by default.

To start working with a DropDownList control, drag and drop a control from the toolbox into your web form.

Appending List Items to the DropDownList Control

The following figure shows how a DropDownList control looks like when it is bound with data. Note that by default, the selected index of the DropDownList control is 0, that is, the first list item in the control is selected.

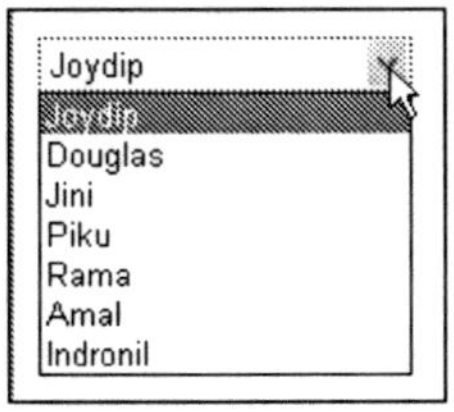

This section discusses how we can add list items to a DropDownList control. You populate data in a DropDownList control using the list items. You can add the list items through the .aspx page as shown in the following code snippet:

```
<asp:DropDownList ID="ddlEmployee" runat="server" Width="147px">
        <asp:ListItem Value="1">Joydip</asp:ListItem>
        <asp:ListItem Value="2">Douglas</asp:ListItem>
        <asp:ListItem Value="3">Jini</asp:ListItem>
        <asp:ListItem Value="4">Piku</asp:ListItem>
        <asp:ListItem Value="5">Rama</asp:ListItem>
        <asp:ListItem Value="6">Amal</asp:ListItem>
        <asp:ListItem Value="7">Indronil</asp:ListItem>
</asp:DropDownList>
```

Similar to the ListBox control, you can also add list items to the DropDownList control using the `Add()` method. This method accepts an object as a parameter and adds it to the Items collection of the control. Refer to the following code snippet which illustrates how this can be accomplished.

```
protected void Page_Load(object sender, EventArgs e)
{
  if (!Page.IsPostBack)
  {
    ddlEmployee.Items.Add("Joydip");
    ddlEmployee.Items.Add("Douglas");
    ddlEmployee.Items.Add("Jini");
    ddlEmployee.Items.Add("Piku");
    ddlEmployee.Items.Add("Rama");
    ddlEmployee.Items.Add("Amal");
    ddlEmployee.Items.Add("Indronil");
  }
}
```

Alternatively, you can also add `ListItems` to a DropDownList control and set a Value field to each of these items added. Following is the code that shows you how to do this.

```
protected void Page_Load(object sender, EventArgs e)
{
  if (!Page.IsPostBack)
  {
    ddlEmployee.Items.Add(new ListItem("Record 1","Joydip"));
    ddlEmployee.Items.Add(new ListItem("Record 2","Douglas"));
    ddlEmployee.Items.Add(new ListItem("Record 3","Jini"));
    ddlEmployee.Items.Add(new ListItem("Record 4","Piku"));
```

```
        ddlEmployee.Items.Add(new ListItem("Record 5","Rama"));
        ddlEmployee.Items.Add(new ListItem("Record 6","Amal"));
        ddlEmployee.Items.Add(new ListItem("Record 7","Indronil"));
    }
}
```

Selecting a List Item

The SelectedItem.Text property of the DropDownList control would give you the text of the selected list item. The following code snippet illustrates how you can display the selected text from a DropDownList control in a Label control on your web form.

```
protected void Button1_Click(object sender, EventArgs e)
    {
        lblEmployeeName.Text = ddlEmployee.SelectedItem.Text;
    }
```

You can select any `ListItem` in the DropDownList by its `Text` or by its `Value` property. The following code snippets illustrate how you can do this.

```
ddlEmployee.SelectedIndex = ddlEmployee.Items.
  IndexOf(ddlEmployee.Items.FindByText("Joydip"));
```

or

```
ddlEmployee.SelectedIndex = ddlEmployee.Items.
  IndexOf(ddlEmployee.Items.FindByValue("Record 1"));
```

You might require adding an extra ListItem to a DropDownList control and displaying a custom message similar to, "--Click to Select--". In such situations, the ListItem added should be the first one among the other ListItems in the DropDownList control. In other words, the ListIndex for such a ListItem should be typically be zero.

The following code shows how you can accomplish this:

```
dropDownList.Items.Add("--Click to Select--");
```

Removing List Items from the DropDownList Control

To remove a specific list item from the list item collection of the DropDownList control, use the `RemoveAt()` method of the Items collection property of the control as shown in the following code snippet:

```
DropDownList1.Items.RemoveAt(0);
```

To remove all the list items from the DropDownList control, use the following code:

```
DropDownList1.Items.Clear();
```

Here, `DropDownList1` is the name of the DropDownList control.

Binding Data to the DropDownList Control

Like the ListBox control, you can bind data to the DropDownList control in either of the following ways:

- Declarative
- Programmatic

We have already discussed how we can bind static data to the DropDownList control declaratively through the `.aspx` page.

For programmatic data binding we can use the `DataManager` class that we designed in the Chapter 1. To bind data to the DropDownList control programmatically, we need to set the `DataTextField` and the `DataValueField` properties appropriately and then make a call to the `DataBind()` method shown as follows:

```
protected void Page_Load(Object sender, EventArgs e)
{
  if (!IsPostBack)
  {
     DataManager dataManager = new DataManager();
     DropDownList1.DataSource = dataManager.GetDataFromArrayList();
     DropDownList1.DataValueField = "EmpCode";
     DropDownList1.DataTextField = "EmpName";
     DropDownList1.DataBind();
   }
}
```

Handling DropDownList Control Events

The `SelectedIndexChanged` event in the **DropDownList** class is executed whenever the index of the selected item, that is the, `SelectedIndex` property in the **DropDownList**, changes. The following code snippet illustrates how this event can be used.

```
private void dropDownList_SelectedIndexChanged(object sender, System.
EventArgs e)
 {
//Custom code to handle the event
 }
```

The section that follows illustrates how you can handle events when working with the DropDownList control.

Associating Event Handlers to a dynamically generated DropDownList Control

What happens when you want to associate event handler to a dynamically generated **DropDownList Control**, that is, a **DropDownList Control** that has been created at run time rather than at design time and the ListItems of it have been populated dynamically.

Let us first have a look at the output once you execute the application. The following is the screenshot of what we actually are looking for:

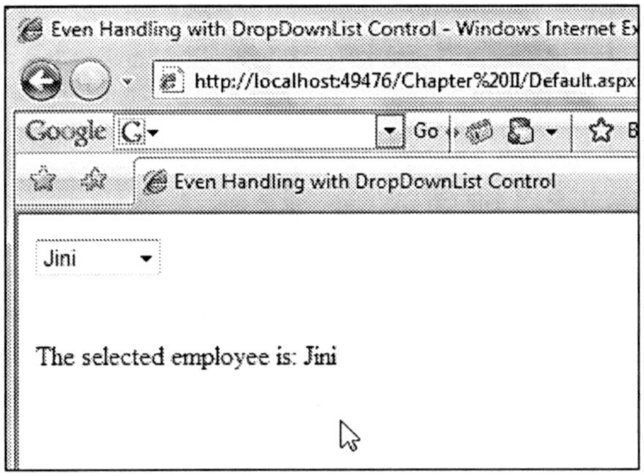

Once you select any of the List Items in the DropDownList control displayed in the screen shot above, an event handler is fired and the selected employee's name is displayed in a TextBox control just beneath the DropDownList.

Simple, just take a `PlaceHolder` to store your dynamically created DropDownList control. Next, add the List Items using the `Add()` method of the `Items` collection of the control. Finally, associate the event handler. That's it!

Following is the code that shows how to accomplish this task:

```
public partial class _Default : System.Web.UI.Page
{
    DropDownList ddlEmployee = null;
    protected void Page_Load(object sender, EventArgs e)
    {
        ddlEmployee = new DropDownList();
        ddlEmployee.Items.Add(new ListItem("Joydip","Record 1"));
```

```
        ddlEmployee.Items.Add(new ListItem("Douglas","Record 2"));
        ddlEmployee.Items.Add(new ListItem("Jini","Record 3"));
        ddlEmployee.Items.Add(new ListItem("Piku","Record 4"));
        ddlEmployee.Items.Add(new ListItem("Rama","Record 5"));
        ddlEmployee.Items.Add(new ListItem("Amal","Record 6"));
        ddlEmployee.Items.Add(new ListItem("Indronil","Record 7"));
        ddlEmployee.AutoPostBack = true;
        ddlEmployee.SelectedIndexChanged += new
          EventHandler(ddlEmployee_SelectedIndexChanged);
        PlaceHolder1.Controls.Add(ddlEmployee);
    }
    protected void ddlEmployee_SelectedIndexChanged(object sender,
      EventArgs e)
    {
        lblDisplay.Text = "The selected employee is: " +
         ddlEmployee.SelectedItem.Text;
    }
}
```

Following is the code in your `.aspx` file:

```
<form id="form1" runat="server">
     <div>
       <asp:PlaceHolder ID="PlaceHolder1"
         runat="server"></asp:PlaceHolder>
       <br /><br /><br /><asp:Label ID="lblDisplay" runat="server"
         Text=""></asp:Label>
   </div>
    </form>
```

Implementing a Simple Application

The following example makes use of the concepts learnt so far to implement a simple application. The application contains a ListBox, DropDownList control, TextBox and two Button controls that can **Add** and **Remove** list items from the ListBox control at runtime. While the **Add** button can be used to add the text typed in the TextBox control to the ListBox, the **Remove** button can be used to remove the list item that is selected from the ListBox. The **SelectionMode** property of the ListBox control can be set using the DropDownList control that displays Single and Multiple as the possible selection modes.

The output of the sample application is shown as follows:

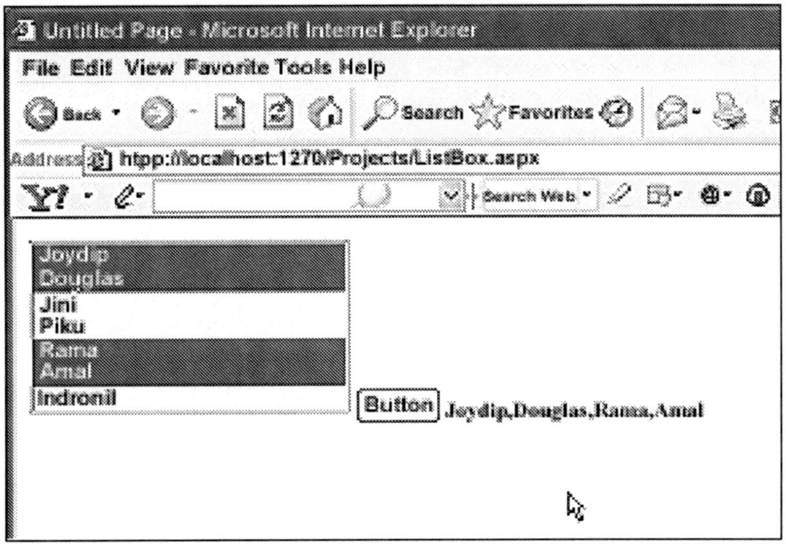

The source code for this simple application is given as follows:

```
public partial class ListBox : System.Web.UI.Page
{
    protected void Page_Load(object sender, EventArgs e)
    {
        if (!IsPostBack)
        {
            DropDownList1.Items.Add("Single");
            DropDownList1.Items.Add("Multiple");
            DropDownList1.SelectedIndex = 0;
            ListBox1.Items.Add("Joydip");
            ListBox1.Items.Add("Douglas");
            ListBox1.Items.Add("Jini");
            ListBox1.Items.Add("Piku");
            ListBox1.Items.Add("Rama");
            ListBox1.Items.Add("Amal");
            ListBox1.Items.Add("Indronil");
            ListBox1.SelectionMode = ListSelectionMode.Single;
        }
    }
    protected void DropDownList1_SelectedIndexChanged(object sender,
      EventArgs e)
    {
```

```
            if (DropDownList1.SelectedIndex == 0)
                ListBox1.SelectionMode = ListSelectionMode.Single;
            else
                ListBox1.SelectionMode = ListSelectionMode.Multiple;
        }
        protected void Add_Click(object sender, EventArgs e)
        {
            ListBox1.Items.Add(TextBox1.Text);
        }
        protected void Remove_Click(object sender, EventArgs e)
        {
            ListBox1.Items.RemoveAt(ListBox1.SelectedIndex);
        }
    }
```

Working with the CheckBoxList Control

The CheckBoxList control consists of a group of check boxes that actually provides a multi-selection checkbox with the capability of selecting one or more items from the list of items. Compared to the CheckBox control, a CheckBoxList control is a preferred choice in cases where you might require creation of a series of check boxes and populate them with data from a data store like, a database table, an Xml file or even a web service that fetches data.

Appending List Items to the CheckBoxList Control

The following figure shows how a **CheckBoxList** control looks like at runtime when it is bound with data.

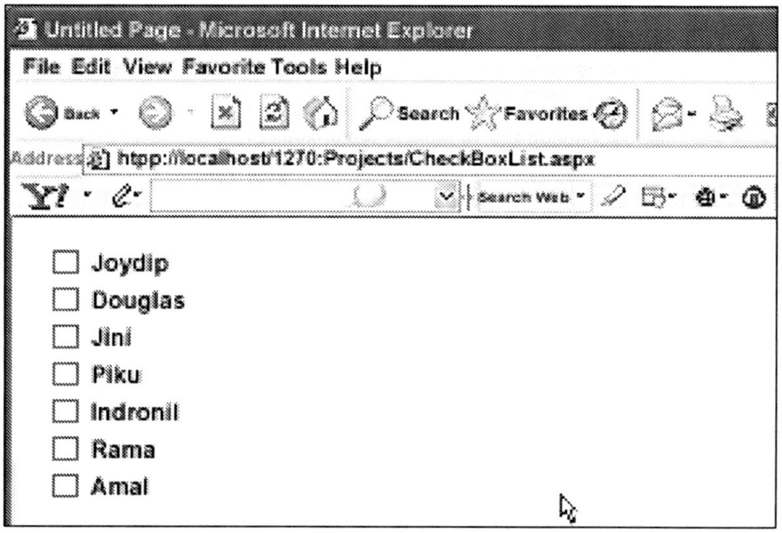

This section discusses how you can accomplish the above, that is, add list items to the CheckBoxList control. You can create a CheckBoxList control and add static data to it using list items as shown in the following code snippet:

```
<asp:checkboxlist id="dept" runat="server">
  <asp:listitem id="1" runat="server" value="IT" />
  <asp:listitem id="2" runat="server" value="Sales" />
  <asp:listitem id="3" runat="server" value="Admin" />
  <asp:listitem id="4" runat="server" value="HR" />
</asp:checkboxlist>
```

You can also add items to the `CheckBoxList` control programmatically. Refer to the following code snippet:

```
protected void Page_Load(object sender, EventArgs e)
    {
        if (!IsPostBack)
        {
            CheckBoxList1.AutoPostBack = true;
            CheckBoxList1.RepeatColumns = 1;
            CheckBoxList1.RepeatDirection = RepeatDirection.Vertical;
            CheckBoxList1.RepeatLayout = RepeatLayout.Flow;
            CheckBoxList1.TextAlign = TextAlign.Right;
            CheckBoxList1.Items.Add(new ListItem("Joydip"));
            CheckBoxList1.Items.Add(new ListItem("Douglas"));
            CheckBoxList1.Items.Add(new ListItem("Jini"));
            CheckBoxList1.Items.Add(new ListItem("Piku"));
            CheckBoxList1.Items.Add(new ListItem("Indronil"));
            CheckBoxList1.Items.Add(new ListItem("Rama"));
            CheckBoxList1.Items.Add(new ListItem("Amal"));
        }
    }
```

Selecting One or More List Items

You can find out which item in this list has been selected by iterating through the items collection of this control. The following code snippet illustrates how you can retrieve the list items that have been selected from `CheckBoxList` control called dept by iterating through and checking the `Selected` property of each list item.

```
string message = String.Empty;
for(int i=0; i<dept.Items.COunt;i++)
{
  if(dept.Items[i].Selected)
     message += dept.Items[0].Text + <br/>;
}
lblDept.Text = message;
```

Note that the `CheckBoxList` class does not contain a SelectedItems property. How about implementing a Custom CheckBoxList control that contains a `SelectedItems` property that can be used to select one or more list items from the control? We will design and implement a Custom CheckBoxList control to accomplish this later in this chapter.

Removing List Items from the CheckBoxList Control

To remove a specific list item from the list item collection of the CheckBoxList control, use the `RemoveAt()` method of the `Items` collection property of the control as shown in the following code snippet:

```
CheckBoxList1.Items.RemoveAt(0);
```

To remove all the list items from the **CheckBoxList** control, use the following code:

```
CheckBoxList1.Items.Clear();
```

Here, `CheckBoxList1` is the name of the CheckBoxList control.

Binding Data to the CheckBoxList Control

Like the ListBox control, you can bind data to the CheckBoxList control in either of the following ways:

- Declarative
- Programmatic

We have already discussed how we can bind data to this control declaratively. For programmatic data binding to the CheckBoxList control you have to use a valid data source and the `DataBind()` method. As usual, you need to specify the `DataTextField` and the `DataValueField` properties to specify the Text and Value properties of each of the list items in the control. You can also set the `Checked` property of the all the CheckBox controls in the list to either true or false programmatically. When a `Checked` property of any of the CheckBox controls in this list is set to true, the control is checked, that is, a check-mark appears in the control. When the same property is false, the control is unchecked.

We have already discussed how we can bind static data to the CheckBoxList control declaratively through the `.aspx` page.

The following code snippet illustrates how you can bind data to this with data from an external data source programmatically.

```
protected void Page_Load(Object sender, EventArgs e)
{
  if (!IsPostBack)
  {
    DataManager dataManager = new DataManager();
    checkBoxList.DataSource = dataManager.GetDataFromArrayList();
    checkBoxList.DataTextField="EmpName";
    checkBoxList.DataValueField="EmpCode";
    checkBoxList.DataBind();
  }
}
```

Handling CheckBoxList Control Events

The `SelectedIndexChanged` event of the CheckBoxList control is fired whenever you select any check box in the list, that is, the SelectedIndex of the control changes. The following code snippet shows how this event can be used for this control:

```
private void checkBoxList_SelectedIndexChanged(object sender,
 System.EventArgs e)
{
//Custom code to handle this event
}
```

In the section that follows, we will take a look at how we can handle events with a CustomCheckBoxList control that we will implement by extending the `CheckBoxList` control.

Implementing a CustomCheckBoxList Control

In this section, we will learn how to design and implement a CustomCheckBoxList control that will enable you to retrieve the values and texts of a multi selection CheckBoxList control. We will implement a `CustomCheckBoxList` class that will contain a `SelectedItems` property. This property returns a collection of items, which are the selected items—it just goes through the list of items and adds the selected ones to its list.

This control will extend the CheckBoxList control and attach this functionality to it. Added to methods and properties of the CheckBoxList class that it automatically inherits on virtue of inheritance, it has two new methods, that is, the `GetCheckedItemValues()` and the `GetCheckedItemText()` methods.

Method `GetCheckedItemValues` is used to return a string array containing all the item values that are checked. Following is the code for this method:

```
public string[] GetCheckedItemValues()
{
      string _selectedValues = String.Empty;
      foreach (System.Web.UI.WebControls.ListItem LI in this.Items)
      {
      if (LI.Selected)
      {
                if (_selectedValues.Equals(String.Empty))
                   _selectedValues = LI.Value;
                else
             _selectedValues = _selectedValues + "," + LI.Value;
      }
      }
      _checkedItemList = _selectedValues.Split(',');
     return _checkedItemList;
 }
```

This method uses a loop on all the items in the current `CheckBoxList` control and finds the items that have been checked. For Items that have been checked, the values of the `Value` property are collected into a string array. This array is then returned back.

The method `GetCheckedItemText()` returns all the `Text` values in a string array. The code for this method is same as the above except that `Text` values are collected into the array instead of the values of the `Value` property. The code snippet for this method is as follows:

```
public string[] GetCheckedItemText()
{
string _selectedText = String.Empty;
foreach (System.Web.UI.WebControls.ListItem LI in this.Items)
      {
            if (LI.Selected)
            {
                if (_selectedText.Equals(String.Empty))
                      _selectedText = LI.Text;
                    else
                      _selectedText = _selectedText + "," + LI.Text;
            }
      }
      _checkedItemList = _selectedText.Split(',');
      return _checkedItemList;
}
```

Let us take a look at how to use this control.

Once the CustomCheckBoxList control is built, you can find it in the toolbox. Just drag it on to the design view mode or you can go to the source view and key in. By dragging the control, it is automatically registered onto the page. You can also register it by writing the following code in your .aspx file:

```
<%@ Register TagPrefix="Sample" Namespace="Samples.Controls"%>
```

Now either add the items from the Design View or bind the data from the database. This is a sample, therefore just added the items from the source view.

```
<Sample:CustomCheckBoxList ID="checkBoxList" runat="server">
            <asp:ListItem Value="0">Sunday</asp:ListItem>
            <asp:ListItem Value="1">Monday</asp:ListItem>
            <asp:ListItem Value="2">Tuesday</asp:ListItem>
            <asp:ListItem Value="3">Wednesday</asp:ListItem>
            <asp:ListItem Value="4">Thursday</asp:ListItem>
            <asp:ListItem Value="5">Friday</asp:ListItem>
            <asp:ListItem Value="6">Saturday</asp:ListItem>
</Sample:CustomCheckBoxList>
```

Following is a view of the CustomCheckBoxList control in design view mode.

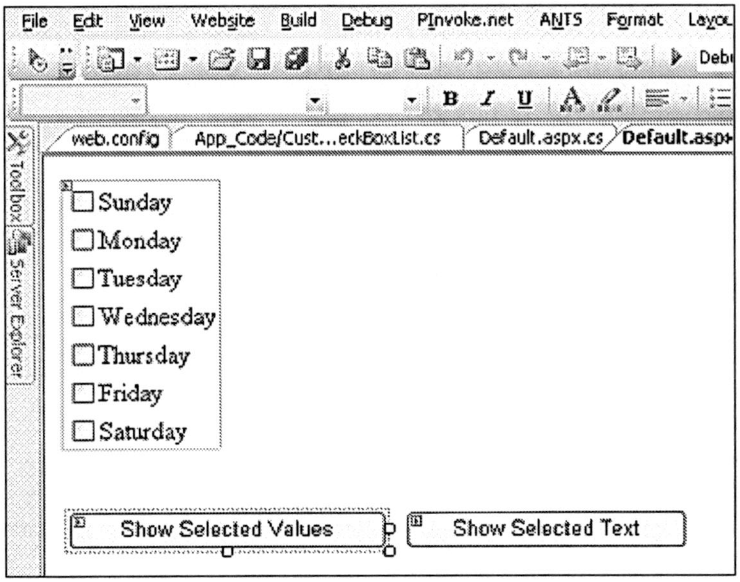

We have two buttons **Show Selected Values** and **Show Selected Text**. When you click on any of these **Button** controls, the respective event handlers of these controls will be invoked.

Let us have a look at the event handlers of these two buttons.

```
protected void btnValues_Click(object sender, EventArgs e)
    {
        string[] checkedItems = checkBoxList.GetCheckedItemValues();
        string printString = "The Selected Values are : <br>";
        foreach (string strSelect in checkedItems)
        {
            printString += strSelect + "<br>";
        }
        Response.Write(printString);
    }

    protected void btnText_Click(object sender, EventArgs e)
    {
        string[] checkedItems = checkBoxList.GetCheckedItemText();
        string printString = "The Selected Text : <br>";
        foreach (string strSelect in checkedItems)
        {
            printString += strSelect + "<br>";
        }
        Response.Write(printString);
    }
```

These event handlers just call the methods of the CustomCheckBoxList control. The `string` array returned is just concatenated in a string by iterating in a loop and displaying it to the user.

Working with the BulletedList Control

The BulletedList control in ASP.NET contains a collection of bulleted list items that are arranged in ordered or unordered fashion. The list items can be any one of the following:

- Text
- Hyperlink
- Link Buttons

You can bind any number of these list items to this control either through your `.aspx` page or using any external data source.

[Note that if you want to make the list items in the BulletedList control either HyperLink or LinkButton type, you need to specify this mode using the DisplayMode property of the control.]

Similarly, you can change the style of the BulletedList control by specifying your required style through the BulletStyle property of the control. These bullet styles can be one of the following:

- NotSet
- Numbered
- CustomImage
- Disc
- Circle
- Square
- LowerAlpha
- UpperAlpha
- LowerRoman
- UpperRoman
- UpperAlpha

Appending List Items to the BulletedList Control

The following figure displays how the BulletedList control looks like when it is bound with data.

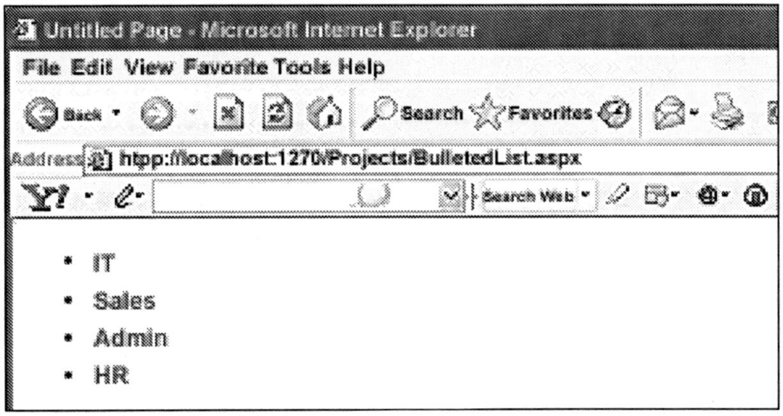

We will now discuss how we can add list items to this control. Refer to the following code snippet that illustrates how such a control can be constructed from your `.aspx` page to display a list of static list items.

```
<asp:BulletedList ID="bListDept" DisplayMode="LinkButton"
runat="server" OnClick="bListDept_Click">
        <asp:listitem Selected = "True" text = "IT" value="IT" />
        <asp:listitem text = "Sales" value="Sales" />
        <asp:listitem text= "Admin" value="Admin" />
        <asp:listitem text = "HR" value="HR" />
</asp:BulletedList>
```

The above code snippet illustrates how the BulletedList control named `bListDept` can be declared in your `.aspx` web page in ASP.NET. Note that the `Selected` property of the control is used to set the default selected list item from among the collection of list items in the control.

You can also add list items to this control programmatically. Following is the code:

```
protected void Page_Load(object sender, EventArgs e)
    {
        if (!IsPostBack)
        {
            bListDept.Items.Add(new ListItem("IT"));
            bListDept.Items.Add(new ListItem("Sales"));
            bListDept.Items.Add(new ListItem("Admin"));
            bListDept.Items.Add(new ListItem("HR"));
            bListDept.Items[0].Selected = true;
        }
    }
```

Selecting a List Item

Drag-and-drop a Label control onto your web form. In the `Click` event of the BulletedList control, write the following code to retrieve the text of the selected list item in the control.

```
protected void bListDept_Click(object sender, BulletedListEventArgs
 e)
{
Label1.Text = "You have clicked: "+bListDept.Items[e.Index].Text;
}
```

Removing List Items from the BulletedList Control

To remove a specific list item from the list item collection of the BulletedList control, use the `RemoveAt()` method of the Items collection property of the control, as shown in the following code snippet:

```
BulletedList1.Items.RemoveAt(0);
```

To remove all the list items from the BulletedList control, use the following code:

```
BulletedList1.Items.Clear();
```

Here, `BulletedList1` is the name of the BulletedList control.

Binding Data to the BulletedList Control

Like the earlier list controls, you can bind data to the BulletedList control in either of the following ways:

- Declarative
- Programmatic

We have already seen how we can bind static data to this control declaratively through the `.aspx` file. This section discusses how you can bind data to this control programmatically.

You can bind data to the BulletedList control using a valid data source and the `DataBind()` method. Like the other list controls that we have already discussed, you need to specify the `DataTextField` and the `DataValueField` properties to specify the Text and Value properties of each of the list items in the control.

The following code snippet shows how you can bind data to this control with data from an external data source:

```
protected void Page_Load(Object sender, EventArgs e)
{
  if (!IsPostBack)
  {
    DataManager dataManager = new DataManager();
    bulletedList.DataSource = dataManager.GetDataFromArrayList();
    bulletedList.DataTextField="EmpName";
    bulletedList.DataValueField="EmpCode";
    bulletedList.DataBind();
  }
}
```

Handling BulletedList Control Events

The `SelectedIndexChanged` event of the BulletedList control is fired whenever you click on any list item in the control. The following code snippet shows how you can use this event in your applications.

```
private void bulletedList_SelectedIndexChanged(object sender,
 System.EventArgs e)
{
//Usual code to handle the event
}
```

Working with the RadioButtonList Control

The RadioButtonList control in ASP.NET is used to display a collection of radio buttons that provide the user a multiple set of choices to choose from. You can select any one of the radio buttons from this list of radio buttons. You can bind data statically or programmatically to this control. The SelectedItem property of this control can be used to retrieve the radio button that has been selected.

Appending List Items to the RadioButtonList Control

The following figure displays the RadioButtonList control bound with data.

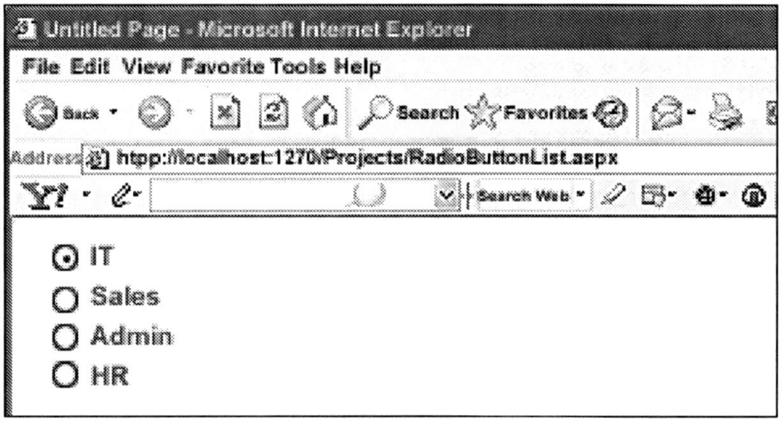

Note that the first list item, that is, the list item at index 0 is selected. This section would discuss how we can add list items to this control.

The following code snippet illustrates how you can create a `RadioButtonList` control in your `.aspx` page populated with list items that contain static data:

```
<asp:RadioButtonList ID="rbListDept" runat="server">
        <asp:listitem Selected = "True" text = "IT" value="IT" />
        <asp:listitem text = "Sales" value="Sales" />
        <asp:listitem text= "Admin" value="Admin" />
        <asp:listitem text = "HR" value="HR" />
</asp:RadioButtonList>
```

Note that the `Selected` property of the control is used to set the default selected list item from among the collection of list items in the control.

You can also append the list items programmatically. Refer to the following code snippet given:

```
protected void Page_Load(object sender, EventArgs e)
    {
        if (!IsPostBack)
        {
            rbListDept.Items.Add(new ListItem("IT"));
            rbListDept.Items.Add(new ListItem("Sales"));
            rbListDept.Items.Add(new ListItem("Admin"));
            rbListDept.Items.Add(new ListItem("HR"));
            rbListDept.Items[0].Selected = true;
        }
    }
```

Selecting a List Item

Drag-and-drop a button and a Label control onto your web form. In the `Click` event of the Button control, write the following code to retrieve the text of the selected list item in the RadioButtonList control.

```
protected void Button1_Click(object sender, EventArgs e)
 {
Label1.Text = "You selected: " + rbListDept.SelectedItem.Text;
 }
```

Removing List Items from the RadioButtonList Control

To remove a specific list item from the list item collection of the RadioButtonList control, use the `RemoveAt()` method of the Items collection property of the control as shown in the following code snippet:

```
RadioButtonList1.Items.RemoveAt(0);
```

To remove all the list items from the RadioButtonList control, use the following code:

```
RadioButtonList1.Items.Clear();
```

Here, `RadioButtonList1` is the name of the RadioButtonList control.

Binding Data to the RadioButtonList Control

We already have had a look at how we can bind static data to this control declaratively. This section discusses how we can bind data to this control programmatically.

You can bind data to the RadioButtonList control using a valid data source and the `DataBind()` method. Like the other list controls that we have already discussed, you need to specify the `DataTextField` and the `DataValueField` properties to specify the `Text` and `Value` properties of each of the list items in the control.

The following code snippet shows how you can bind data to this control with data from an external data source:

```
protected void Page_Load(Object sender, EventArgs e)
{
  if (!IsPostBack)
  {
    DataManager dataManager = new DataManager();
    radioButtonList.DataSource = dataManager.GetDataFromArrayList();
    radioButtonList.DataTextField="EmpName";
    radioButtonList.DataValueField="EmpCode";
    radioButtonList.DataBind();
  }
}
```

Handling RadioButtonList Control Events

The `SelectedIndexChanged` event of the RadioButtonList control is fired whenever you click on any of the list items in the control. The following code snippet shows how this event can be used in your applications.

```
private void rButtonList_SelectedIndexChanged(object sender,
 System.EventArgs e)
{
//Custom code to handle the event
}
```

Summary

This chapter has had a detailed look at the various list controls available in ASP.NET and how we can Add, Remove and Select list items from each of these controls with sample code examples wherever appropriate. I have also demonstrated how to design and implement a `CustomCheckBoxList` class in this chapter. We will discuss the Repeater control and how we can use it to perform various CRUD operations with it in the next chapter. We will also discuss when and why we will choose a Repeater control in place of a DataGrid control in our applications.

3

Working with the Repeater Control

In Chapter 2, we looked at the List controls in ASP.NET and how we can use these controls to bind and display data in our applications. We discussed how we can add, display, select and delete the items of each of the List controls and how to handle events when working with them. We also looked at how we can implement a Custom List control.

In this chapter we will discuss how we can use the Repeater control in ASP.NET. Both Repeater and DataList controls in ASP.NET allow you to display data quickly, and both support only templates for displaying data. We will discuss the DataList and the other related data-bound controls in the forthcoming chapters of the book.

In this chapter, we will cover the ASP.NET Repeater control. We will learn about:

- Using the Repeater control
- Display data using the Repeater control
- Paging, sorting, and filtering data
- Handling Repeater control events

The ASP.NET Repeater Control

The Repeater control in ASP.NET is a data-bound container control that can be used to automate the display of a collection of repeated list items. These items can be bound to either of the following data sources:

- Database Table
- XML File

In a Repeater control, the data is rendered as DataItems that are defined using one or more templates. You can even use HTML tags such as `<li>`, `<ul>`, or `<div>` if required. Similar to the DataGrid, DataList, or GridView controls (we try each of these controls in detail in Chapters 4 and 5), the Repeater control has a DataSource property that is used to set the DataSource of this control to any ICollection, IEnumerable, or IListSource instance. Once this is set, the data from one of these types of data sources can be easily bound to the Repeater control using its `DataBind()` method.

However, the Repeater control by itself does not support paging or editing of data. Unlike the DataGrid control that will be covered in Chapter 5 of this book, the Repeater control is light weight and does not contain so many features as the former contains. However, it enables you to place HTML code in its templates. We will learn what templates in a Repeater control are. It is great in situations where you need to display the data quickly and format the data to be displayed easily. We will be covering the DataGrid control later in this book.

Using the Repeater Control

The Repeater control is a data-bound control that uses templates to display data. It does not have any built-in support for paging, editing, or sorting of the data that is rendered through one or more of its templates. The Repeater control works by looping through the records in your data source and then repeating the rendering of one of its templates called the ItemTemplate, one that contains the records that the control needs to render. We will learn more about the templates of the Repeater control in this section. Before we learn about the templates and how to use them, let us take a look at how we can get started with this control.

To use this control, drag and drop the control in the design view of the web form onto a web form from the toolbox. Refer to the following screenshot:

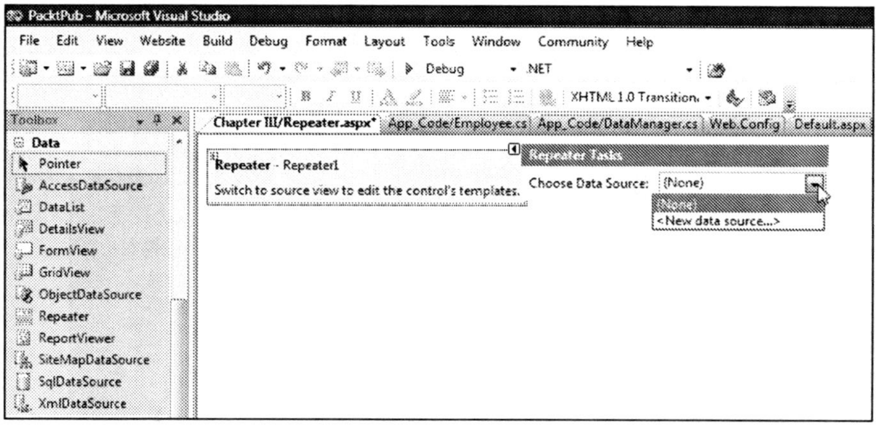

You can also drag and drop the **Repeater** control from the toolbox onto the source view directly. This is shown in the following screenshot:

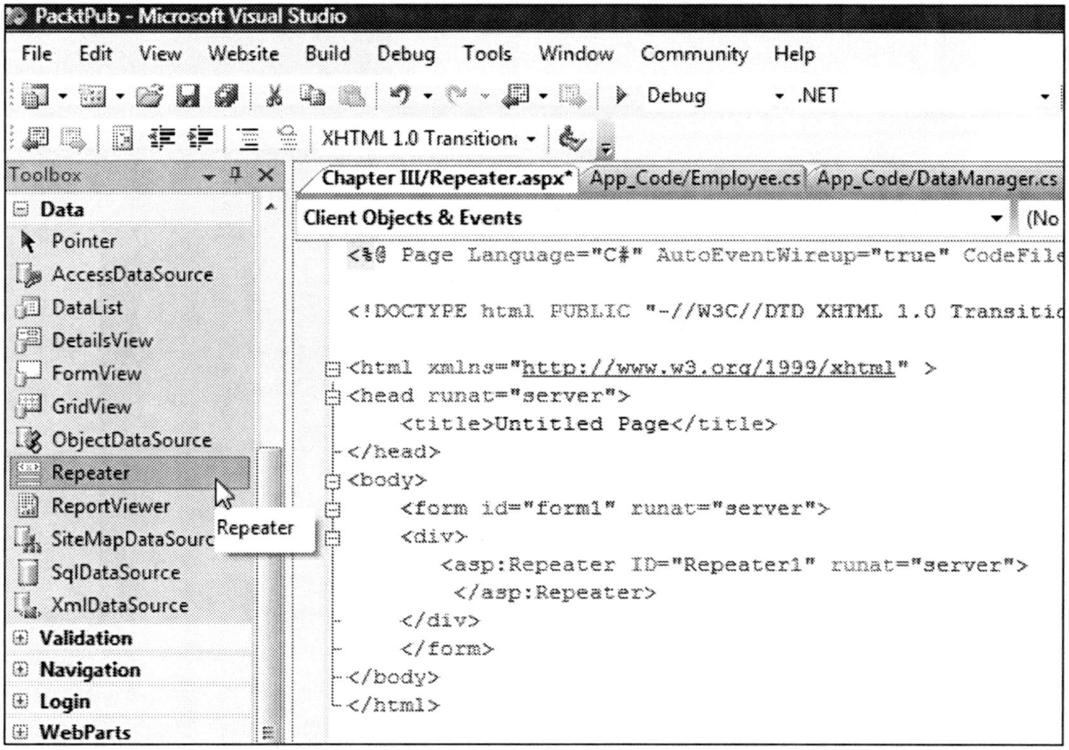

For customizing the behavior of this control, you have to use the built-in templates that this control comes with. These templates are actually blocks of HTML code. The Repeater control contains the following five templates:

1. HeaderTemplate
2. ItemTemplate
3. AlternatingItemTemplate
4. SeparatorTemplate
5. FooterTemplate

The following screenshot shows how a Repeater control looks when populated with data.

Employee Code	Employee Name	Employee Salary	Department Name
3	Joydip	2000	IT
4	Douglas	75000	IT
5	Jini	15500	MKTG
6	Rama	18500	HR
7	Amal	22000	FINANCE
8	Piku	9000	PERSONNEL
9	Indronil	19000	MKTG
27	Bapila	32500	FINANCE
Total Records: 8			

Note that the templates (Header, Item, Footer, Alternate and Separator) have all been used.

The following code snippet is an example of the order in which the templates of the `Repeater` control are used.

```
<asp:Repeater id="repEmployee" runat="server">
<HeaderTemplate>
...
</HeaderTemplate>
<ItemTemplate>
</ItemTemplate>
<FooterTemplate>
...
</FooterTemplate>
</asp:Repeater>
```

When the `Repeater` control is bound to a data source, the data from the data source is displayed using the `ItemTemplate` element and any other optional elements, if used. Note that the contents of the `HeaderTemplate` and the `FooterTemplate` are rendered once for each Repeater control. The contents of the `ItemTemplate` are rendered for each record in the control.

You can also use the additional `AlternatingItemTemplate` element after the `ItemTemplate` element for specifying the appearance of each alternate record. You can also use the `SeparatorTemplate` element between each record for specifying the separators for the records.

Displaying Data Using the Repeater Control

This section discusses how we can display data using the Repeater control. As discussed earlier, the Repeater control uses templates for formatting the data that it displays. The following code snippet displays the code in an `.aspx` file that contains a Repeater control.

> Note that we would be making use of templates and that the data would be bound to the control from the code-behind file using the `DataManager` class.

```
<asp:Repeater ID="Repeater1" runat="server">
  <HeaderTemplate>
    <table border="1">
      <tr>
        <th>
          <asp:Label id="Emp_Code" Text="Employee Code"
            runat="server" /></th>
        <th>
          <asp:Label id="Emp_Name" Text="Employee Name"
            runat="server" /></th>
        <th>
          <asp:Label id="Emp_Salary" Text="Employee Salary"
            runat="server" /></th>
        <th>
         <asp:Label id="Dept_Code" Text="Department Name"
            runat="server" /> </th>
      </tr>
  </HeaderTemplate>
  <ItemTemplate>
    <tr bgcolor="#0xbbcc">
      <td>
        <%# DataBinder.Eval(Container.DataItem, "EmpCode")%>
      </td>
      <td>
        <%# DataBinder.Eval(Container.DataItem, "EmpName")%>
```

```
        </td>
        <td>
          <%# DataBinder.Eval(Container.DataItem, "Salary")%>
        </td>
        <td>
          <%# DataBinder.Eval(Container.DataItem, "DeptName")%>
        </td>
      </tr>
    </ItemTemplate>
    <SeparatorTemplate>
      <tr bgcolor="#ffbbcc">
        <td>
          <hr>
        </td>
        <td>
          <hr>
        </td>
        <td>
          <hr>
        </td>
        <td>
          <hr>
        </td>
      </tr>
    </SeparatorTemplate>
    <AlternatingItemTemplate>
      <tr bgcolor=»#ccaabb»>
        <td>
          <%# DataBinder.Eval(Container.DataItem, «EmpCode»)%>
        </td>
        <td>
          <%# DataBinder.Eval(Container.DataItem, «EmpName»)%>
        </td>
        <td>
          <%# DataBinder.Eval(Container.DataItem, «Salary»)%>
        </td>
        <td>
          <%# DataBinder.Eval(Container.DataItem, «DeptName»)%>
        </td>
        </tr>
    </AlternatingItemTemplate>
    <FooterTemplate>
      <table border=»1»>
        <tr bgcolor=»#0xffaa»>
          <td> Total Records: <%#totalRecords%> </td>
        </tr>
      </table>
      </table>
    </FooterTemplate>
  </asp:Repeater>
```

The `Repeater` control is populated with data in the `Page_Load` event by reusing the `DataManager()`, which we used in Chapters 1 and 2 .

```
public int totalRecords;
    protected void Page_Load(object sender, EventArgs e)
    {
      DataManager dataManager = new DataManager();
      Repeater1.DataSource = dataManager.GetEmployees();
      totalRecords = dataManager.GetEmployees().Count;
      Repeater1.DataBind();
    }
```

Note how the `SeparatorTemplate` and the `AlternatingItemTemplate` have been used in the previous code example. Further, the `DataBinder.Eval()` method has been used to display the values of the corresponding fields from the data container, (in our case, the `DataSet` instance) in the `Repeater` control. The `FooterTemplate` uses the `Total Records` variable and substitutes its value to display the total number of records displayed by the control.

The following is the output on execution.

Employee Code	Employee Name	Employee Salary	Department Name
3	Joydip	2000	IT
4	Douglas	75000	IT
5	Jini	15500	MKTG
6	Rama	18500	HR
7	Amal	22000	FINANCE
8	Piku	9000	PERSONNEL
9	Indronil	19000	MKTG
27	Bapila	32500	FINANCE
Total Records: 8			

> The Header and the Footer templates of the Repeater control are still rendered even if the data source does not contain any data. If you want to suppress their display, you can use the `Visible` property of the Repeater control and use it to suppress the display of these templates with a simple logic. Here is how you specify the `Visible` property of this control in your `.aspx` file to achieve this:
>
> ```
> Visible="<%# Repeater1.Items.Count > 0 %>"
> ```
>
> When you specify the `Visible` property as shown here, the Repeater is made visible only if there are records in your data source.

Displaying Checkboxes in a Repeater Control

Let us now understand how we can display checkboxes in a **Repeater Control** and retrieve the number of checked items. We will use a Button control and a Label control in our page. When you click on the Button control, the number of checked items in the **Repeater Control** will be displayed in the Label control. The output on execution is similar to what is shown in the following screenshot:

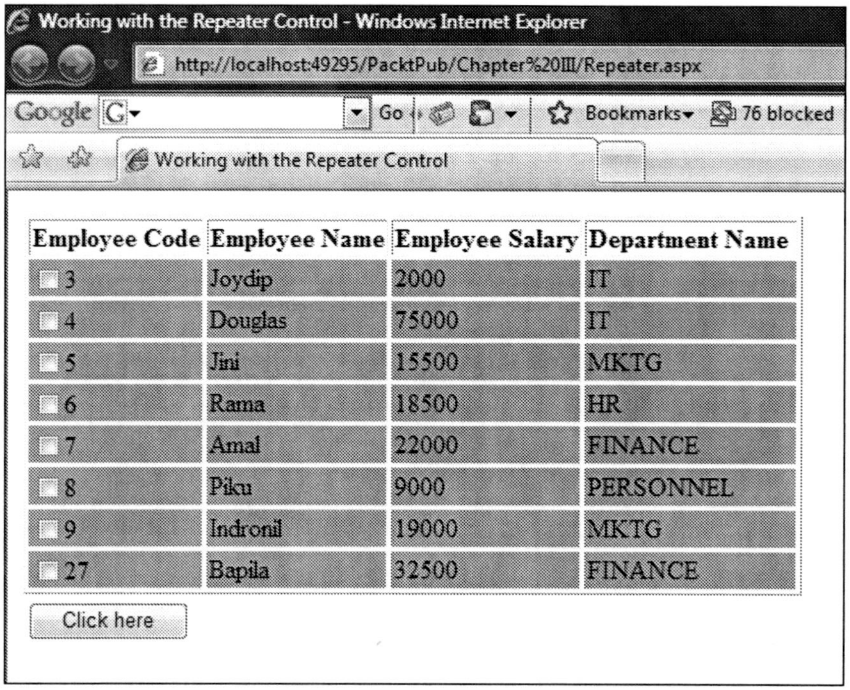

Employee Code	Employee Name	Employee Salary	Department Name
3	Joydip	2000	IT
4	Douglas	75000	IT
5	Jini	15500	MKTG
6	Rama	18500	HR
7	Amal	22000	FINANCE
8	Piku	9000	PERSONNEL
9	Indronil	19000	MKTG
27	Bapila	32500	FINANCE

Here is the code that we will use in the .aspx file to display checkboxes in a Repeater control.

```
<form id="form1" runat="server">
    <asp:Repeater ID="Repeater1" runat="server">
    <HeaderTemplate>
      <table border="1">
        <tr>
           <th>
             <asp:Label id="Emp_Code" Text="Employee Code"
               runat="server" /></th>
           <th>
             <asp:Label id="Emp_Name" Text="Employee Name"
               runat="server" /></th>
           <th>
             <asp:Label id="Emp_Salary" Text="Employee Salary"
               runat="server" /></th>
           <th>
             <asp:Label id="Dept_Code" Text="Department Name"
               runat="server" /> </th>
         </tr>
    </HeaderTemplate>
    <ItemTemplate>
      <tr bgcolor="#0xbbcc">
        <td>
          <asp:CheckBox id="chkbox1" runat="server"
            Checked="false" Text = '<%#
            DataBinder.Eval(Container.DataItem,
            "EmpCode")%>'></asp:CheckBox>
        </td>
        <td>
          <%# DataBinder.Eval(Container.DataItem, "EmpName")%>
        </td>
        <td>
          <%# DataBinder.Eval(Container.DataItem, "Salary")%>
        </td>
        <td>
          <%# DataBinder.Eval(Container.DataItem, "DeptName")%>
        </td>
      </tr>
    </ItemTemplate>
</asp:Repeater>
     <table border="0" width="300px">
      <tr>
```

```
            <td>
              <asp:Button ID="btnClick" runat="server" Width="100px"
               Text="Click here" OnClick="btnClick_Click" /></td>
            <td>
              <asp:Label ID="lblDisplay" runat="server"
                Width="200px"></asp:Label> </td>
          </tr>
    </form>
```

The data is bound to the `Repeater` control in the `Page_Load` event as follows:

```
public int totalRecords;
  protected void Page_Load(object sender, EventArgs e)
  {
    if (!IsPostBack)
    {
      DataManager dataManager = new DataManager();
      Repeater1.DataSource = dataManager.GetEmployees();
      totalRecords = dataManager.GetEmployees().Count;
      Repeater1.DataBind();
    }
  }
```

Note that we have used the `Page.IsPostBack` to check whether the page has posted back in the `Page_Load` method. If you don't bind data by checking whether the page has posted back, the Repeater control will be rebound to data once again after a postback and all the checkboxes in your web page will be reset to the unchecked state.

The source code for the click event of the Button control that we have used is as follows:

```
protected void btnClick_Click(object sender, EventArgs e)
{
    int counter = 0;
    foreach (RepeaterItem r in Repeater1.Items)
    {
      CheckBox chk = (CheckBox)r.FindControl("chkbox1");
        if (chk.Checked) counter++;
    }
     lblDisplay.Text = " No of checked records is: " +
       counter.ToString();
}
```

When you execute the application, the Repeater control is displayed with records from the employee table. Now you check one or more of the checkboxes and then click on the Button control just beneath the Repeater control as follows:

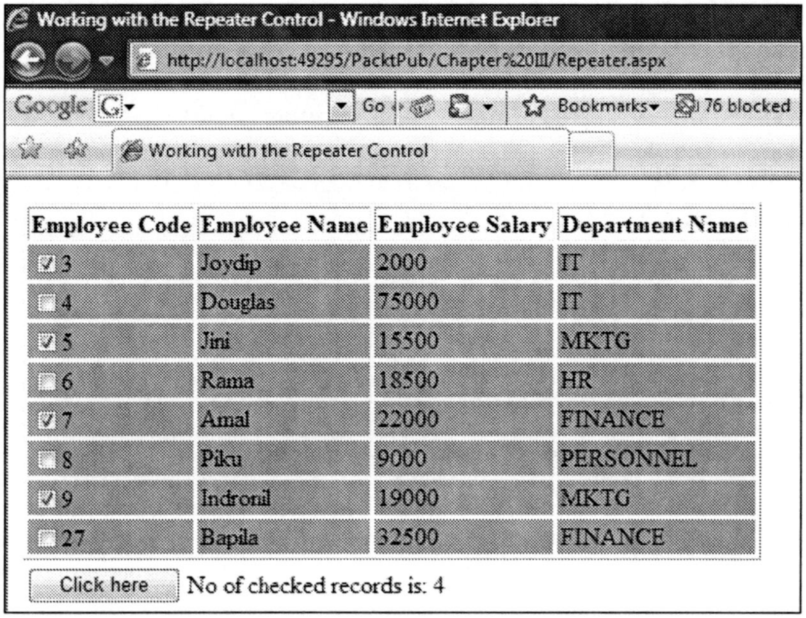

Note that the number of checked records is displayed in the Label control.

Implementing Data Paging Using the Repeater Control

Data paging is a concept that allows you to retrieve a specified number of records and display them in the user interface. The data is displayed *one page* at a time. You can use data paging to split the data rendered to the user into multiple pages for faster download of pages, provide a flexible user interface, and minimize the load on the database server. You use paging when the volume of data to be displayed is huge and you need to divide it into pages of data for efficient display of the records.

We have had a look at how we can display data using the Repeater control. Let us now understand how we can display data using the Repeater control *one page* at a time, using the PagedDataSource class. It should be noted that the Repeater control does not support paging by default. Hence, we need to implement our custom paging logic for data paging with this control.

We will first add four integer variables, namely: `currentPageIndex`, `PAGESIZE`, `totalRecords`, and `maxNumberOfPages`. The following code snippet displays these variables. Note that the `PAGESIZE` variable is constant because its value will not change throughout the execution of the application. You can, however, change the value of this variable manually if you so desire. As we have few records in our employee table, the value of this variable is set to `3`. This implies that each page of records that will be displayed will contain 3 records. The maximum number of pages that would be displayed is determined by the variable called `maxNumberOfPages`. The variable `currentPageIndex` implies the index of the current page being displayed. Though the value of this index has been set to 0 in the code, its value when displayed to the user will be 1. The variable `totalRecords` indicates the total number of records in the result set.

```
public static int currentPageIndex = 0;
public const int PAGESIZE = 3;
public static int totalRecords;
public static int maxNumberOfPages;

private static String sortColumn = String.Empty;
```

Note the case difference for the variable `PAGESIZE` above. It is just to imply that it is a constant variable. In the `Page_Load` event we make calls to the methods `InitializePaging()` and `BindPagedData()`. While the former initializes the above variables, the later is responsible for binding data to the Repeater control, one page at a time.

The `InitializePaging()` method is shown below.

```
private void InitializePaging()
{
    currentPageIndex = 0;
    totalRecords = GetTotalRecordCount();
    maxNumberOfPages = totalRecords / PAGESIZE;
}
```

The above method initializes the `currentPageIndex`, `totalRecords`, and `maxNumberOfPages` variables. The `currentPageIndex` is set to a value of 0 and the `GetTotalRecordCount()` method is called to retrieve the total number of records in the result set. The `maxNumberOfPages` variable determines the total number of pages that will be displayed. This is calculated using the values of the `totalRecords` and the `PAGESIZE` variables.

The following is the source code for the `GetTotalRecordCount()` method:

```
private int GetTotalRecordCount()
{
    DataManager dataManager = new DataManager();
    return dataManager.GetEmployees().Count;
}
```

This method makes use of the `DataManager` class to determine the total number of records in the employee result set.

In the `Page_Load` event, the `InitializePaging()` and the `BindPagedData()` methods are called as follows:

```
protected void Page_Load(object sender, EventArgs e)
{
    if (!IsPostBack)
    {
       InitializePaging();
       BindPagedData(currentPageIndex, PAGESIZE);
    }
}
```

The following section discusses the `BindPagedData()` method, that is, a method that actually binds the data from the employee result set to the repeater control in a paged fashion.

The BindPagedData() Method

The `BindPagedData()` method that follows accepts the current page index and the page size as parameters. A DataSet instance is populated with data using the DataManager class (remember, we used the same class in Chapters 1 and 2 to bind data to the data controls). Next, an instance of the PagedDataSource class is created and the DataSet instance is set to the DataSource property of an instance of the PagedDataSource class. Note that you cannot store an object of any type in a PagedDataSource; it has to be an enumerable object only. Once the DataSource property of the PagedDataSource instance is set, the next step is to set the DataSource property of the Repeater control with the instance of the PagedDataSource class. Refer to the following code snippet:

```
private void BindPagedData(int currentPageIndex, int pageSize)
{
    DataManager dataManager = new DataManager();
    PagedDataSource pagedDataSource = new PagedDataSource();
    pagedDataSource.PageSize =
    pageSize;pagedDataSource.CurrentPageIndex =
    currentPageIndex;pagedDataSource.AllowPaging = true;
    pagedDataSource.DataSource = dataManager.GetEmployees();
    Repeater1.DataSource = pagedDataSource;
    Repeater1.DataBind();
}
```

Fine, but how do we navigate from one page of data to another? Well, the next section discusses how we can tune our user interface so that it will have the navigation links so as to enable us to navigate from one page of data to another.

Navigating through the Pages

We will now add four Link Buttons to the Repeater control that we created earlier. For this, add the following code to the Repeater control in the `.aspx` file.

```
<asp:LinkButton id="First" Text="<< First" OnClick="FirstPage"
    runat="server"/>;
<asp:LinkButton id="Prev" Text="< Previous" OnClick="PreviousPage"
    runat="server"/>;
<asp:LinkButton id="Next" Text="Next >" OnClick="NextPage"
    runat="server"/>;
<asp:LinkButton id="Last" Text=">> Last" OnClick="LastPage"

    runat="server"/>
```

These controls correspond to the following operations on the data to be displayed:

1. Display the Records of the First Page
2. Display the Records of the Previous Page (Relative)
3. Display the Records of the Next Page (Relative)
4. Display the Records of the Last Page

All the above Link Buttons invoke the respective event handlers in their `OnClick` events. These event handlers are responsible for setting the `currentPageIndex` appropriately and then displaying the data for the page selected by the user. To accomplish this, the necessary logic to set the `currentPageIndex` is used and then the `BindPagedData()` method called with the `currentPageIndex` and the `PAGESIZE` as parameters.

The following is the source code for these event handlers that would be triggered as and when we click on the navigation links in the user interface.

```
protected void FirstPage(object sender, EventArgs e)
{
    currentPageIndex = 0;
    BindPagedData(currentPageIndex, PAGESIZE);
}
protected void LastPage(object sender, EventArgs e)
{
```

```
        currentPageIndex = maxNumberOfPages;
        BindPagedData(currentPageIndex, PAGESIZE);
    }
    protected void PreviousPage(object sender, EventArgs e)
    {
        currentPageIndex--;
          if (currentPageIndex < 0)
            currentPageIndex = 0;
            BindPagedData(currentPageIndex, PAGESIZE);
    }
    protected void NextPage(object sender, EventArgs e)
    {
        currentPageIndex++;
          if (currentPageIndex > maxNumberOfPages)
            currentPageIndex = maxNumberOfPages;
            BindPagedData(currentPageIndex, PAGESIZE);
    }
```

We are done! The following screenshot displays the output on execution.

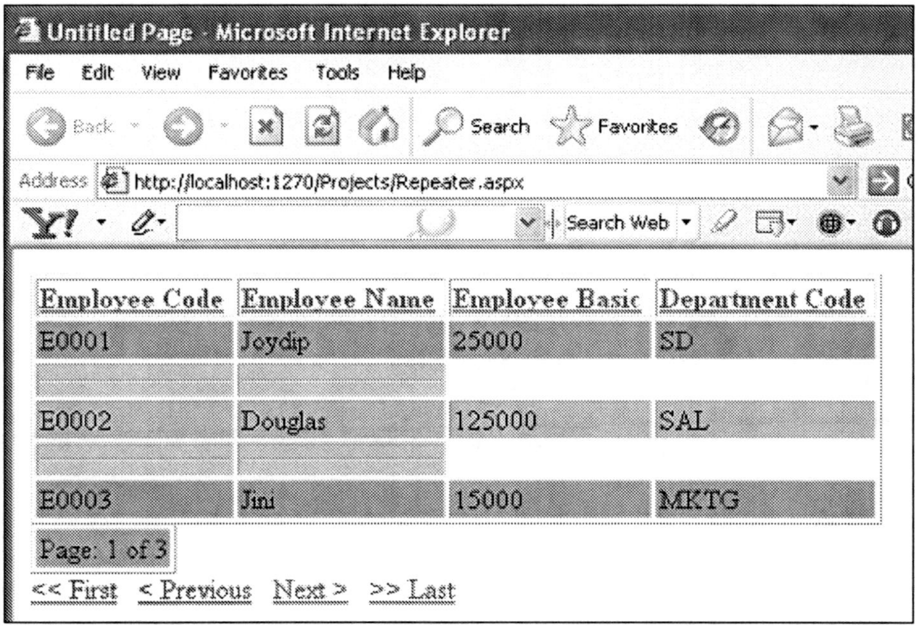

You can navigate to any of the pages by clicking on the links that correspond to the **First**, **Previous**, **Next**, or the **Last** pages. The next section discusses how we can implement custom sorting with that Repeater control.

Sorting Data Using the Repeater Control

For sorting data, we have links that correspond to the columns in the employee result set, in the header section of the Repeater control.

```
<tr>
  <th>
    <asp:LinkButton id="Emp_Code" OnClick="EmpCodeSort"
      Text="Employee Code" runat="server" /></th>
  <th>
    <asp:LinkButton id="Emp_Name" OnClick="EmpNameSort"
      Text="Employee Name" runat="server" /></th>
  <th>
    <asp:LinkButton id="Emp_Basic" OnClick="EmpBasicSort"
      Text="Employee Basic" runat="server" /></th>
  <th>
    <asp:LinkButton id="Dept_Code" OnClick="DeptCodeSort"
      Text="Department Code" runat="server" /></th>
</tr>
```

All of these link buttons have associated event handlers that get called on their `OnClick` events. These event handlers set the `sortColumn` variable to the name of the column on which the sort has to be performed. Refer to the following code snippets:

```
protected void EmpCodeSort(object sender, EventArgs e)
{
    sortColumn = "EmpCode";
    currentPageIndex = 0;
    BindPagedData(currentPageIndex, PAGESIZE);
}
protected void EmpNameSort(object sender, EventArgs e)
{
    sortColumn = "EmpName";
    currentPageIndex = 0;
    BindPagedData(currentPageIndex, PAGESIZE);
}
protected void EmpBasicSort(object sender, EventArgs e)
{
    sortColumn = "Basic";
    currentPageIndex = 0;
    BindPagedData(currentPageIndex, PAGESIZE);
}
protected void DeptCodeSort(object sender, EventArgs e)
```

```
{
    sortColumn = "DeptCode";
    currentPageIndex = 0;
    BindPagedData(currentPageIndex, PAGESIZE);
}
```

Revisiting the DataManager Class

We will now add a method in the DataManager class that will return a sorted result set based on the name of the sort column, that is, the column on which to sort the data. The code for this method is as follows:

```
public ArrayList GetSortedEmployees(string sortColumn)
{
    SqlConnection conn = null;
    ArrayList employeeList = null;
    try
    {
      conn = new SqlConnection(connectionString);
      conn.Open();
      string sql = "select EmpCode, EmpName, Basic,
         JoiningDate, DeptCode from employee e, Department d
         where e.DeptID = d.DeptID" + " Order By "+sortColumn;
      SqlCommand cmd = new SqlCommand(sql, conn);
      SqlDataReader dr = cmd.ExecuteReader();
      employeeList = new ArrayList();
      while (dr.Read())
      {
        Employee emp = new Employee();
        if (dr["EmpCode"] != DBNull.Value)
          emp.EmpCode = dr["EmpCode"].ToString();
        if (dr["EmpName"] != DBNull.Value)
          emp.EmpName = dr["EmpName"].ToString();
        if (dr["Basic"] != DBNull.Value)
          emp.Basic = Convert.ToDouble(dr["Basic"].ToString());
        if (dr["JoiningDate"] != DBNull.Value)
          emp.JoiningDate =
             Convert.ToDateTime(dr["JoiningDate"].ToString());
        if (dr["DeptCode"] != DBNull.Value)
          emp.DeptCode = dr["DeptCode"].ToString();
          employeeList.Add(emp);
          emp = null;
      }
    }
```

```
        catch
        {
          throw;
        }
        finally
        {
              Dr.Close(); conn.Close();
        }
          return employeeList;
  }
```

Once you are done with the DataReader, you must always close it by calling the `Close()` method on the DataReader instance. Unless you close a DataReader, you cannot execute any commands using the Connection instance on which the DataReader has been used.

You should not use the `Finalize()` method of your class to close a database connection or a DataReader instance due to the non-deterministic nature of finalization in Microsoft .NET. To learn more on when and how you can use `Dispose()` and `Finalize()` efficiently, refer to my article at:

`http://www.devx.com/dotnet/Article/33167`

The `GetSortedEmployees()` method needs to be called in place of the `GetEmployees()` method for displaying the sorted employee data in the user interface based on the sort column selected by the user.

Now we have to make the following change in the `BindPagedData()` method to incorporate the sorting functionality:

```
if(sortColumn == String.Empty)
pagedDataSource.DataSource = dataManager.GetEmployees();
else
pagedDataSource.DataSource = dataManager.GetSortedEmployees(sortColum
n);
```

We are done! You can now click on any of the links on the header (those that correspond to the respective columns in the employee result set) and see the data being displayed in the Repeater control in a sorted manner.

Filtering Data Using the Repeater Control

This section discusses how we can implement custom filtering of the data displayed in the Repeater control. For filtering data from the employee result set, we will use a DropDownList that is populated with the department names and, depending on the user's selection, the employee records for the selected department will be displayed in the Repeater control. The code that creates a DropDownList in the `.aspx` file follows:

```
<asp:DropDownList ID="drpDept" AutoPostBack = true runat="server"

   OnSelectedIndexChanged="drpDept_SelectedIndexChanged"> </asp:
DropDownList>
```

This control is bound to data using the DataManager class as usual.

```
protected void BindDepartmentList()
    {
        drpDept.DataSource = new DataManager().GetDepartmentList();
        drpDept.DataTextField = "DeptName";
        drpDept.DataValueField = "DeptCode";
        drpDept.DataBind();
        drpDept.Items.Insert(0, "All");
    }
```

The string value `All` is stored in the initial index of the control, i.e., index 0. Hence, selection of the first index would imply that the employee data of all the departments would be displayed.

We will now take a variable called `filterCondition` that will contain the condition based on which the data needs to be filtered.

```
private static String filterCondition = String.Empty;
```

The above variable is set to the appropriate department name based on the user's selection in the DropDownList control.

The event handler `drpDept_SelectedIndexChanged` is called whenever the selected index of the DropDownList control is changed. The source code for this event handler is as follows:

```
protected void drpDept_SelectedIndexChanged(object sender, EventArgs
    e)
    {
        if (drpDept.SelectedIndex == 0)
        {
            filterCondition = String.Empty;
```

```
                BindPagedData(currentPageIndex, PAGESIZE);
            }
            else
            {
                filterCondition = drpDept.SelectedValue;
                BindPagedData(currentPageIndex, PAGESIZE);
            }
        }
```

The value of the `SelectedValue` property of the DropDownList control actually contains the name of the selected department. Accordingly, the variable `filterCondition` is set to this value in the `drpDept_SelectedIndexChanged` event handler.

The updated `BindPagedData()` method that incorporates the filtering, paging, and sorting functionality (all in one) is as follows:

```
    private void BindPagedData(int currentPageIndex, int pageSize)
        {
            ArrayList dataList = null;
            DataManager dataManager = new DataManager();
            PagedDataSource pagedDataSource = new PagedDataSource();
            pagedDataSource.PageSize = pageSize;
            pagedDataSource.CurrentPageIndex = currentPageIndex;
            pagedDataSource.AllowPaging = true;
            if (sortColumn == String.Empty)
            {
                dataList = dataManager.GetEmployees();
                pagedDataSource.DataSource = dataList;
                totalRecords = dataList.Count;
                maxNumberOfPages = totalRecords / PAGESIZE;
            }
            else
            {
                if (filterCondition == String.Empty)
                {
                    dataList =
                       dataManager.GetSortedEmployees(sortColumn);
                    pagedDataSource.DataSource = dataList;
                    totalRecords = dataList.Count;
                    maxNumberOfPages = totalRecords / PAGESIZE;
                }
                else
                {
                    dataList =
```

```
                dataManager.GetEmployeeByDept(filterCondition);
            pagedDataSource.DataSource = dataList;
            totalRecords = dataList.Count;
            maxNumberOfPages = totalRecords / PAGESIZE;
        }
    }
    Repeater1.DataSource = pagedDataSource;
    Repeater1.DataBind();
}
```

The filter condition is checked and if the value of the variable `filterCondition` is non-empty, the `GetEmployeeByDept()` method of the `DataManager` class is called.

The figure below shows the output of the sample application with filtering functionality. The user can select a department of his/her choice based on which the employee data for that department would be displayed in the Repeater control.

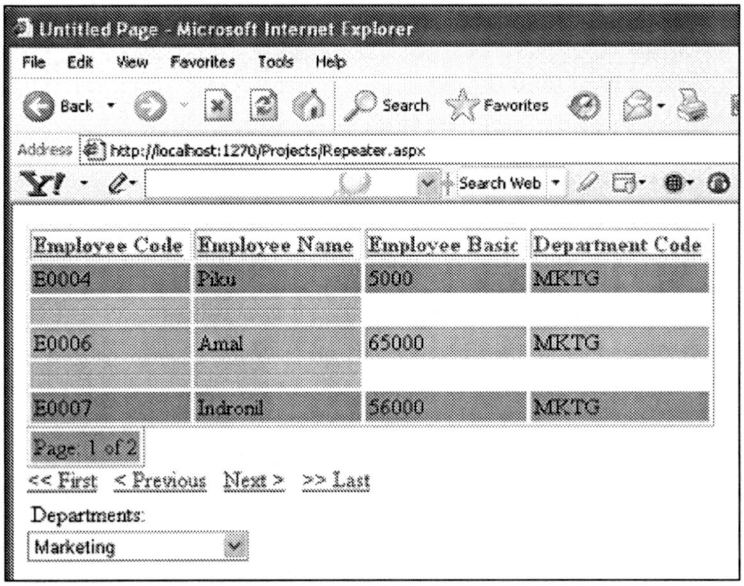

The complete code for our `Repeater` class (that contains all the functionality that we have discussed so far) in the `Repeater.aspx.cs` file is shown here, for reference:

```
using System;
using System.Data;
using System.Configuration;
using System.Collections;
using System.Web;
using System.Web.Security;
```

```
using System.Web.UI;
using System.Web.UI.WebControls;
using System.Web.UI.WebControls.WebParts;
using System.Web.UI.HtmlControls;
public partial class Repeater:System.Web.UI.Page
{
    public static int currentPageIndex;
    public const int PAGESIZE = 3;
    public static int totalRecords = 0;
    public static int maxNumberOfPages = 0;
    private static String sortColumn = String.Empty;
    private static String filterCondition = String.Empty;
    protected void PageLoad(object sender, EventArgs e)
    {
        if (!IsPostBack)
        {
            InitializePaging();
            BindPagedData(currentPageIndex, PAGESIZE);
            BindDepartmentList();
        }
    }
    private void InitializePaging()
    {
        currentPageIndex = 0;
        totalRecords = GetTotalRecordCount();
        maxNumberOfPages = totalRecords / PAGESIZE;
    }
    private int GetTotalRecordCount()
    {
        DataManager dataManager = new DataManager();
        return dataManager.GetEmployees().Count;
    }
    protected void FirstPage(object sender, EventArgs e)
    {
        currentPageIndex = 0;
        BindPagedData(currentPageIndex, PAGESIZE);
    }
    protected void LastPage(object sender, EventArgs e)
    {
        currentPageIndex = maxNumberOfPages;
        BindPagedData(currentPageIndex, PAGESIZE);
    }
    protected void PreviousPage(object sender, EventArgs e)
```

```
{
    currentPageIndex--;
    if (currentPageIndex < 0)
        currentPageIndex = 0;
    BindPagedData(currentPageIndex, PAGESIZE);
}
protected void NextPage(object sender, EventArgs e)
{
    currentPageIndex++;
    if (currentPageIndex > maxNumberOfPages)
        currentPageIndex = maxNumberOfPages;
    BindPagedData(currentPageIndex, PAGESIZE);
}
private void BindPagedData(int currentPageIndex, int pageSize)
{
    ArrayList dataList = null;
    DataManager dataManager = new DataManager();
    PagedDataSource pagedDataSource = new PagedDataSource();
    pagedDataSource.PageSize = pageSize;
    pagedDataSource.CurrentPageIndex = currentPageIndex;
    pagedDataSource.AllowPaging = true;
    if (sortColumn == String.Empty)
    {
        dataList = dataManager.GetEmployees();
        pagedDataSource.DataSource = dataList;
        totalRecords = dataList.Count;
        maxNumberOfPages = totalRecords / PAGESIZE;
    }
    else
    {
        if (filterCondition == String.Empty)
        {
            dataList =
               dataManager.GetSortedEmployees(sortColumn);
            pagedDataSource.DataSource = dataList;
            totalRecords = dataList.Count;
            maxNumberOfPages = totalRecords / PAGESIZE;
        }
        else
        {
            dataList =
               dataManager.GetEmployeeByDept(filterCondition);
            pagedDataSource.DataSource = dataList;
            totalRecords = dataList.Count;
```

```
                maxNumberOfPages = totalRecords / PAGESIZE;
            }
        }
        Repeater1.DataSource = pagedDataSource;
        Repeater1.DataBind();
    }
    protected void BindDepartmentList()
    {
        drpDept.DataSource = new DataManager().GetDepartmentList();
        drpDept.DataTextField = "DeptName";
        drpDept.DataValueField = "DeptCode";
        drpDept.DataBind();
        drpDept.Items.Insert(0, "All");
    }
    protected void EmpCodeSort(object sender, EventArgs e)
    {
        sortColumn = "EmpCode";
        currentPageIndex = 0;
        BindPagedData(currentPageIndex, PAGESIZE);
    }
    protected void EmpNameSort(object sender, EventArgs e)
    {
        sortColumn = "EmpName";
        currentPageIndex = 0;
        BindPagedData(currentPageIndex, PAGESIZE);
    }
    protected void EmpBasicSort(object sender, EventArgs e)
    {
        sortColumn = "Basic";
        currentPageIndex = 0;
        BindPagedData(currentPageIndex, PAGESIZE);
    }
    protected void DeptCodeSort(object sender, EventArgs e)
    {
        sortColumn = "DeptCode";
        currentPageIndex = 0;
        BindPagedData(currentPageIndex, PAGESIZE);
    }
   protected void drpDept_SelectedIndexChanged(object sender,
    EventArgs e)
    {
        if (drpDept.SelectedIndex == 0)
        {
```

```
                filterCondition = String.Empty;
                BindPagedData(currentPageIndex, PAGESIZE);
            }
            else
            {
                filterCondition = drpDept.SelectedValue;
                BindPagedData(currentPageIndex, PAGESIZE);
            }
        }
    }
```

This concludes our discussion on how we can implement custom paging, sorting, and filtering using the Repeater control. The next and concluding section discusses the salient events of the Repeater control and their applicability.

Handling Repeater Control Events

Similar to the other data-bound controls in ASP.NET, you can use the Repeater control to handle events raised by user actions. Apart from the other regular events, the most notable events of the Repeater control are:

- DataBinding
- ItemCreated
- ItemDataBound
- ItemCommand

The DataBinding event is fired when the Repeater control is bound to a data source. While the ItemCreated event is fired each time an item in the control is created, the ItemDataBound event gets fired when each of the items in the collection is bound to data from the data source. Lastly, the ItemCommand event is fired whenever a control within the Repeater raises an event. It should be noted that the ItemDataBound event creates a collection of primary keys and stores them in the ViewState. The DataBinding event on the other hand deletes these keys as and when the Repeater control is rebound to the data source. This is required in cases where you need to perform CRUD (Create, Read, Update, and Delete) operations using the Repeater control and then re-bind the control to refresh the data contained within.

The following code example illustrates how you can use panels within a Repeater control and then use the `ItemDataBound` event of the control to turn the visibility of the panels on or off, depending on your requirements.

Here is the code for the Repeater control in your `.aspx` file:

```
<asp:Repeater ID="Repeater1" runat="server"
     OnItemDataBound="Repeater1_ItemDataBound">
        <ItemTemplate>
            <asp:Panel ID="Panel1" runat="server" Visible="false"
              BackColor="DodgerBlue">
               <div>
                    <asp:Label ID="lblEmployeeCode" runat="server"
                      Text="Code"
                          Width="50px"/>
                   <asp:Label ID="lblEmployeeName" runat="server"
                     Text="Employee Name"
                          Width="200px"/>
                   <asp:Label ID="lblSalary" runat="server"
                     Text="Salary"
                          Width="100px"/>
                   <asp:Label ID="lblDepartment" runat="server"
                     Text="Department"
                          Width="100px"/>
               </div>
            </asp:Panel>
            <asp:Panel ID="Panel2" runat="server" Visible="false"
              BackColor="BurlyWood">
               <div>
                    <asp:Label ID="Label1" runat="server" Text="Code"
                      Width="50px"/>
                   <asp:Label ID="Label2" runat="server"
                     Text="Employee Name"
                          Width="200px"/>
                   <asp:Label ID="Label3" runat="server"
                     Text="Salary"
                          Width="100px"/>
                   <asp:Label ID="Label4" runat="server"
                     Text="Department"
                          Width="100px"/>
               </div>
            </asp:Panel>
        </ItemTemplate>
</asp:Repeater>
```

The event handler method shows how you can set the `Visible` property of the Panels within the Repeater control to true or false based on your requirements.

```
protected void Repeater1_ItemDataBound(object sender,
 System.Web.UI.WebControls.RepeaterItemEventArgs e)
{
if (e.Item.ItemType == ListItemType.Item)
{
   Panel first = (Panel)e.Item.FindControl("Panel1");
   Panel second = (Panel)e.Item.FindControl("Panel2");
   //Write your custom code to set the Visible property of the Panels
   //to true or false as shown below.
   //first.Visible = false; second.Visible = true;
   //or
   //first.Visible = true; second.Visible = false;
  }
 }
```

Note how we have used the `FindControl()` method to retrieve references to the Panels contained within the Repeater control.

Summary

This chapter discussed the Repeater control and how we can use it in our ASP.NET applications. It has demonstrated how we can use this control for custom paging, sorting, and filtering of data. Though this control does not support all the functionalities of other data controls, like DataGrid and GridView, it is still a good choice if you want faster rendering of data as it is light weight, and is very flexible. You can still write your own code to implement paging, sorting, or editing functionalities.

4
Working with the DataList Control

In Chapter 3, we saw the Repeater control in ASP.NET and how we can use it to bind and unbind data in our applications. In this chapter, we will discuss the DataList control, which, like the Repeater control, can be used to display a list of repeated data items.

In this chapter, we will cover the ASP.NET DataList control. We will learn about the following:

- Using the DataList control
- Binding images to a DataList control dynamically
- Displaying data using the DataList control
- Selecting, editing and delete data using this control
- Handling the DataList control events

The ASP.NET DataList Control

The DataList control like the Repeater control is a template driven, light weight control, and acts as a container of repeated data items. The templates in this control are used to define the data that it will contain. It is flexible in the sense that you can easily customize the display of one or more records that are displayed in the control. You have a property in the DataList control called **RepeatDirection** that can be used to customize the layout of the control.

The RepeatDirection property can accept one of two values, that is, Vertical or Horizontal. The RepeatDirection is Vertical by default. However, if you change it to Horizontal, rather than displaying the data as rows and columns, the DataList control will display them as a list of records with the columns in the data rendered displayed as rows.

This comes in handy, especially in situations where you have too many columns in your database table or columns with larger widths of data. As an example, imagine what would happen if there is a field called Address in our Employee table having data of large size and you are displaying the data using a Repeater, a DataGrid, or a GridView control. You will not be able to display columns of such large data sizes with any of these controls as the display would look awkward. This is where the DataList control fits in.

In a sense, you can think the DataList control as a combination of the DataGrid and the Repeater controls. You can use templates with it much as you did with a Repeater control and you can also edit the records displayed in the control, much like the DataGrid control of ASP.NET. The next section compares the features of the three controls that we have mentioned so far, that is, the Repeater, the DataList, and the DataGrid control of ASP.NET.

When the web page is in execution with the data bound to it using the Page_Load event, the data in the DataList control is rendered as DataListItem objects, that is, each item displayed is actually a DataListItem. Similar to the Repeater control, the DataList control does not have Paging and Sorting functionalities built into it.

Using the DataList Control

To use this control, drag and drop the control in the design view of the web form onto a web form from the toolbox.

Refer to the following screenshot, which displays a **DataList** control on a web form:

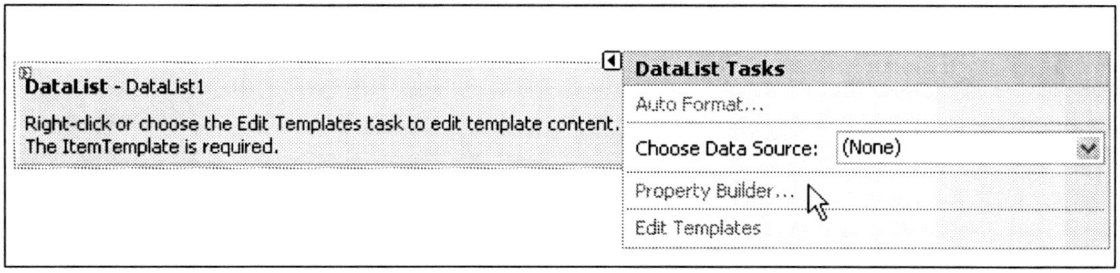

The following list outlines the steps that you can follow to add a **DataList** control in a web page and make it working:

1. Drag and drop a **DataList** control in the web form from the toolbox.
2. Set the **DataSourceID** property of the control to the data source that you will use to bind data to the control, that is, you can set this to an SQL Data Source control.
3. Open the `.aspx` file, declare the `<ItemTemplate>` element and define the fields as per your requirements.
4. Use data binding syntax through the `Eval()` method to display data in these defined fields of the control.

You can bind data to the DataList control in two different ways, that is, using the DataSourceID and the DataSource properties. You can use the inbuilt features like selecting and updating data when using the DataSourceID property. Note that you need to write custom code for selecting and updating data to any data source that implements the ICollection and IEnumerable data sources. We will discuss more on this later. The next section discusses how you can handle the events in the DataList control.

Displaying Data

Similar to the Repeater control that we looked at in Chapter 3, the DataList control contains a template that is used to display the data items within the control. Since there are no data columns associated with this control, you use templates to display data. Every column in a DataList control is rendered as a `<span>` element.

A DataList control is useless without templates. Let us now lern what templates are, the types of templates, and how to work with them. A template is a combination of HTML elements, controls, and embedded server controls, and can be used to customize and manipulate the layout of a control. A template comprises HTML tags and controls that can be used to customize the look and feel of controls like Repeater, DataGrid, or DataList. There are seven templates and seven styles in all. You can use templates for the DataList control in the same way you did when using the Repeater control. The following is the list of templates and their associated styles in the DataList control.

The Templates are as follows:

1. ItemTemplate
2. AlternatingItemTemplate
3. EditItemTemplate

4. FooterTemplate
5. HeaderTemplate
6. SelectedItemTemplate
7. SeparatorTemplate

The following screenshot illustrates the different templates of this control.

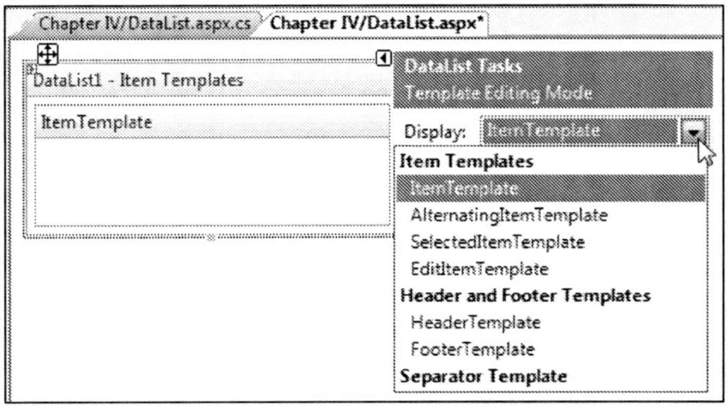

As you can see from this figure, the templates are grouped under three broad categories. These are:

1. Item Templates
1. Header and Footer Templates
2. Separator Template

Note that out of the templates given above, the **ItemTemplate** is the one and only mandatory template that you have to use when working with a **DataList** control. Here is a sample of how your `DataList` control's templates are arranged:

```
<asp:DataList id="dlEmployee" runat="server">
<HeaderTemplate>
...
</HeaderTemplate>
<ItemTemplate>
...
</ItemTemplate>
<AlternatingItemTemplate>
...
</AlternatingItemTemplate>
<FooterTemplate>
...
</FooterTemplate>
</asp:DataList>
```

The following screenshot displays a DataList control populated with data and with its templates indicated.

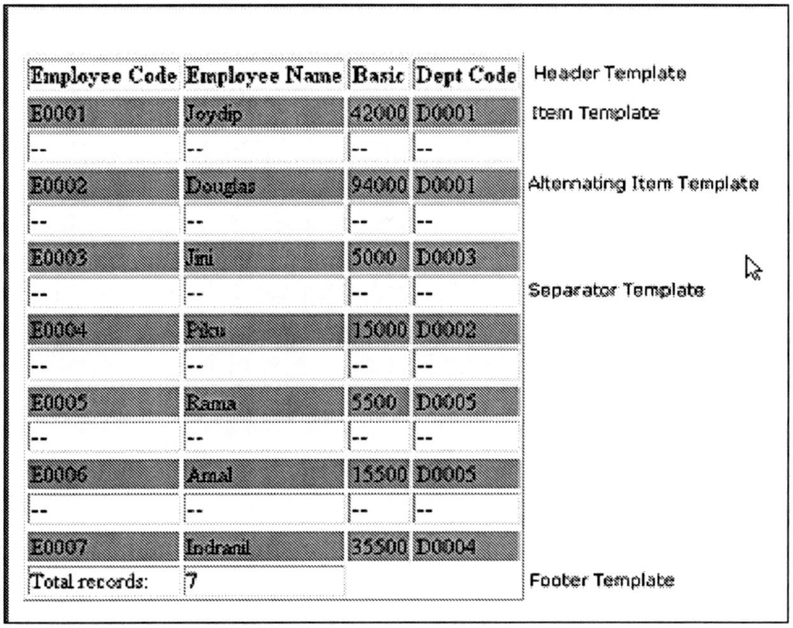

Customizing a DataList control at run time

You can customize the DataList control at run time using the ListItemType property in the ItemCreated event of this control as follows:

```
private void DataList1_ItemCreated(object
sender, ..........System.Web.UI.WebControls.
DataListItemEventArgs e)
{
   switch (e.Item.ItemType)
   {
      case System.Web.UI.WebControls.ListItemType.Item :
         e.Item.BackColor = Color.Red;
         break;
      case System.Web.UI.WebControls.ListItemType.
         AlternatingItem : e.Item.BackColor = Color.Blue;
         break;
      case System.Web.UI.WebControls.ListItemType.
         SelectedItem : e.Item.BackColor = Color.Green;
         break;
      default :
         break;
      }
}
```

The Styles that you can use with the DataList control to customize the look and feel are:

1. AlternatingItemStyle
2. EditItemStyle
3. FooterStyle
4. HeaderStyle
5. ItemStyle
6. SelectedItemStyle
7. SeparatorStyle

You can use any of these styles to format the control, that is, format the HTML code that is rendered.

You can also use layouts of the DataList control for formatting, that is, further customization of your user interface. The available layouts are as follows:

- FlowLayout
- TableLayout
- VerticalLayout
- HorizontalLayout

You can specify your desired flow or table format at design time by specifying the following in the `.aspx` file.

```
RepeatLayout = "Flow"
```

You can also do the same at run time by specifying your desired layout using the `RepeatLayout` property of the DataList control as shown in the following code snippet:

```
DataList1.RepeatLayout = RepeatLayout.Flow
```

In the code snippet, it is assumed that the name of the DataList control is `DataList1`.

Let us now understand how we can display data using the DataList control. For this, we would first drag and drop a DataList control in our web form and specify the templates for displaying data. The code in the `.aspx` file is as follows:

```
<asp:DataList ID="DataList1" runat="server">
            <HeaderTemplate>
                <table border="1">
                    <tr>
                        <th>
```

```
                        Employee Code
                    </th>
                    <th>
                        Employee Name
                    </th>
                    <th>
                        Basic
                    </th>
                    <th>
                        Dept Code
                    </th>
                </tr>
        </HeaderTemplate>
        <ItemTemplate>
            <tr bgcolor="#0xbbbb">
                <td>
                    <%# DataBinder.Eval(Container.DataItem,
                        "EmpCode")%>
                </td>
                <td>
                    <%# DataBinder.Eval(Container.DataItem,
                        "EmpName")%>
                </td>
                <td>
                    <%# DataBinder.Eval(Container.DataItem,
                        "Basic")%>
                </td>
                <td>
                    <%# DataBinder.Eval(Container.DataItem,
                        "DeptCode")%>
                </td>
            </tr>
        </ItemTemplate>
        <FooterTemplate>
        </FooterTemplate>
</asp:DataList>
```

The `DataList` control is populated with data in the `Page_Load` event of the web form using the `DataManager` class as usual.

```
protected void Page_Load(object sender, EventArgs e)
    {
        DataManager dataManager = new DataManager();
        DataList1.DataSource = dataManager.GetEmployees();
        DataList1.DataBind();
    }
```

Note that the `DataBinder.Eval()` method has been used as usual to display the values of the corresponding fields from the data container in the DataList control. The data container in our case is the DataSet instance that is returned by the `GetEmployees ()` method of the `DataManager` class.

When you execute the application, the output is as follows:

Employee Code	Employee Name	Salary	Dept Name
3	Joydip	20000	IT
4	Douglas	75000	IT
5	Jini	15500	MKTG
6	Rama	18500	HR
7	Amal	22000	FINANCE
8	Piku	9000	PERSONNEL
9	Indronil	19000	MKTG
27	Bapila	32500	FINANCE

Handling Events

The Repeater, DataList, and DataGrid controls support event bubbling. What is *event bubbling*? Event Bubbling refers to the ability of a control to capture the events in a child control and bubble up the event to the container whenever an event occurs. The DataList control supports the following six events:

- ItemCreated
- ItemCommand
- EditCommand
- UpdateCommand
- DeleteCommand
- CancelCommand

We will now discuss how we can work with the events of the DataList control. In order to handle events when working with a DataList control, include a Button or a LinkButton control in the DataList control. These controls have click events that can be used to bubble up the triggered event to the container control, that is, the DataList.

The following code snippet illustrates how you can attach a handler to an `ItemCommand` event of a `DataList` control:

```
<asp:DataList ID="DataList1" runat="server" onItemCommand =
        "ItemCommandEventHandler"/>
```

The corresponding handler that gets called whenever the event is fired is as follows:

```
void ItemCommandEventHandler (Object src, DataListCommandEventArgs e
....)
{
    //Some event handling code
}
```

Similarly, you can handle the `ItemCreated` event by specifying the handler in the `.aspx` file as follows:

```
<asp:DataList ID="DataList1" runat="server" onItemCreated =
        "ItemCreatedEventHandler" />
```

The corresponding handler that is triggered whenever this event occurs is as follows.

```
void ItemCreatedEventHandler ( Object src, DataListCommandEventArgs e
)
{
    //Some event handling code
}
```

Similarly, you can use the `CancelCommand` event by specifying the event handler in your `.aspx` file as follows:

```
<asp:DataList ID="DataList1" runat="server" onCancelCommand =
.........."CancelCommandEventHandler" />
```

The corresponding event handler that would get fired is as follows:

```
void CancelCommandEventHandler ( Object src, DataListCommandEventArgs
 e )
{
    //Some event handling code
}
```

You can handle any of the other events similarly and execute your event handlers appropriately. We will discuss more about using these events to Select, Edit, and Delete data using the DataList control later in this chapter.

We will explore how we can display images using the DataList control in the next section.

Binding Images Dynamically

Let us now see how we can display images using the DataList control. Here is a situation where this control scores over the other data-bound controls as you can set the RepeatDirection property of this control to `Horizontal` so that we can display the columns of a particular record in one single row.

The following screenshot illustrates how the output of the application would look when it is executed:

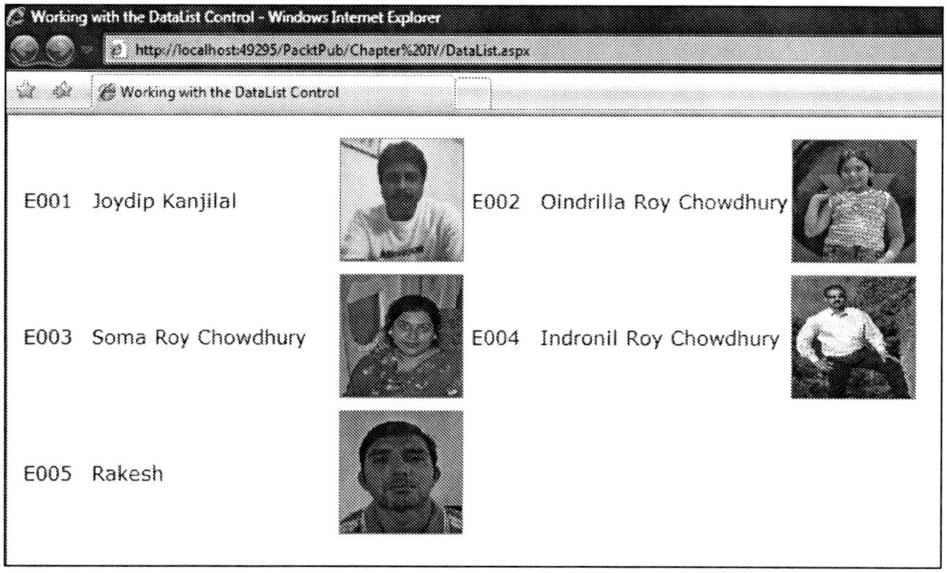

We will now discuss how we can implement this application that displays the employee details, like code, name, and the individual's photo. We need an Image control that we will use inside the ItemTemplate of the DataList control in use. Here is how you can use the Image control.

```
<img src='<%# DataBinder.Eval(Container.DataItem, "EmpName") %>.png'
style="height:100px;width:100px;border:1px solid gray;"/>
```

Note that all the images have a primary name corresponding to the employee's name with a `.png` extension. The complete source code of the DataList control in your `.aspx` file would be similar to what follows:

```
<asp:DataList ID="DataList1" runat="server" RepeatColumns="2"
  RepeatDirection="Horizontal">
        <ItemTemplate>
```

```
        <table id="Table1" cellpadding="1" cellspacing="1"
        visible ="true">
        <tr>
        <td width="50px">
        <p align="left">
            <asp:Label ID="lblEmpCode" runat ="server"
              CssClass="LabelStyle" Text=' <%#
              DataBinder.Eval(Container.DataItem,
              "EmpCode")%>'></asp:Label>
        </p>
        <td>
        <td width="200px">
         <p align="left">
           <asp:Label ID="lblEmpName" runat ="server"
             CssClass="LabelStyle" Text=' <%#
             DataBinder.Eval(Container.DataItem,
             "EmpName")%>'></asp:Label>
         </p>
         </td>
         <td width="100px">
         <p align="left">
         <img src='<%# DataBinder.Eval(Container.DataItem, "EmpName")
          %>.png' style="height:100px;width:100px;border:1px
          solid gray;"/>
         </td>
         </p>
        </td>
        </table>
        </ItemTemplate>
</asp:DataList>
```

Note the use of the properties `RepeatColumns` and `RepeatDirection` in this code snippet. While the former implies the number of columns that you would like to display per record in the rendered output, the later implies the direction of the rendered output, that is, horizontal or vertical.

Binding data to the control is simple. You need to bind the data to this control in the Page_Load event of this control in your code-behind file. Here is how you do the binding:

```
DataManager dataManager = new DataManager();
DataList1.DataSource = dataManager.GetEmployees();
DataList1.DataBind();
```

Wow! When you execute the application, the images are displayed along with the employee's details. The output is similar to what we have seen in the screenshot earlier in this section.

In the following sections, we will explore how to Select, Edit, and Delete data using the DataList control.

Selecting Data

You need to specify the event handler that will be invoked in the `OnItemCommand` event as follows:

```
OnItemCommand = "Employee_Select"
```

You also need to specify a `LinkButton` that the user would have to click on to select a particular row of data in the DataList control. This command button would be specified in the ItemTemplate as shown here:

```
<asp:LinkButton ID="lnkSelect" runat="server" CommandName="Select" >
Select </asp:LinkButton>
```

The reason why we choose to use the ItemTemplate to place the command button to select data is that the contents of this template are rendered once for each row of data in the DataList control. The code for the event handler is as follows:

```
protected void Employee_Select(object source,
                                DataListCommandEventArgs e)
    {
        DataList1.EditItemIndex = e.Item.ItemIndex;
        DataList1.DataBind();
    }
```

The output on execution is shown in the following screenshot.

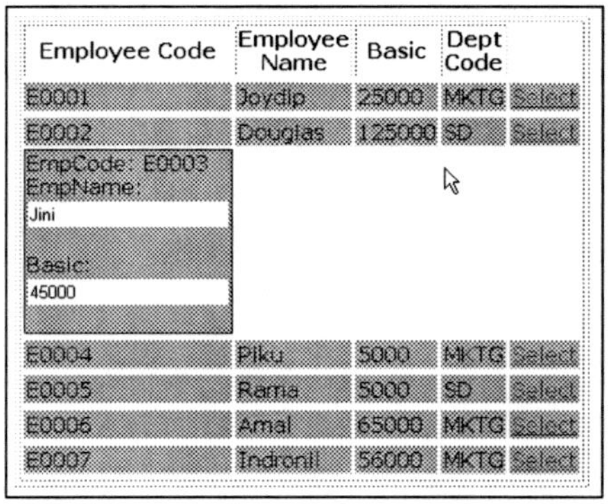

Resizing a DataList control when the browser's size changes

When you change the width or height of a browser that has a DataList control in it, the size of the DataList doesn't change. Here is a workaround to this.

Create a CSS class that you will use in as the control's `CssClass` as shown below.

```
<script type="text/css">
  .ResizeDataList
  {
    height:100%;width:100%;
  }
</script>
Next, use this CSS class in the DataList control as
shown here.
<asp:DataList ID="dl" runat="server" CssClass="ResizeDa
taList">
<!-- Usual code here -->
</asp:DataList>
```

Editing data

The DataList control can be used to edit your data, bound to this control from a data store. This section discusses how we can edit data using this control. You can edit data using the DataList control by providing a command-type button control in the ItemTemplate of the DataList control. These command-type button can be one of the following.

- Button
- LinkButton
- ImageButton

In our example, we will be using an ImageButton control. Further, you need to specify the OnEditCommand event and the corresponding event handler that will be triggered whenever the user wants to edit data in the DataList control by clicking on the ImageButton meant for editing the data.

Note that whenever the user clicks on the command button for editing the data, the data items in the DataList control are set to editable mode to enable the user to edit the data. This is accomplished by the use of the EditItemTemplate. It should be noted that the EditItemTemplate is rendered for a data item that is currently in the edit mode of operation.

The following code listing shows how your .aspx code for this control with edit mode enabled would look:

```
<asp:DataList ID="DataList1" DataKeyField = "EmpCode" GridLines =
            "Both" CellPadding="3"
            CellSpacing="0"
            Font-Names="Verdana"
            Font-Size="12pt"
            Width="150px"
            OnEditCommand = "Employee_Edit" runat="server">
            <HeaderTemplate>
                <table border="1">
                    <tr>
                        <th>
                            Employee Code
                        </th>
                        <th>
                            Employee Name
                        </th>
                        <th>
                            Basic
                        </th>
                        <th>
                            Dept Code
                        </th>
                    </tr>
            </HeaderTemplate>
                <EditItemTemplate>
                EmpCode: <asp:Label ID="lblEmpCode" runat="server"
                         Text='<%# Eval("EmpCode") %>'>
                    </asp:Label>
                <br />
                EmpName: <asp:TextBox ID="txtEmpName" runat="server"
                           Text='<%#
                           DataBinder.Eval(Container.DataItem,
                           "EmpName") %>'>
                      </asp:TextBox>
                <br />
                Basic: <asp:TextBox ID="txtBasic"
                         runat="server"
                        Text='<%# DataBinder.Eval(Container.DataItem,
                        "Basic") %>'>
                     </asp:TextBox>
                <br />
```

```
            </EditItemTemplate>
            <ItemTemplate>
                <tr bgcolor="#0xbbbb">
                    <td>
                        <%# DataBinder.Eval(Container.DataItem,
                         "EmpCode")%>
                    </td>
                    <td>
                        <%# DataBinder.Eval(Container.DataItem,
                         "EmpName")%>
                    </td>
                    <td>
                        <%# DataBinder.Eval(Container.DataItem,
                         "Basic")%>
                    </td>
                    <td>
                        <%# DataBinder.Eval(Container.DataItem,
                         "DeptCode")%>
                    </td>
                    <td>
                <asp:LinkButton ID=»lnkEdit» runat=»server»
                    CommandName=»Edit» >
                    Edit
                </asp:LinkButton>
                </td>
                </tr>
            </ItemTemplate>
        </asp:DataList>
```

The corresponding event handler to handle the edit operation, `Employee_Edit`, is defined as follows:

```
protected void Employee_Edit(object source, DataListCommandEventArgs
 e)
    {
        DataList1.EditItemIndex = e.Item.ItemIndex;
        DataList1.DataBind();
    }
```

The `.ItemIndex` property of the `DataListCommandEventArgs` instance gives us the **row index** of the DataList control that is being edited. This index starts with a value of zero, that is, the index for the first row of data that is rendered in the DataList control is 0.

The following screenshot shows the output on execution.

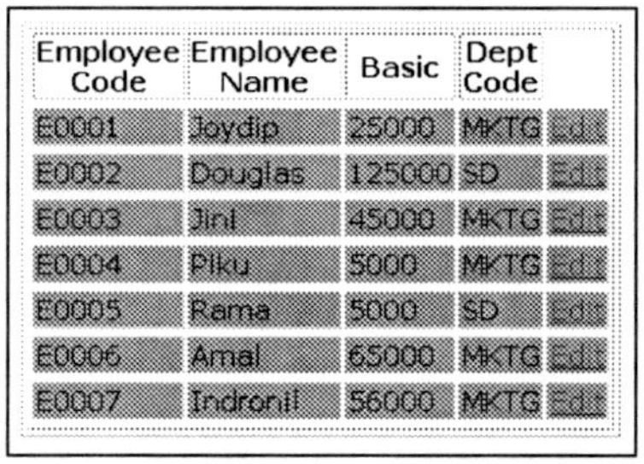

Note that the Edit command button is rendered for each of the rows of the DataList control. Now, when you click on this button on any of the rows to edit the data for that row, the output is as follows:

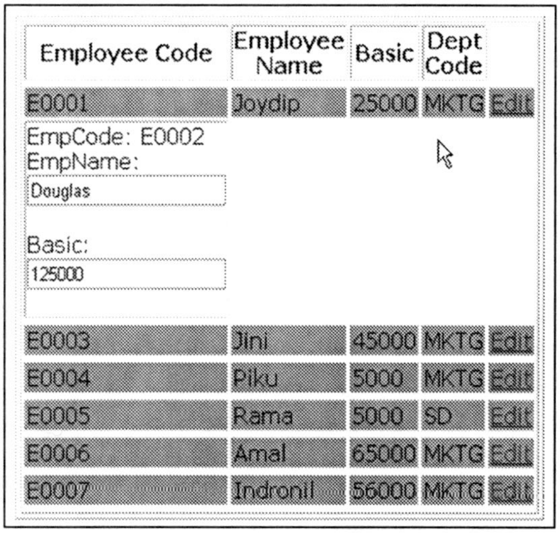

Note that the second record is set to editable mode on clicking the **Edit** command button that corresponds to the second record.

> **How to enable/disable an embedded control within the DataList control**
>
> To enable or disable any control contained within the DataList control, use the following technique in the ItemDataBound event of the control.

```
DataListProduct_ItemDataBound(object sender,
  System.Web.UI.WebControls.DataListItemEventArgs e)
{
  if ( e.Item.ItemType == ListItemType.Item || e.Item.ItemType ==
    ListItemType.AlternatingItem )
    {
      TextBox txtBox = e.Item.FindControl("txtEmpName") as TextBox;
      txtBox.Visble=false;
    }
}
```

Deleting Data

This section discusses how we can delete data using the DataList control. Similar to what we have done in the previous section for editing data using the DataList control, you need to specify the event handler that will be triggered for the delete operation in the `.aspx` file. You also require a LinkButton as usual.

The following code snippet illustrates the code that you need to write for the `.aspx` file to specify the event handler that will be invoked for the delete operation.

```
OnDeleteCommand = "Employee_Delete"
```

The code for the `Employee_Delete` event handler that you need to write in the code-behind file, that is, `DataList.aspx.cs`, is as follows:

```
protected void Employee_Delete(object source,
DataListCommandEventArgs e)
    {
        DataList1.EditItemIndex = e.Item.ItemIndex;
        //Code to delete the row represented by ItemIndex
        DataList1.EditItemIndex = -1; //Reset the index
        DataList1.DataBind();
    }
```

The following is the output on execution.

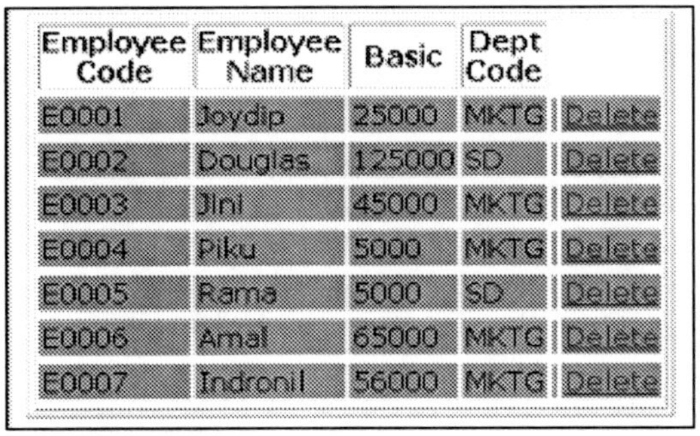

Employee Code	Employee Name	Basic	Dept Code	
E0001	Joydip	25000	MKTG	Delete
E0002	Douglas	125000	SD	Delete
E0003	Jini	45000	MKTG	Delete
E0004	Piku	5000	MKTG	Delete
E0005	Rama	5000	SD	Delete
E0006	Amal	65000	MKTG	Delete
E0007	Indronil	56000	MKTG	Delete

As is apparent from the given screenshot, you just need to click the **Delete** Link Button that corresponds to the employee record that you need to delete. Once you do so, the specific record gets deleted.

Summary

We have had a bird's eye view of the DataList control in this chapter and how we can use it in our ASP.NET applications. We have discussed how to select, edit, and delete data with this control and how to work with the events of this control. We also discussed how we can bind images to the DataList control programmatically. The next chapter will discuss the DataGrid control, one of the most widely used data controls in ASP.NET.

5

Working with the DataGrid Control in ASP.NET

In Chapter 4, we had a look at the DataList control in ASP.NET, and how we can use it to bind and unbind data in our applications. In this chapter, we will discuss the DataGrid control and implement a sample application that would contain all the necessary operations that we generally require with this control.

In this chapter, we will learn about the following:

- Creating a DataGrid control
- Implementing a sample application using the DataGrid control
- Displaying data using the DataGrid control
- Styling the DataGrid control
- Appending data using the DataGrid control
- Editing data using the DataGrid control
- Deleting data using the DataGrid control
- Paging using the DataGrid control

Note that we will cover how to bind data using master detail relationships in the chapter on GridView control. Also note that we will be reusing our DataManager class throughout this chapter. You can also use SQLDataSource, AccessDataSource, or an XmlDataSource to retrieve data. We have already discussed these controls in the first chapter.

The ASP.NET DataGrid Control

The DataGrid control in ASP.NET is a very powerful and flexible control that can be used to display data in a tabular fashion. It allows you to format your data the way you want it. Note that in ASP.NET 2.0, you won't find this control in the toolbox. You have to embed HTML code, in the code behind it. Rather, in ASP.NET 2.0, you have the GridView control in place of DataGrid that is more like an improved version of the DataGrid control. This control is more in use amongst the ASP.NET community compared to its earlier counterpart. We will discuss the GridView control in the next chapter.

Note that the output of the DataGrid control, like other data list controls, is in HTML format. The next section discusses how we can get started with a DataGrid control in ASP.NET.

Creating a DataGrid Control

Follow these simple steps to create a DataGrid control.

1. Start Visual Studio .NET.
2. Next, create a new ASP.NET web application project and name it of your choice.
3. Then in the web form file, that is, the `.aspx` file, paste the following code within the Form tag of the web form.

```
<asp:datagrid runat="server" id="dgEmployee"/>
```

You are done! This will create a **DataGrid** control that has an ID of `dgEmployee`. The following screenshot illustrates how the control looks in the design view of the web form:

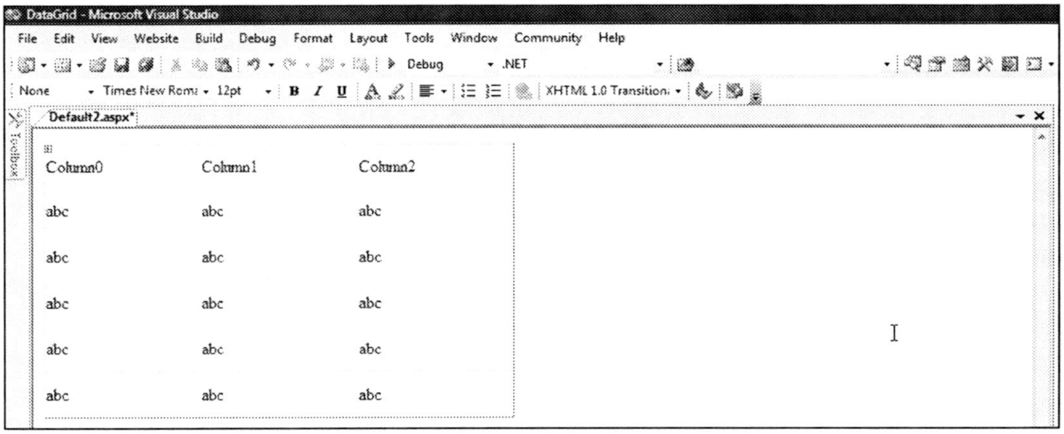

Implementing a Sample Application Using DataGrid Control

I will now talk about how we can implement a sample application using the **DataGrid** control. This sample application will initially display the records from the **Employee** table with provisions to perform all **CRUD** operations. You can append, edit and delete records using the user interface that gets displayed once you invoke the application.

The following screenshot displays the output on execution of the application:

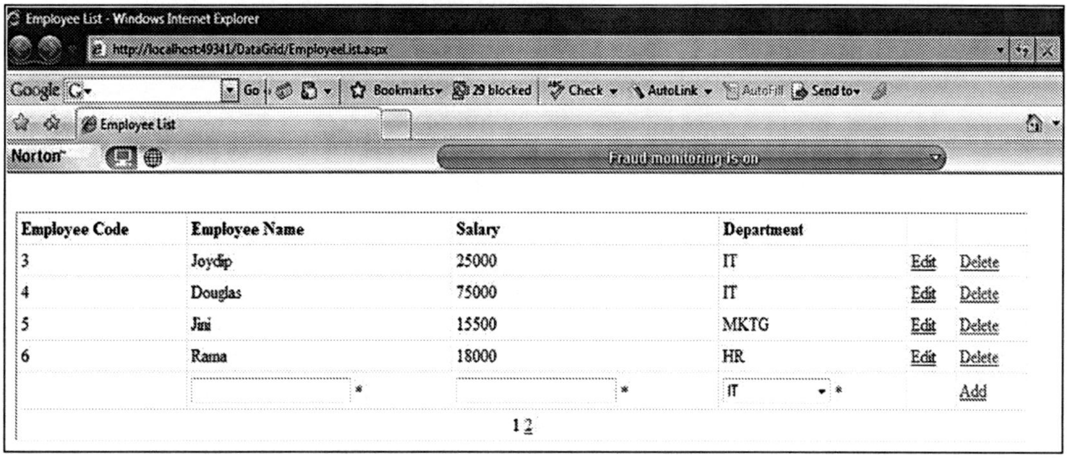

I will now run through the steps that you can follow for implementing this sample application. Follow these simple steps in the same sequence that is given below.

Step 1: Create a **DataGrid** control either by dragging and dropping in your web form from the toolbox, or by writing code in the `.aspx` file. Here is how we can use a `TemplateColumn` in our **DataGrid**.

```
<asp:TemplateColumn HeaderText="Employee Code">
<ItemTemplate>
<asp:Label Text='<%# Convert.ToString(DataBinder.Eval(Container.
DataItem,"EmpCode")) %>'
runat="server" ID="lblEmpCode"></asp:Label>
<asp:TextBox runat="server" ID="txtEmpCode" Visible="False"
MaxLength="30" Text='<%# Convert.ToString(DataBinder.Eval(Container.
DataItem,"EmpCode")) %>'
Width="40">
</asp:TextBox>
</ItemTemplate>
</asp:TemplateColumn>
```

Step 2: Repeat the same for the other columns, that is, `Employee Name`, `Salary` and `Department Name`. Here is how the columns tag of the **DataGrid** control will look like after you have used `TemplateColumn` for each of the above fields.

```
<Columns>
                    <asp:TemplateColumn HeaderText="Employee Code">
                        <ItemTemplate>
                            <asp:Label Text='<%# Convert.
ToString(DataBinder.Eval(Container.DataItem,"EmpCode")) %>'
                                runat="server" ID="lblEmpCode">
                            </asp:Label>
                            <asp:TextBox runat="server"
ID="txtEmpCode" Visible="False" MaxLength="30" Text='<%# Convert.
ToString(DataBinder.Eval(Container.DataItem,"EmpCode")) %>'
                                Width="40">
                            </asp:TextBox>
                        </ItemTemplate>
                     </asp:TemplateColumn>
                    <asp:TemplateColumn HeaderText="Employee Name">
                        <ItemTemplate>
                            <asp:Label Text='<%# Convert.
ToString(DataBinder.Eval(Container.DataItem,"EmpName")) %>'
                                runat="server" ID="lblEmpName">
                            </asp:Label>
                        </ItemTemplate>
                    </asp:TemplateColumn>
                    <asp:TemplateColumn HeaderText="Salary">
                        <ItemTemplate>
                            <asp:Label Text='<%# Convert.
ToString(DataBinder.Eval(Container.DataItem,"Basic")) %>'
                                runat="server" ID="lblBasic">
                            </asp:Label>
                        </ItemTemplate>

                    </asp:TemplateColumn>
                    <asp:TemplateColumn HeaderText="Department">
                      <ItemTemplate>
                         <asp:Label Text='
                            <%# Convert.ToString(DataBinder.
                             Eval(Container.DataItem,"DeptName")) %>'
                             runat="server" ID="lblDeptCode">
                            </asp:Label>
                        </ItemTemplate>
                        </asp:TemplateColumn>
                </Columns>
```

Here is how the **DataGrid** will now look with template columns bound to it:

Employee Code	Employee Name	Salary	Department
Databound	Databound	Databound	Databound
Databound	Databound	Databound	Databound
Databound	Databound	Databound	Databound
Databound	Databound	Databound	Databound
Databound	Databound	Databound	Databound

Step 3: Now you need to use `EditItemTemplate` to make the data in the **DataGrid** control editable. Here is the updated columns tag of the **DataGrid** control with `EditItemTemplate` used for editing its fields based on selection of a particular employee. Here is an example of how to use the `EditItemTemplate` in the **DataGrid** control.

```
<EditItemTemplate>
 <asp:TextBox runat="server" ID="txtEmpName_Edit" MaxLength="30"
Text='<%# Convert.ToString(DataBinder.Eval(Container.
DataItem,"EmpName")) %>'
 Width="150">
 </asp:TextBox>
 <font color="red">*</font>
 </EditItemTemplate>
```

Note that the `TextBox` control is used to allow the user to type in the editable data. Repeat this for all the other fields. Here is how the columns tag of the **DataGrid** control will look after the `EditItemTemplate` has been used for the other fields.

```
<Columns>
         <asp:TemplateColumn HeaderText="Employee Code">
           <ItemTemplate>
             <asp:Label Text= '<%# Convert.ToString(DataBinder
              .Eval(Container.DataItem,"EmpCode")) %>'
               runat="server" ID="lblEmpCode">
             </asp:Label>
             <asp:TextBox runat="server" ID="txtEmpCode"
               Visible="False" MaxLength="30" Text='<%# Convert
               ToString(DataBinder.
               Eval(Container.DataItem,"EmpCode")) %>'
               Width="40">
              </asp:TextBox>
            </ItemTemplate>
              <FooterTemplate>
              </FooterTemplate>
```

```
        <EditItemTemplate>
          <asp:TextBox runat="server" ID="txtEmpCode_Edit"
            MaxLength="30" Convert
            Text='<%#.ToString(DataBinder.
            Eval(Container.DataItem,"EmpCode")) %>'
            Width="40" Enabled="false">
          </asp:TextBox>
            <font color="red">*</font>
        </EditItemTemplate>
          </asp:TemplateColumn>
<asp:TemplateColumn HeaderText="Employee Name">
  <ItemTemplate>
    <asp:Label Text='<%# Convert.ToString (DataBinder.
      Eval(Container.DataItem,"EmpName")) %>'
      runat="server" ID="lblEmpName">
    </asp:Label>
  </ItemTemplate>
      <FooterTemplate>
         <asp:TextBox ID="txtEmpName_Add" Width="150"
           MaxLength="30" runat="server" />
             <font color="red">*</font>
      </FooterTemplate>
      <EditItemTemplate>
         <asp:TextBox runat="server"
           ID="txtEmpName_Edit" MaxLength="30"
           Text='<%# Convert.ToString(DataBinder.
           Eval(Container.DataItem,"EmpName")) %>'
           Width="150">
          </asp:TextBox>
              <font color="red">*</font>
       </EditItemTemplate>
</asp:TemplateColumn>
<asp:TemplateColumn HeaderText="Salary">
  <ItemTemplate>
    <asp:Label Text='<%# Convert.ToString(DataBinder.
      Eval(Container.DataItem,"Basic")) %>'
      runat="server" ID="lblBasic">
    </asp:Label>
  </ItemTemplate>
       <FooterTemplate>
          <asp:TextBox ID="txtBasic_Add"
            Width="150" MaxLength="30"
            runat="server" />
             <font color="red">*</font>
        </FooterTemplate>
```

```
            <EditItemTemplate>
               <asp:TextBox runat="server"
                 ID="txtBasic_Edit" MaxLength="30"
                 Text='<%# Convert.ToString(DataBinder.
                 Eval(Container.DataItem,"Basic")) %>'
                 Width="150">
                </asp:TextBox>
                   <font color="red">*</font>
                    </EditItemTemplate>
      </asp:TemplateColumn>
      <asp:TemplateColumn HeaderText="Department">
        <ItemTemplate>
          <asp:Label Text='<%# Convert.ToString(DataBinder
           .Eval(Container.DataItem,"DeptName")) %>'
            runat="server" ID="lblDeptCode">
          </asp:Label>
         </ItemTemplate>
            <FooterTemplate>
               <asp:DropDownList ID="ddlDeptCode_Add"
                 runat="server" DataValueField="DeptCode"
                 DataTextField="DeptName" DataSource='<%#
                 FillDept()%>'></asp:DropDownList>
                  <font color="red">*</font>
            </FooterTemplate>
                <EditItemTemplate>
                   <asp:DropDownList ID="ddlDeptCode_Edit"
                     runat="server" DataValueField="DeptCode"
                     DataTextField="DeptName" DataSource='<%#
                     FillDept()%>'></asp:DropDownList>
                      <font color="red">*</font>
                </EditItemTemplate>
      </asp:TemplateColumn>
         <asp:EditCommandColumn ButtonType="LinkButton"
           UpdateText="Save" CancelText="Cancel"
           EditText="Edit"></asp:EditCommandColumn>
      <asp:TemplateColumn>
        <ItemTemplate>
          <asp:LinkButton CommandName="Delete" Text="Delete"
            ID="btnDelete" runat="server" />
        </ItemTemplate>
            <FooterTemplate>
               <asp:LinkButton CommandName="Insert" Text="Add"
                 ID="btnAdd" runat="server" />
            </FooterTemplate>
      </asp:TemplateColumn>
</Columns>
```

Note how we have used links for editing and deleting data in the **DataGrid** control, as shown in the previous code snippet.

Here is how our **DataGrid** control looks with `ItemTemplate` and `EditItemTemplate` used for each of its fields:

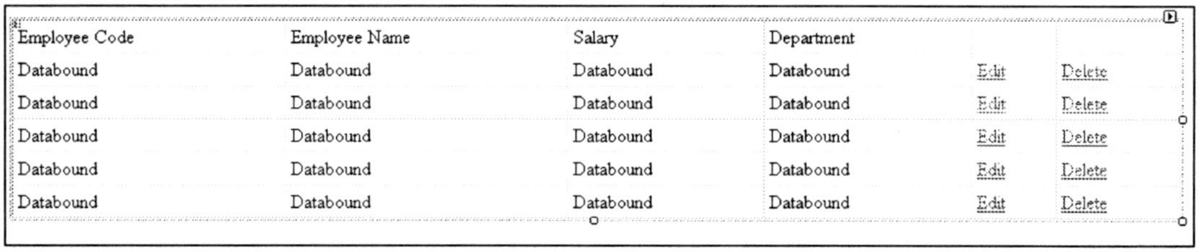

Note the **Edit** and **Delete** links in this screenshot.

Step 4: The next step is binding data to the **DataGrid** control in the `Page_Load` event handler of our web page using the `DataManager` class and invoking the `GetEmployees()` method of the class.

This is shown in the code snippet that follows.

```
protected void Page_Load(object sender, EventArgs e)
    {
        if (!Page.IsPostBack)
            this.BindGrid();
        this.lblMessage.Text = String.Empty;
    }
```

The `BindGrid()` method shown above, is responsible for binding data to the **DataGrid** by reusing the `DataManager` class. `BindGrid()` method is given as follows:

```
public void BindGrid()
{
    DataManager dataManager = new DataManager();
    ArrayList arrayList = dataManager.GetEmployees();
    dgEmployees.DataSource = arrayList;
    dgEmployees.DataBind();
}
```

Note the usage of the **Label** control named `lblMessage` in the above code snippet. We will discuss the usage of the **Label** control used later in this section.

Step 5: We will now incorporate **Paging** in the **DataGrid** control and apply some custom styles for its rows, header, and footer. We will also use the `OnItemCommand`, `OnEditCommand`, and `OnDeleteCommand` events of the **DataGrid** control to invoke respective event handlers to perform the actual `Select`, `Add`, `Edit`, or `Delete` operations using the control. These event handlers will be discussed in the next section of this chapter.

The following is the complete HTML source code of the control looks with all the event handlers set.

```
<body>
    <form id="frmEmployeeList" runat="server">
      <div>
        <asp:Label ID="lblMessage" runat="server" ForeColor="red"
          Font-Italic="true" Font-Bold="true"></asp:Label></div>
        <br/>
      <div>
        <asp:DataGrid ID="dgEmployees" runat="server"
          BorderStyle="None" PageSize="4" AllowPaging="True"
          OnItemCommand="onAdd" OnDeleteCommand="onDelete"
          OnUpdateCommand="onUpdate" OnCancelCommand="onCancel"
          OnEditCommand="onEdit" DataKeyField="EmpCode"
          ShowFooter="True" AutoGenerateColumns="False"
          CellPadding="4" BorderWidth="1px" BorderColor="#333366"
          BackColor="White" Width="80%"
          OnItemDataBound="dgEmployees_ItemDataBound"
          OnPageIndexChanged="dgEmployees_PageIndexChanged">
           <SelectedItemStyle Font-Bold="True" ForeColor="#663399"
               BackColor="#FFCC66">
           </SelectedItemStyle>
             <ItemStyle ForeColor="#330099"
               BackColor="White">
             </ItemStyle>
               <HeaderStyle Font-Bold="True"></HeaderStyle>
               <FooterStyle VerticalAlign="Middle"></FooterStyle>
                 <Columns>
                   <asp:TemplateColumn HeaderText="Employee Code">
                     <ItemTemplate>
                       <asp:Label Text='<%#
                         Convert.ToString(DataBinder.
                         Eval(Container.DataItem,"EmpCode")) %>'
                         runat="server" ID="lblEmpCode">
                       </asp:Label>
                       <asp:TextBox runat="server" ID="txtEmpCode"
```

```
              Visible="False" MaxLength="30" Text='<%#
              Convert.ToString(DataBinder
             .Eval(Container.DataItem,"EmpCode")) %>'
              Width="40">
            </asp:TextBox>
          </ItemTemplate>
<FooterTemplate>
</FooterTemplate>
   <EditItemTemplate>
     <asp:TextBox runat="server" ID="txtEmpCode_Edit"
       MaxLength="30" Text='<%# Convert.ToString
      (DataBinder.Eval(Container.DataItem,"EmpCode"))
       %>'
       Width="40" Enabled="false">
     </asp:TextBox>
        <font color="red">*</font>
   </EditItemTemplate>
     </asp:TemplateColumn>
     <asp:TemplateColumn HeaderText="Employee Name">
       <ItemTemplate>
         <asp:Label Text='<%# Convert.ToString
           (DataBinder.Eval(Container.DataItem,
           "EmpName")) %>'
           runat="server" ID="lblEmpName">
         </asp:Label>
       </ItemTemplate>
<FooterTemplate>
  <asp:TextBox ID="txtEmpName_Add" Width="150"
    MaxLength="30" runat="server" />
     <font color="red">*</font>
</FooterTemplate>
   <EditItemTemplate>
     <asp:TextBox runat="server" ID="txtEmpName_Edit"
       MaxLength="30" Text='<%# Convert.ToString
      (DataBinder.Eval(Container.DataItem,"EmpName"))
       %>'
       Width="150">
     </asp:TextBox>
       <font color="red">*</font>
   </EditItemTemplate>
     </asp:TemplateColumn>
     <asp:TemplateColumn HeaderText="Salary">
       <ItemTemplate>
          <asp:Label Text='<%# Convert.ToString
```

```
            (DataBinder.Eval(Container.DataItem,
            "Basic")) %>'
            runat="server" ID="lblBasic">
          </asp:Label>
        </ItemTemplate>
<FooterTemplate>
  <asp:TextBox ID="txtBasic_Add" Width="150"
    MaxLength="30" runat="server" />
        <font color="red">*</font>
</FooterTemplate>
   <EditItemTemplate>
     <asp:TextBox runat="server" ID="txtBasic_Edit"
       MaxLength="30" Text='<%# Convert.ToString
       (DataBinder.Eval(Container.DataItem,"Basic"))
       %>'
       Width="150">
     </asp:TextBox>
       <font color="red">*</font>
   </EditItemTemplate>
     </asp:TemplateColumn>
     <asp:TemplateColumn HeaderText="Department">
       <ItemTemplate>
         <asp:Label Text='<%# Convert.ToString
          (DataBinder.Eval(Container.DataItem,
          "DeptName")) %>'
          runat="server" ID="lblDeptCode">
         </asp:Label>
       </ItemTemplate>
<FooterTemplate>
  <asp:DropDownList ID="ddlDeptCode_Add"
    runat="server" DataValueField="DeptCode"
    DataTextField="DeptName" DataSource='<%#
    FillDept()%>'></asp:DropDownList>
        <font color="red">*</font>
</FooterTemplate>
   <EditItemTemplate>
      <asp:DropDownList ID="ddlDeptCode_Edit"
        runat="server" DataValueField="DeptCode"
        DataTextField="DeptName" DataSource='<%#
        FillDept()%>'></asp:DropDownList>
         <font color="red">*</font>
     </EditItemTemplate>
     </asp:TemplateColumn>
     <asp:EditCommandColumn ButtonType="LinkButton"
```

```
                        UpdateText="Save" CancelText="Cancel"
                        EditText="Edit"></asp:EditCommandColumn>
                      <asp:TemplateColumn>
                        <ItemTemplate>
                          <asp:LinkButton CommandName="Delete"
                            Text="Delete" ID="btnDelete" OnClick
                            ="fnCheckDelete();" runat="server" />
                        </ItemTemplate>
                 <FooterTemplate>
                    <asp:LinkButton CommandName="Insert" Text="Add"
                      ID="btnAdd" runat="server" />
                 </FooterTemplate>
                      </asp:TemplateColumn>
                  </Columns>
            <PagerStyle HorizontalAlign="Center"
              Mode="NumericPages"></PagerStyle>
         </asp:DataGrid>
      </div>
    </form>
  </body>
```

Step 6: Before any of the records are deleted, we should prompt the user for confirmation. Note that in the code snippet shown above, the **JavaScript** method, `fnCheckDelete()` is called, as shown here:

```
<asp:LinkButton CommandName="Delete" Text="Delete" ID="btnDelete"
    OnClick ="fnCheckDelete();" runat="server" />
```

Let us now incorporate a **JavaScript** method in our `.aspx` file that will be invoked each time you click on the **Delete** link in the user interface.

```
function fnCheckDelete()
{
  if (confirm("Are you sure you want to delete this record ?"))
    return true;
    return false;
}
```

Note that the department names are displayed using a **DropDownList** control within the **DataGrid** control. The above method actually prompts for confirmation from the user prior to deleting the selected record.

We will see more on this as we proceed further.

Step 7: Now we need to populate the **DropDownList** control with data from the Department table. Let us now incorporate the `FillDept()` method in the code behind file to bind data to this control from the department table.

```
public DataTable FillDept()
{
        DataManager dataManager = new DataManager();
        return dataManager.GetDepartmentList().Tables[0];
}
```

When you run the application for the first time, you will see a list of records displayed. This concludes our discussion on how data is bound to the **DataGrid,** inclusive of the **DropDownList** control that displays the department names within the **DataGrid** control. In the sections that follow, we'll discuss how we can perform various operations using the **DataGrid** control.

> Suppose you want to display the record number of each row in a **DataGrid** control. You can use a `TemplateColumn` for this and display the value of the `ItemIndex` property, as shown below.
>
> ```
> <asp:templatecolumn HeaderText="Record No">
>  <itemtemplate>
>  <%# Container.ItemIndex + 1 %>
>  </itemtemplate>
> </asp:templatecolumn>
> ```
>
> Note that the value of the `ItemIndex` property starts with a value of zero, to which we have added 1, as shown in the code snippet above.

Displaying Data

Let us now learn how we can display data in our web forms using the **DataGrid** control. This is how the **DataGrid** will look once you bind data to it.

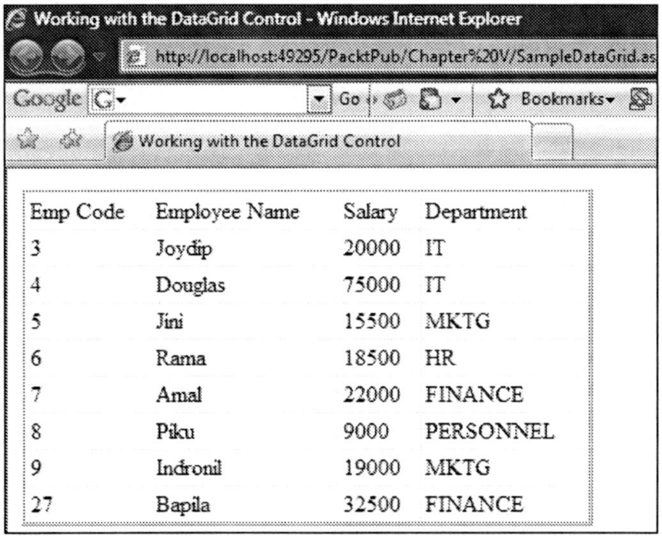

How do we accomplish this? It's really simple. Just drag-and-drop the control from the toolbox (if you are using ASP.NET 1.1) or write the code for the control in the `.aspx` file manually (if you are using ASP.NET 2.0 or higher).

> Based on how data is bound in the columns of a **DataGrid** control, you can have either a `BoundColumn` or a `TemplateColumn`. A `BoundColumn` implies one where the data is bound directly and you do not have control of customizing it using custom HTML code. In contrast, you can customize the markup as per your requirements when using a `TemplateColumn`. You can use the syntax of both HTML and Web Controls in a `TemplateColumn`. You generally use a `TemplateColumn` when you need to edit data in a **DataGrid** control.

Here is how we have used the `BoundColumn` in the following code snippet:

```
<asp:BoundColumn DataField="EmpCode"
   HeaderText="Emp Code"></asp:BoundColumn>
<asp:BoundColumn DataField="EmpName"
   HeaderText="Employee Name"></asp:BoundColumn>
<asp:BoundColumn DataField="Salary"
   HeaderText="Salary"></asp:BoundColumn>
<asp:BoundColumn DataField="DeptName"
   HeaderText="Department"></asp:BoundColumn>
```

Each of the `BoundColumn`, as shown in the code snippet above, is used to bind data retrieved from the database to the respective columns of the **DataGrid** control.

Here is the how you can declaratively write code to create a **DataGrid** control with its data bound columns:

```
<asp:DataGrid id="dgEmployee" HeaderStyle-CssClass="Header"
    runat="server" Width="100%" AutoGenerateColumns="False"
    CellPadding="3">
<ItemStyle CssClass="GridRow"></ItemStyle>
<HeaderStyle CssClass="GridHeader"></HeaderStyle>
  <Columns>
      <asp:BoundColumn DataField="EmpCode"
        HeaderText="Emp Code"></asp:BoundColumn>
      <asp:BoundColumn DataField="EmpName"
        HeaderText="Employee Name"></asp:BoundColumn>
      <asp:BoundColumn DataField="Salary"
        HeaderText="Salary"></asp:BoundColumn>
      <asp:BoundColumn DataField="DeptName"
        HeaderText="Department"></asp:BoundColumn>
  </Columns>
</asp:DataGrid>
```

We will retrieve data in the code behind, using the `DataManager` class and bind the data to our **DataGrid** control from the code behind file for our web page. For this, we will call the `GetEmployees()` method of this class in the `Page_Load` event, shown as follows:

```
protected void Page_Load(object sender, EventArgs e)
    {
        if (!IsPostBack)
        {
            DataManager dataManager = new DataManager();
            dgEmployee.DataSource = dataManager.GetEmployees();
            dgEmployee.DataBind();
        }
    }
```

The **DataGrid** that we have just created lacks a good look and feel. We can apply custom styles or even use style sheets in the **DataGrid** control to improve the look and feel of it. The next section discusses how we can do this.

Styling the DataGrid Control

In this section, we will learn how we can apply styles to the **DataGrid** control. We will explore how we can customize the look and feel of our **DataGrid** control using **Cascading Style Sheets**. We will display the records from the employee table and customize the header and the row style of the control using the style sheet. We will also display a horizontal bar that displays an employee's salary graphically, relative to the max salary. Here is the stylesheet that we will use.

```
body{
}
GridHeader
{
      font-family :Verdana ;
      font-size :12;
      color :White ;
      background-color :Black ;
}
GridRow
{
      font-family:Verdana ;
      font-size :11;
      background-color : White ;
}
SalaryBar
```

```
{
        font-family:Verdana ;
        font-size :10;
        background-color : Red ;
}
```

The CSS classes correspond to the `Header`, `Row` and the `Bar` that we will use in the DataGrid control. Following is the output of the application when you execute it.

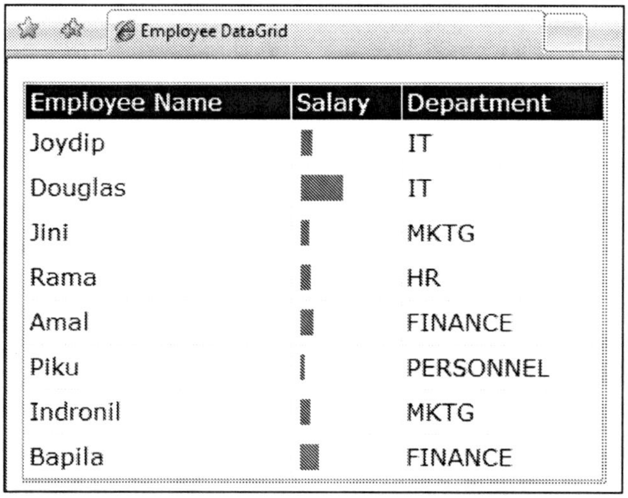

When you move your mouse on any of the bars shown above, the employee's salary is displayed as a tool tip. The following screenshot illustrates this:

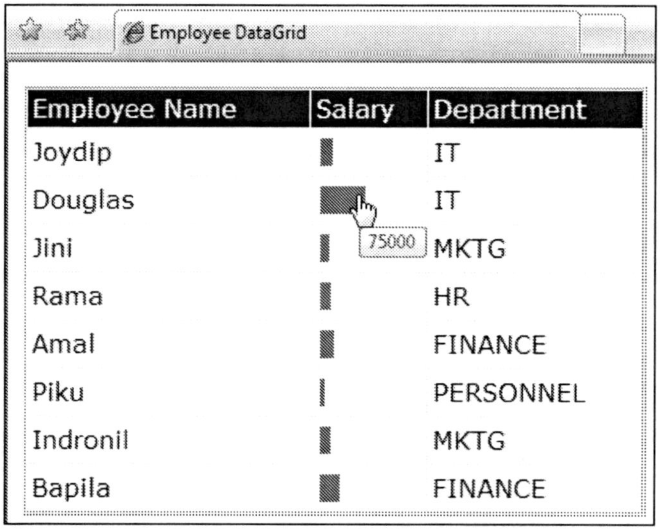

Wow! Note that when you place the mouse cursor on top of the **Salary** bar for the employee **Douglas**, the salary is displayed as a tool tip.

Now we will discuss how we can implement such an application. Here is the source code of the `.aspx` file that contains the **DataGrid** control, its templates, and the styles that have been applied to the control.

```
<form id="Form1" method="post" runat="server">
  <table id="Table1" cellspacing="0" cellpadding="0" width="400"
    border="1">
    <tr>
      <td>
        <asp:DataGrid id="dgEmployee".HeaderStyle-
          CssClass="Header"runat="server" Width="100%"
          AutoGenerateColumns="False" CellPadding="3">
            <ItemStyle.CssClass="GridRow">
            </ItemStyle>
            <HeaderStyle CssClass="GridHeader">
            </HeaderStyle>
              <Columns>
        <asp:BoundColumn DataField="EmpName" HeaderText="Employee
          Name"></asp:BoundColumn>
        <asp:TemplateColumn HeaderText="Salary">
           <ItemTemplate>
             <table width="100%">
               <tr>
                 <td>
                   <a title='<%#
                     DataBinder.Eval(Container.DataItem,"Salary").ToS
                     tring()%>' style="cursor:hand">
                   <div class="SalaryBar" style="width:
                     <%#((int.Parse(DataBinder.Eval(Container
                     DataItem,"Salary").ToString())*100)/MAXSALARY
                     )%>%;"></div>
                   </a>
                 </td>
                 <td style="width:<%# 100-
                   ((int.Parse(DataBinder.Eval(Container.DataItem,
                   "Salary").ToString())*100)/ MAXSALARY)%> +
                   MAXSALARY %;"></td>
             </tr>
           </table>
         </ItemTemplate>
        </asp:TemplateColumn>
        <asp:BoundColumn DataField="DeptName" HeaderText
```

```
            ="Department"></asp:BoundColumn>
             </Columns>
          </asp:DataGrid></td>
      </tr>
    </table>
  </form>
```

Note how the styles have been applied using the style sheet given earlier in this section. We have used the `SalaryBar` class of our style sheet to customize the `<td>` tag that relates to salary. Here is the source code that illustrates how you will bind data to the **DataGrid** control.

```
protected double MAXSALARY;
    private void Page_Load(object sender, System.EventArgs e)
    {
        if (!IsPostBack)
        {
            DataManager dataManager = new DataManager();
            MAXSALARY = double.Parse(dataManager.GetMaxSalary());
            dgEmployee.DataSource = dataManager.GetEmployees();
            dgEmployee.DataBind();
        }
    }
```

The `GetMaxSalary()` has been introduced new to our `DataManager` class. The intent of this method is returning the maximum salary of all the employees in the table. Following is the source code for the method.

```
public String GetMaxSalary()
    {
        SqlConnection conn = null;
        try
        {
            conn = new SqlConnection(connectionString);
            conn.Open();
            string sql = "Select Max(Salary) from Employee";
            SqlCommand cmd = new SqlCommand(sql, conn);
            return cmd.ExecuteScalar().ToString();
        }
        catch
        {
            throw;
        }
        finally
        {
            conn.Close();
        }
    }
```

For formatting the date type values in a **DataGrid** control you can use `DataFormatString` as shown below.

```
<asp:BoundColumn DataField="JoinDate"
HeaderText="Joining Date"
        DataFormatString="{0:MM-dd-yyyy}"/>
```

Appending Data Using the DataGrid Control

A blank row is displayed just beneath the last record of the page in view, as shown in the screenshot earlier, in this chapter. You can type in your required data and then click on the **Add** link to append the record in the employee table. Refer to the following screenshot:

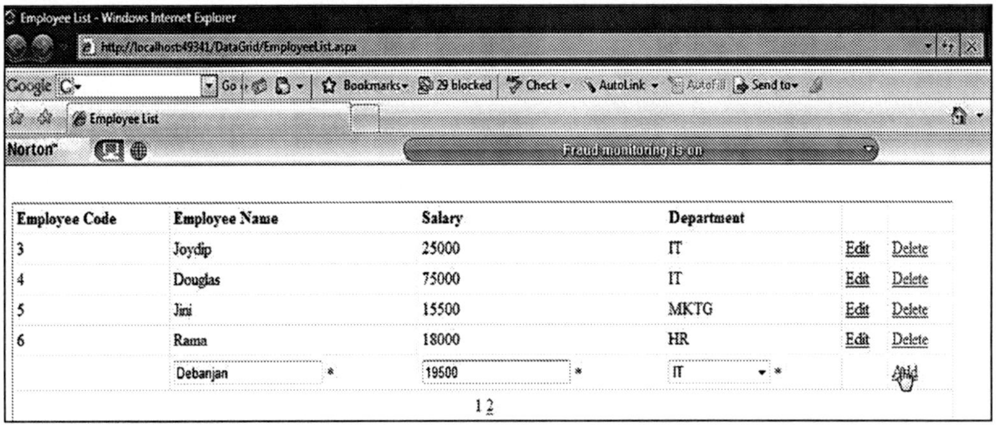

A new record is inserted in the employee table. The following screenshot displays the newly added record:

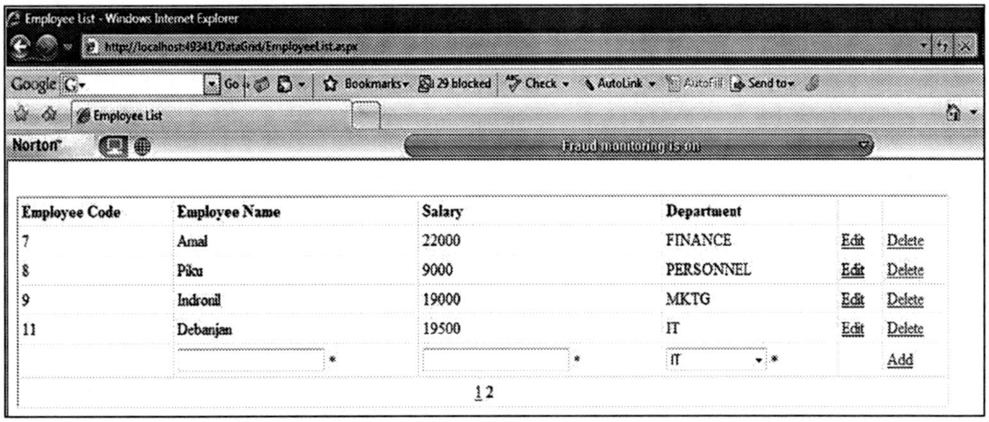

When you click on the Add LinkButton in the user interface, the `onAdd()` event handler is triggered. This has already been set in the `.aspx` file using the following statement:

```
OnItemCommand="onAdd"
```

The command name for the `Add LinkButton` has already been specified using the following statement in the `.aspx` file.

```
<asp:LinkButton CommandName="Insert" Text="Add" ID="btnAdd"
   runat="server" />
```

Next, the `FindControl()` method is called to retrieve the control instances within the **DataGrid** control. Here is the code that we will use the `FindControl()` method, in our code behind file, to retrieve the reference to the controls `txtEmpName_Add` and `txtBasic_Add` that are contained within the **DataGrid** control.

```
if (e.CommandName == "Insert")
     {
      if (((TextBox)e.Item.FindControl("txtEmpName_Add")).Text == "")
         {
            this.lblMessage.Text = "** Please Enter Employee Name **";
            return;
         }
     if (((TextBox)e.Item.FindControl("txtBasic_Add")).Text == "")
        {
          this.lblMessage.Text = "** Please Enter Employee Basic **";
          return;
        }
```

First we need to check the command name as shown in the source code given above. Note that in the code snippet shown above, that is, an instance of `DataGridCommandArgs`.

The complete source code for the `onAdd()` method is shown below:

```
public void onAdd(object source, DataGridCommandEventArgs e)
{
     if (e.CommandName == "Insert")
     {
      if (((TextBox)e.Item.FindControl("txtEmpName_Add")).Text == "")
         {
            this.lblMessage.Text = "** Please Enter Employee Name **";
            return;
         }
     if (((TextBox)e.Item.FindControl("txtBasic_Add")).Text == "")
```

```
        {
          this.lblMessage.Text = "** Please Enter Employee Basic **";
          return;
        }
    Employee employee = new Employee();
    employee.DeptCode = ((DropDownList)e.Item.FindControl
      ("ddlDeptCode_Add")).SelectedValue;
    employee.EmpName = ((TextBox)e.Item.FindControl("txtEmpName_Add"))
        .Text.Replace("'", "");
    employee.Basic = Convert.ToDouble(((TextBox)e
       .Item.FindControl("txtBasic_Add")).Text.Replace("'", ""));
       DataManager dataManager = new DataManager();
       dataManager.AddEmployee(employee);
       this.dgEmployees.EditItemIndex = -1;
       this.BindGrid();
        }
     }
```

As we can see in the code snippet above, once we have retrieved the reference to the controls within our **DataGrid** control, we can easily retrieve the data from these controls using their respective properties. Once done, we can set these values to the respective properties of an instance of our **Business Entity** class called `Employee`. The Employee class contains a list of private variables that correspond to the fields in the employee table. These variables are exposed using their corresponding public properties.

Here is the source code for the `Employee` class.

```
public class Employee
{
    private string empCode = String.Empty;
    private string empName = String.Empty;
    private double basic = 0.0;
    private string deptCode = String.Empty;
    private string deptName = String.Empty;
    private DateTime joiningDate;
    private bool active = false;

    public string EmpCode
    {
        get
        {
            return empCode;
        }
        set
        {
```

```
                empCode = value;
            }
        }
        public string EmpName
        {
            get
            {
                return empName;
            }
            set
            {
                empName = value;
            }
        }
        public double Basic
        {
            get
            {
                return basic;
            }
            set
            {
                basic = value;
            }
        }
        public string DeptCode
        {
            get
            {
                return deptCode;
            }
            set
            {
                deptCode = value;
            }
        }
        public string DeptName
        {
            get
            {
                return deptName;
            }
            set
            {
                deptName = value;
            }
        }
```

```
        public DateTime JoiningDate
        {
            get
            {
                return joiningDate;
            }
            set
            {
                joiningDate = value;
            }
        }
        public bool Active
        {
            get
            {
                return active;
            }
            set
            {
                active = value;
            }
        }
    }
```

As with a typical business entity class, the `Employee` class that represents the **Employee Business Entity** contains private members that are exposed using their corresponding public properties.

Next, an instance of the `DataManager` class is created and the `AddEmployee()` method of the `DataManager` class is called and the Business Entity instance,that is, the instance of the `Employee` class is passed to it as a parameter. The source code for the `AddEmployee()` method is given as follows:

```
    public int AddEmployee(Employee e)
        {
            String sqlString = "insert into Employee(EmployeeName,
              Salary, DepartmentID) values('" + e.EmpName + "', '" +
              e.Basic + "', '" + e.DeptCode + "')";
            SqlConnection sqlConnection = new
             SqlConnection(connectionString);
             sqlConnection.Open();
            SqlCommand sqlCommand = new SqlCommand(sqlString,
             sqlConnection);
            return sqlCommand.ExecuteNonQuery();
        }
```

Editing Data Using the DataGrid Control

You can edit a record using the **Edit** LinkButton, as shown in the following screenshot:

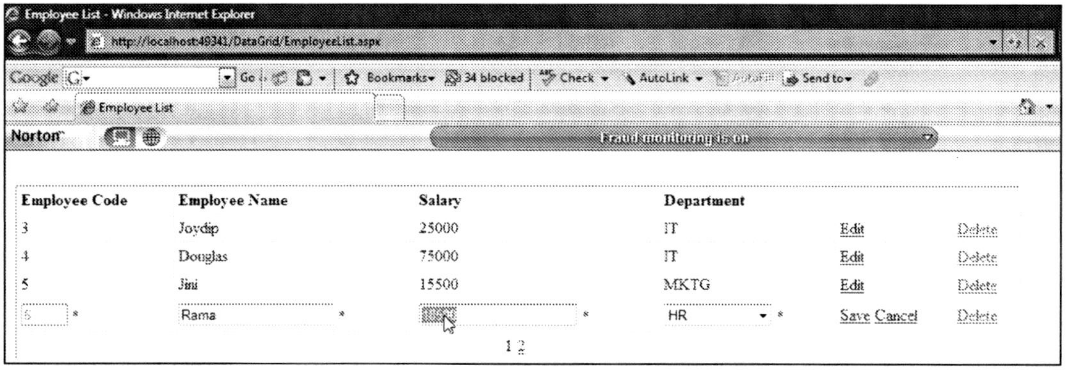

Note that we have changed the basic **Salary** from **18000** to **18500** for the employee **Rama**. Now, when you click on the **Save** LinkButton, the record is saved with these changes. The following screenshot displays the edited record once the page refreshes after the **Save** operation is successful.

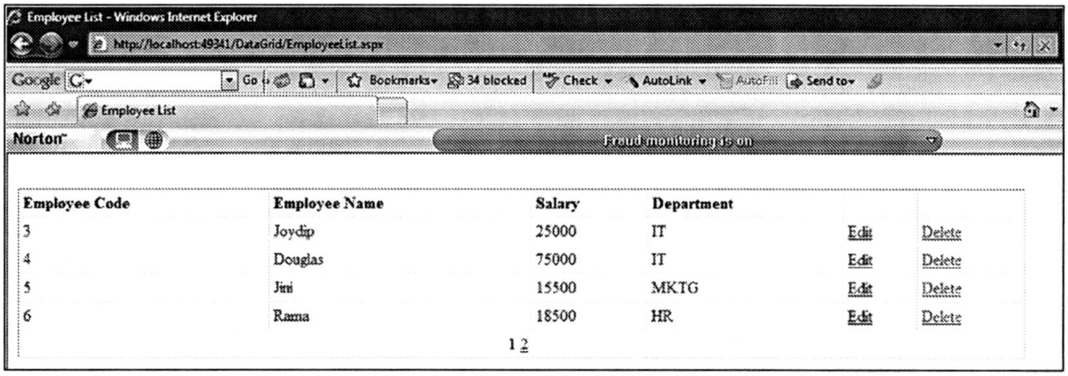

In order to edit data in the **DataGrid** control, we require a *TemplateColumn* called `EditCommandColumn`. The following is the code snippet which illustrates the same:

```
<asp:EditCommandColumn ButtonType="LinkButton" UpdateText="Save"
   CancelText="Cancel" EditText="Edit"></asp:EditCommandColumn>
```

Once defined, we need a method that should be executed to make the record editable. Note that the method to be executed is specified using the `OnEditCommand` attribute of the `DataGrid`, as shown in the following code snippet:

```
<asp:DataGrid ID="dgEmployees" runat="server" BorderStyle="None"
   PageSize="4" AllowPaging="True"
   OnItemCommand="onAdd" OnDeleteCommand="onDelete"
   OnUpdateCommand="onUpdate" OnCancelCommand="onCancel"
   OnEditCommand="onEdit" DataKeyField="EmpCode" ShowFooter="True"
   AutoGenerateColumns="False"
   CellPadding="4" BorderWidth="1px" BorderColor="#333366"
   BackColor="White" Width="80%"
   OnItemDataBound="dgEmployees_ItemDataBound"
   OnPageIndexChanged="dgEmployees_PageIndexChanged">
```

Now, when you click on the **Edit** LinkButton, the `onEdit()` event handler method gets fired. The code for this event handler is as follows:

```
public void onEdit(Object source, DataGridCommandEventArgs e)
    {
        this.dgEmployees.ShowFooter = false;
        this.dgEmployees.EditItemIndex = e.Item.ItemIndex;
        this.BindGrid();
    }
```

Note that when this event is fired, the `EditItemIndex` of the **DataGrid** control is set to the current row. This implies that all fields of the `EditItemTemplate` in the **DataGrid** become active and all the fields of the `ItemTemplate` become hidden. Hence, the controls in the `EditItemTemplate` become editable. Note that we have not made the Employee code field editable as this is the primary key. The following code snippet shows the `EditItemTemplate` of the Employee Name field in our **DataGrid** control.

```
<EditItemTemplate>
<asp:TextBox runat="server" ID="txtEmpName_Edit" MaxLength="30"
   Text='<%# Convert.ToString(DataBinder.Eval
   (Container.DataItem,"EmpName")) %>' Width="150">
</asp:TextBox>
  <font color="red">
  </font>
</EditItemTemplate>
```

Once you are done with the required changes, you can click on either the **Save** LinkButton to update the record, or, the **Cancel** LinkButton to undo the changes made. The `onUpdate()` method shown below is the event handler that is triggered whenever you click on the **Save** LinkButton after editing the selected record. The following is the code for `onUpdate()` method:

```
public void onUpdate(Object source, DataGridCommandEventArgs e)
 {
     if (((TextBox)e.Item.FindControl("txtEmpName_Edit")).Text == "")
         {
           this.lblMessage.Text = "** Please Enter Employee Name **";
             return;
         }
     if (((TextBox)e.Item.FindControl("txtBasic_Edit")).Text == "")
         {
           this.lblMessage.Text = "** Please Enter Employee Basic **";
             return;
         }
    Employee employee = new Employee();
    employee.EmpCode = ((TextBox)e
      Item.FindControl("txtEmpCode_Edit")).Text;
      employee.DeptCode ((DropDownList)e
     =.Item.FindControl("ddlDeptCode_Edit")).SelectedValue;
     employee.EmpName = ((TextBox)e.
       Item.FindControl("txtEmpName_Edit")).Text.Replace("'", "");
     employee.Basic = Convert.ToDouble(((TextBox)e.
       Item.FindControl("txtBasic_Edit")).Text.Replace("'", ""));
     DataManager dataManager = new DataManager();
      dataManager.UpdateEmployee(employee);
      this.dgEmployees.EditItemIndex = -1;
      this.BindGrid();
     }
```

Note that we make a call to the `UpdateEmployee()` method of the `DataManager` to update the record in the employee table. The following is the source code for the `UpdateEmployee()` method:

```
public int UpdateEmployee(Employee e)
{
    string sqlString = "update Employee set EmployeeName =  '" +
     e.EmpName + "', Salary = '" + e.Basic + "', DepartmentID = '" +
     e.DeptCode + "' where EmployeeID = '" + e.EmpCode + "'";
    SqlConnection sqlConnection = new SqlConnection(connectionString);
    sqlConnection.Open();
    SqlCommand sqlCommand = new SqlCommand(sqlString, sqlConnection);
    return sqlCommand.ExecuteNonQuery();
}
```

The `BindGrid()` method is called to rebind data to the **DataGrid** control so as to refresh the display after the edited record has been saved to the table.

Deleting Data Using the DataGrid Control

You can delete a record by clicking on the **Delete** LinkButton next to a record, as shown in the following screenshot:

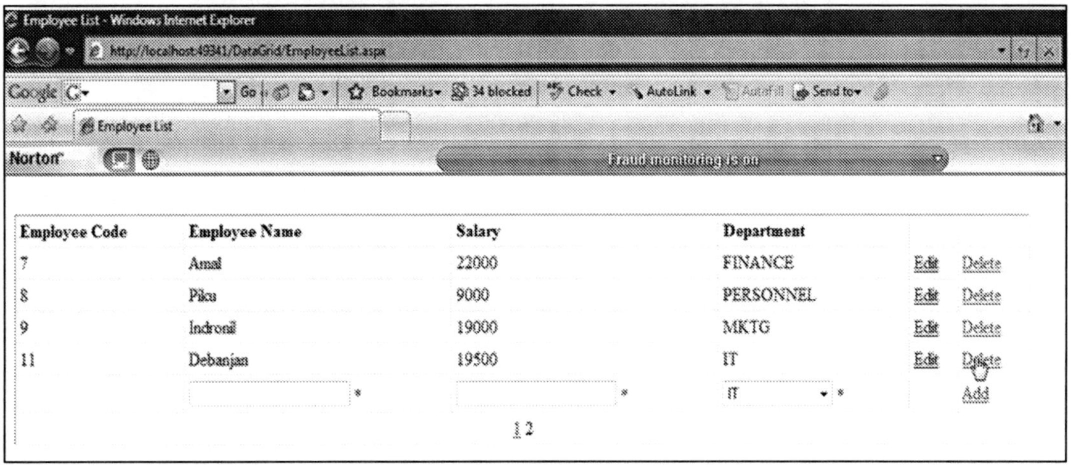

When you click on the **Delete** LinkButton, a dialog box pops up and prompts for confirmation. Refer to the following screenshot:

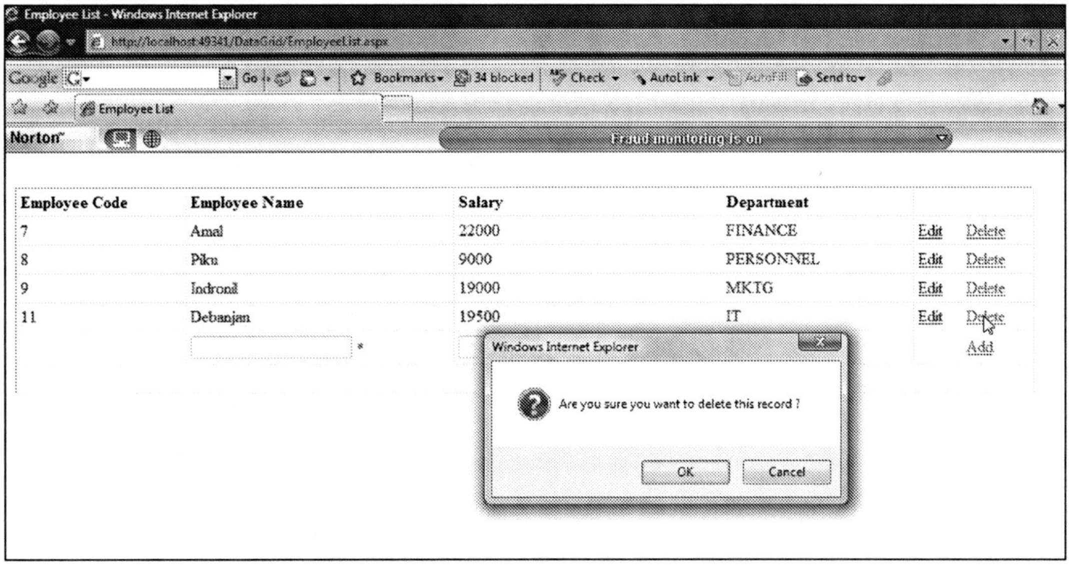

Now, click on the **OK** button to delete this record. The following screenshot captures the output after the record is deleted:

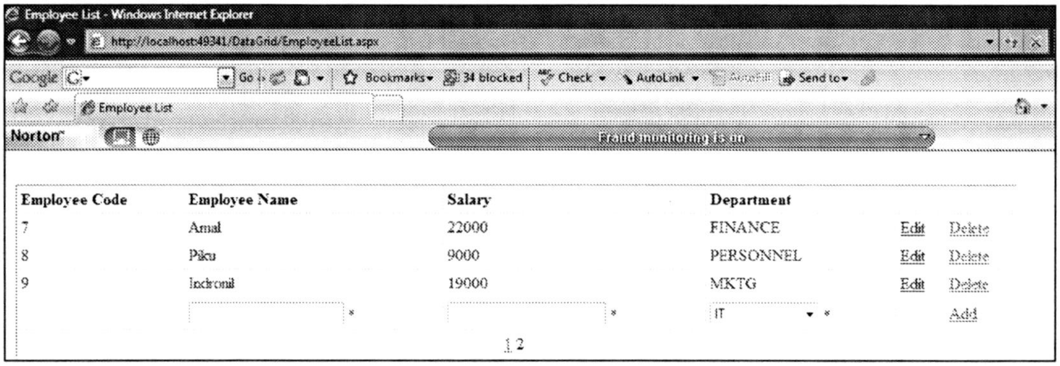

Once the record is deleted, the page refreshes and you can see that the record you just deleted, that is, the employee called **Debanjan** with an **Employee Code 11**, is no longer displayed in the **DataGrid**.

The following is the source code for the `onDelete()` event handler method that is fired once you click on the **Delete** LinkButton.

```
public void onDelete(object source, DataGridCommandEventArgs e)
{
   String employeeCode = dgEmployees.DataKeys
     [e.Item.ItemIndex].ToString().Replace("'", "");
   DataManager dataManager = new DataManager();
   dataManager.DeleteEmployee(employeeCode);
   this.dgEmployees.EditItemIndex = -1;
   this.BindGrid();
}
```

The above event handler method makes use of the `DataManager` class, as usual, to delete an employee record. The following is the source code for the `DeleteEmployee()` method of the `DataManager` class.

```
public int DeleteEmployee(String empCode)
{
    string sqlString = "Delete from Employee where EmployeeID = '" +
      empCode + "'";
    SqlConnection sqlConnection = null;
    sqlConnection = new SqlConnection(connectionString);
    sqlConnection.Open();
    SqlCommand sqlCommand = new SqlCommand(sqlString, sqlConnection);
    return sqlCommand.ExecuteNonQuery();
}
```

> If you want to provide the user a confirmation alert before he or she deletes the record, you can use the `RowDataBound` event for this. The code snippet given below illustrates that you can achieve this.
>
> ```
> protected void dgEmployee_RowDataBound (object sender,
> System.Web.UI.WebControls.GridViewRowEventArgs e)
>    {
>       if (e.Row.RowType == DataControlRowType.DataRow)
>       {
>          ((LinkButton)(e.Row.Cells[0].Controls[5])).
>           Attributes.Add("onclick",
>             "return confirm('Please confirm before the
>              record is deleted');");
>       }
>    }
> ```

When you click on the **Cancel** LinkButton in the dialog box, the `EditItemIndex` is set to `1` to make the record non-editable. Once this is done, the `EditItemTemplate` is hidden and the `ItemTemplate` is made active.

Paging Using the DataGrid Control

You can also use paging with the **DataGrid** control. To enable paging, you need to set the `AllowPaging` property of the control, as shown in the following code snippet:

```
AllowPaging="True"
```

The event handler that should be called whenever the page index changes is also set in the `.aspx` file as shown here.

```
OnPageIndexChanged="dgEmployees_PageIndexChanged"
```

The `dgEmployees_PageIndexChanged()` event handler is called each time the data results are changed by clicking on the links that correspond to the page numbers. Refer to the first screenshot in this chapter. The source code for this event handler is as follows:

```
protected void dgEmployees_PageIndexChanged(object source,
   System.Web.UI.WebControls.DataGridPageChangedEventArgs e)
{
   this.dgEmployees.CurrentPageIndex = e.NewPageIndex;
   this.BindGrid();
}
```

The `BindGrid()` method is called and the `CurrentPageIndex` property, that holds the index of the most recent page in use, is set to the value of the `NewPageIndex` property of the instance of the `DataGridPageChangedEventArgs` class.

The source code for the `dgEmployees_ItemDataBound()` event handler is as follows.

```
protected void dgEmployees_ItemDataBound(object sender,
   System.Web.UI.WebControls.DataGridItemEventArgs e)
{
   if (e.Item.ItemType == ListItemType.Item || e.Item.ItemType ==
     ListItemType.AlternatingItem || e.Item.ItemType ==
     ListItemType.EditItem)
{
   ((LinkButton)e.Item.FindControl("btnDelete")).
      Attributes["onClick"] = "return fnCheckDelete()";
}
if (e.Item.ItemType == ListItemType.EditItem)
{
   try
   {
       ((DropDownList)e.Item.FindControl
         ("ddlDeptCode_Edit")).Items.FindByValue
         (Convert.ToString(DataBinder.Eval(e.Item.DataItem,
         "DeptCode"))).Selected = true;
   }
    catch { }
}
}
```

Summary

In this chapter we discussed the **DataGrid** control and how we can implement a sample application that contains all the necessary functionalities, like display, append, edit, and delete data using this control. We have discussed how we can work with the events of **DataGrid** control. In addition, we looked at how we can style our **DataGrid** using CSS classes in a sample application. In the next two chapters, we will learn how we can work with the DataView, GridView, FormView, DetailsView, and the TreeView controls in ASP.NET. In the concluding chapter of this book, we will discuss how we can bind data to the new data controls of Orcas using LINQ.

6

Displaying Views of Data (Part I)

In Chapter 5, we have looked at how we can work with the DataGrid control in ASP.NET. This is the first in the series of two chapters on how we can use the view controls, like, GridView, DetailsView and FormView controls to display different views of data in ASP.NET 2.0. In this chapter, I will present the GridView control and how the data source controls can be used to bind data to it. We will also discuss how we can export data from this control to **Excel** or **Word** documents with sample code in each case.

In this chapter, we will learn the following:

- Using the GridView control
- Displaying data using the GridView control
- Displaying CheckBox and DropDownList inside a GridView control
- Selecting a row inside a GridView control
- Displaying a hierarchical GridView control
- Paging data using the GridView control
- Sorting data using the GridView control
- Inserting, editing and deleting data using the GridView control
- Exporting the GridView control
- Formatting the GridView control

The ASP.NET GridView Control

The idea behind the development of this data control is to display data in one of the simplest ways possible, without having to write even a single line of code. Amazing, isn't it? You only require proper configuration of the data source controls, that is, the **SqlDataSource**, **AccessDataSource**, **ObjectDataSource** or the **XmlDataSource** control and setting this as the data source property of the **GridView** data control. Once the application is executed, this control is rendered as a table tag in HTML. We will learn more on this as we progress through the chapter.

To use the **GridView** web control, you can drag and drop it from the **Toolbox** as shown in the following snapshot:

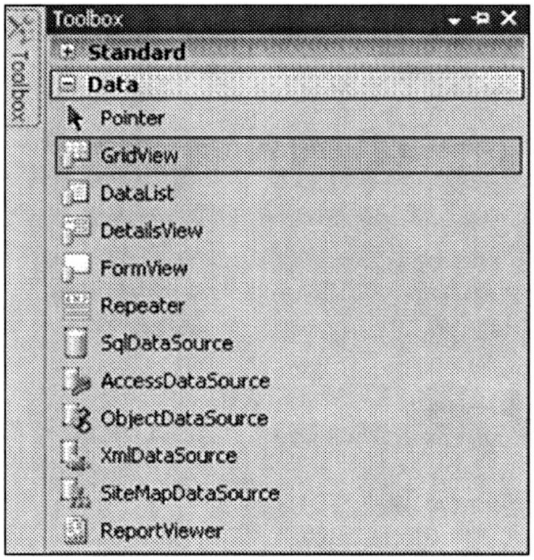

You can also create the **GridView** control programmatically in your `.aspx` file. The complete syntax for using the **GridView** control is shown as follows:

```
<asp:GridView id="value" Runat="Server"
  AllowPaging="True|False"
  AllowSorting="True|False"
  AutoGenerateColumns="True|False"
  Caption="string"
  CaptionAlign="Left|NotSet|Right|Justify"
  CellPadding="n"
  CellSpacing="n"
  DataSourceID="datasourceid"
  EmptyDataText="string"
  GridLines="Both|Horizontal|Vertical|None"
```

```
    PageSize="n"
    ShowHeader="True|False"
    ShowFooter="True|False"
      property="value"
      Style="style"
      HeaderStyle-property="value"
      RowStyle-property="value"
      AlternatingRowStyle-property="value"
      FooterStyle-property="value"
  />
```

You can bind data to this web control using any of the data source controls available with ASP.NET 2.0. We will take **SqlDataSource** control in this chapter. We have already discussed data source controls in Chapter 1 of this book. The following figure displays the **GridView** control in its design view. Note that you have the generic columns associated with the control before you bind any data source to it. These columns have names like **Column0, Column1, Column2**, until a data source is bound to it.

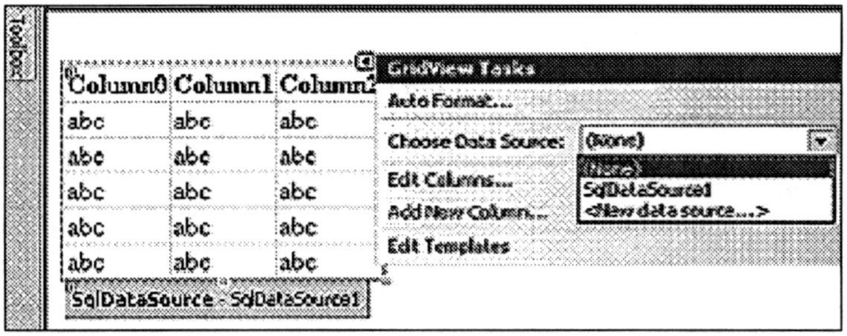

As we have seen in Chapter 1 of this book, you can associate a data source with this control easily from the **New Data Source** option. Once a data source is associated with this control, the control can display data once you execute your web page. The following screenshot shows a **GridView** control with data from our Employee table.

Employee ID	EmployeeName	Joining Date	Department ID	Salary
3	Joydip	08-09-2007	1	Rs. 20,000.00
4	Douglas	08-09-2007	1	Rs. 75,000.00
5	Jini	08-09-2007	2	Rs. 15,500.00
6	Rama	01-09-2007	3	Rs. 18,500.00
7	Amal	10-12-2006	4	Rs. 22,000.00
8	Piku	01-09-2007	5	Rs. 9,000.00
9	Indronil	08-09-2007	2	Rs. 19,000.00
27	Bapila	02-01-2005	4	Rs. 32,500.00

If you look at the above figure, you will observe that the data displayed in the **JoiningDate** and the **Salary** fields are not properly formatted. We will learn how to format data using the **GridView** control later in this chapter.

DataGrid is generally used in ASP.NET 1.1 and not in ASP.NET 2.0. In ASP.NET 2.0, we prefer using the **GridView** control. You need not write much code to render the control. This is what makes the life of a developer much easier.

Our GridView as displayed in the previous figure lacks visual appeal. Let us learn how we can use proper formatting at column level or cell level of this control to produce visually appealing displays.

You have in the GridView control one column per column of the Data Source control that you use. Let us now take a look at the declarative mark-up of the `GridView` control in the source code view, that is, in the `.aspx` file. Refer to the following code snippet that illustrates this:

```
<asp:GridView ID="GridView1" runat="server"
  AutoGenerateColumns="False" DataKeyNames="EmployeeID"
   DataSourceID="SqlDataSource1">
   <Columns>
     <asp:BoundField DataField="EmployeeID" HeaderText="EmployeeID"
       InsertVisible="False" ReadOnly="True"
        SortExpression="EmployeeID" />
     <asp:BoundField DataField="EmployeeName"
       HeaderText="EmployeeName" SortExpression="EmployeeName" />
     <asp:BoundField DataField="JoiningDate" HeaderText="JoiningDate"
       SortExpression="JoiningDate" />
     <asp:BoundField DataField="DepartmentID"
       HeaderText="DepartmentID" SortExpression="DepartmentID" />
     <asp:BoundField DataField="Salary" HeaderText="Salary"
       SortExpression="Salary" />
   </Columns>
</asp:GridView>
```

The corresponding code in the `.aspx` file for the `SqlDataSource` control (that we have used to bind data to this control) is as follows:

```
<asp:SqlDataSource ID="SqlDataSource1" runat="server"
  ConnectionString="Data Source=.;Initial Catalog=Test;User
   ID=sa;Password=sa"
    ProviderName="System.Data.SqlClient" SelectCommand="SELECT
    [EmployeeID], [EmployeeName], [JoiningDate], [DepartmentID],
    [Salary] FROM [Employee]">
</asp:SqlDataSource>
```

Note that these mark-ups are actually rendered as HTML tags when the page is executed. Let us now customize the look and feel of the GridView control. You can customize the GridView control at the control level, that is, the GridView Level, the row level or at the column level.

The following code snippet shows how you can set the background colour at the column level and the `GridView` level for customized display.

```
<asp:GridView ID="GridView1" runat="server" RowStyle-BackColor =
  "CadetBlue" AutoGenerateColumns= "False" DataKeyNames="EmployeeID"
   DataSourceID="SqlDataSource1">
  <Columns>
    <asp:BoundField DataField="EmployeeID" HeaderStyle-BackColor =
      "Aqua" HeaderText="EmployeeID" InsertVisible="False"
       ReadOnly="True" SortExpression="EmployeeID" />
    <asp:BoundField DataField="EmployeeName" HeaderStyle-BackColor =
      "Aqua" HeaderText="EmployeeName" SortExpression="EmployeeName"
    />
    <asp:BoundField DataField="JoiningDate" HeaderStyle-BackColor =
      "Aqua" HeaderText="JoiningDate" SortExpression="JoiningDate"
    />
    <asp:BoundField DataField="DepartmentID" HeaderStyle-BackColor =
      "Aqua" HeaderText="DepartmentID" SortExpression="DepartmentID"
    />
    <asp:BoundField DataField="Salary" HeaderStyle-BackColor =
      "Aqua" HeaderText="Salary" SortExpression="Salary" />
  </Columns>
</asp:GridView>
```

The following screenshot shows the **GridView** control populated with data from the Employee table and with a customized look and feel.

EmployeeID	EmployeeName	JoiningDate	DepartmentID	Salary
3	Joydip	08-09-2007	1	Rs. 20,000.00
4	Douglas	08-09-2007	1	Rs. 75,000.00
5	Jini	08-09-2007	2	Rs. 15,500.00
6	Rama	01-09-2007	3	Rs. 18,500.00
7	Amal	10-12-2006	4	Rs. 22,000.00
8	Piku	01-09-2007	5	Rs. 9,000.00
9	Indronil	08-09-2007	2	Rs. 19,000.00
27	Bapila	02-01-2005	4	Rs. 32,500.00

You can even use your Cascading Style Sheets for customizing the look and feel of the **GridView** control.

Note the use of both paging and sorting functionalities in a GridView control. The sections that follow look at how you can work with the GridView control to implement paging and sorting functionalities.

Comparing DataGrid and GridView Controls

In this section we will discuss how the two data controls DataGrid and GridView differ. While both DataGrid and GridView controls are used for binding and displaying data in tabular format, there are subtle differences between the two as far as their suitability is concerned. When you use a DataGrid control, you need to write your own code for binding, sorting, and paging data. In contrast, these features are inbuilt in the **GridView** control and you can display, insert, edit or delete your data using this control without having to write code. However, some of these pitfalls of the DataGrid control have been addressed with ASP.NET 2.0 and after. Let us take a look at the salient features of the GridView control. These are as follows:

- Support for data source binding using the new Data Source controls available in ASP.NET 2.0 and after
- Advanced event model
- In-built support for paging and sorting of data
- Better design time support and added templates from its earlier counterparts

Displaying DropDownList in a GridView Control

In this section we will learn how to display a DropDownList in a GridView control. We will display the department names of the employees using the DropDownList control. Following is the output when you execute the application:

Rec No	EmployeeName	Department	JoiningDate	Salary
1	Joydip	IT	08-09-2007	Rs. 20,000.00
2	Douglas	IT	08-09-2007	Rs. 75,000.00
3	Jini	MKTG	08-09-2007	Rs. 15,500.00
4	Rama	HR	01-09-2007	Rs. 18,500.00
5	Amal	FINANCE	10-12-2006	Rs. 22,000.00
6	Piku	PERSONNEL	01-09-2007	Rs. 9,000.00
7	Indronil	MKTG	08-09-2007	Rs. 19,000.00
8	Bapila	FINANCE	02-01-2005	Rs. 32,500.00

Following is the code in the .aspx file that illustrates how you can associate a DropDownList control with the department names of an employee.

```
<Columns>
  <asp:TemplateField HeaderText="Rec No" HeaderStyle-BackColor =
    "DarkOrange" Visible="True">
    <ItemTemplate>
       <%# Container.DisplayIndex + 1 %>
    </ItemTemplate>
  </asp:TemplateField>
  <asp:TemplateField Visible="False">
    <ItemTemplate>
       <asp:Label ID="lblDept" runat="server" Text='<%#
         Eval("DepartmentID") %>' />
    </ItemTemplate>
  </asp:TemplateField>
  <asp:BoundField DataField="EmployeeName" HeaderStyle-BackColor =
    "DarkOrange" HeaderText="EmployeeName"/>
  <asp:TemplateField ControlStyle-ForeColor="Black" HeaderStyle-
    BackColor = "DarkOrange" HeaderText="Department">
    <ItemTemplate>
       <asp:DropDownList ID="drpDept" ForeColor="Black"
         BackColor="Khaki" runat="server">
       </asp:DropDownList>
    </ItemTemplate>
  </asp:TemplateField>
  <asp:BoundField DataField="JoiningDate" HeaderStyle-BackColor =
    "DarkOrange" HeaderText="JoiningDate" DataFormatString="{0:d}"/>
  <asp:BoundField DataField="Salary" HeaderStyle-BackColor =
    "DarkOrange" HeaderText="Salary" DataFormatString="{0:C}"/>
</Columns>
```

Refer to the code snippet above. The DisplayIndex property of the Container object has been used to display the record number for each record of the GridView control. The value of this property starts with 0, hence the necessity of adding 1 to it. Note that we have taken a TemplateField to use a DropDownList control called drpDept that will display the department names in the list control. The department to which a particular employee belongs would be selected by default. To achieve this, we need to write the following code in the RowDataBound event handler of the GridView control.

```
protected void GridView1_RowDataBound(object sender,
  GridViewRowEventArgs e)
    {
       if (e.Row.RowType == DataControlRowType.DataRow)
```

```
        {
            String deptID = ((Label)e.Row.
              FindControl("lblDept")).Text;
            DataSet ds = new DataSet();
            ds = dataManager.GetDepartmentList();
            DropDownList ddl =
             (DropDownList)e.Row.FindControl("drpDept");
            ddl.DataSource = ds.Tables[0];
            ddl.DataTextField = "DeptName";
            ddl.DataValueField = "DeptCode";
            ddl.DataBind();
            ddl.SelectedIndex =
             ddl.Items.IndexOf(ddl.Items.FindByValue(deptID));
        }
    }
```

The department name of each employee is actually stored in a hidden label control called `lblDept`. A reference to this control is retrieved using the `FindControl()` method. The `GetDepartmentList()` method returns the department names as a `DataSet`. Using the `FindControl()` method, a reference to the `DropDownList` control called `drpDept`, is retrieved. Next, the `DataTextField` and the `DataValueField` properties of the `DropDownList` control are set properly. The `FindByValue()` method is used to set the `SelectedIndex` property of the control to the appropriate department name.

Displaying CheckBox in a GridView Control

We will now explore how to display a CheckBox in each of the records in a **GridView** control. Following is the output of the application on execution.

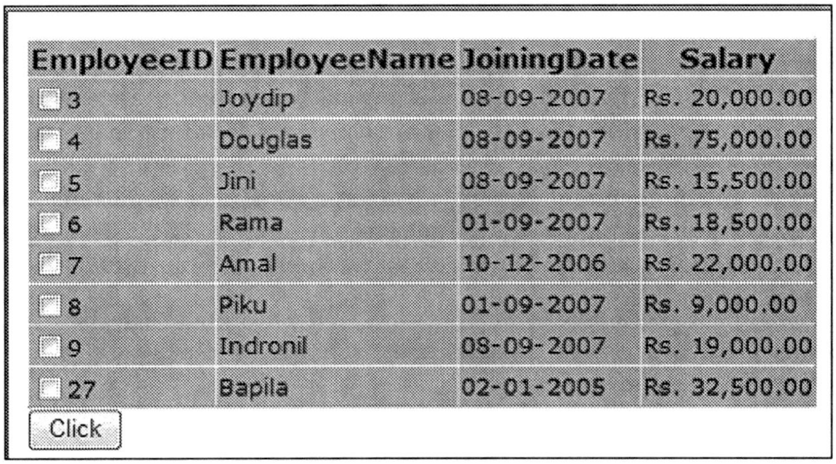

EmployeeID	EmployeeName	JoiningDate	Salary
3	Joydip	08-09-2007	Rs. 20,000.00
4	Douglas	08-09-2007	Rs. 75,000.00
5	Jini	08-09-2007	Rs. 15,500.00
6	Rama	01-09-2007	Rs. 18,500.00
7	Amal	10-12-2006	Rs. 22,000.00
8	Piku	01-09-2007	Rs. 9,000.00
9	Indronil	08-09-2007	Rs. 19,000.00
27	Bapila	02-01-2005	Rs. 32,500.00

Note that there is a CheckBox control in the **EmployeeID** column of the **GridView** control for each of its records displayed. When you select one or more check boxes and click on the **Click** button control beneath the **GridView** control, the employee names for the selected employee records are displayed as shown in the following figure:

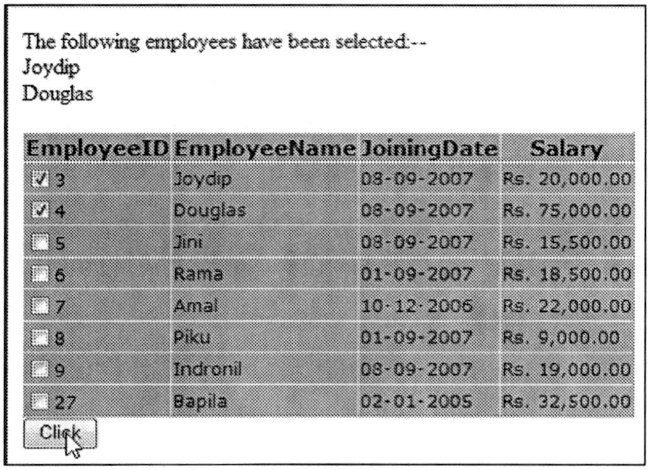

Let us now understand how we can achieve this. To display a CheckBox that is bound to the **EmployeeID** column, we will use a `TemplateField`, as shown in the following code snippet:

```
<asp:TemplateField Visible="True" ControlStyle-ForeColor="Black"
  HeaderStyle-BackColor = "DarkOrange" HeaderText="EmployeeID">
  <ItemTemplate>
    <asp:CheckBox ID="chkSelect" runat="server" Text='<%#
      Eval("EmployeeID") %>'/>
  </ItemTemplate>
</asp:TemplateField>
```

In the `Click` event of the button control, we need to iterate through all the rows of the **GridView** control and check whether the `CheckBox` for that row is checked. If so, the employee name corresponding to that record is displayed. Following is the code for the event handler for the `Click` event of the button control.

```
protected void btnClick_Click(object sender, EventArgs e)
{
        Response.Write("The following employees have been selected:--
         ");
        for (int i = 0; i < GridView1.Rows.Count; i++)
        {
```

```
                if (((CheckBox)GridView1.Rows[i].FindControl
                    ("chkSelect")).Checked)
                {
                    Response.Write("<BR>" + GridView1
                    .Rows[i].Cells[3].Text);
                }
            }
    }
```

Note that we have used the `FindControl()` method as usual to retrieve a reference to the `CheckBox` control of each of the rows of the `GridView` control. In the next section we will learn how we can display tool tips in a GridView control.

Change the Row Color of GridView Control Using JavaScript

We will now explore how we can change the color of a GridViewRow using JavaScript. First, let us understand how we can change the row color in the `Click` event of any particular row of the **GridView** control. Following is a screenshot that illustrates that the color of the clicked row has been changed.

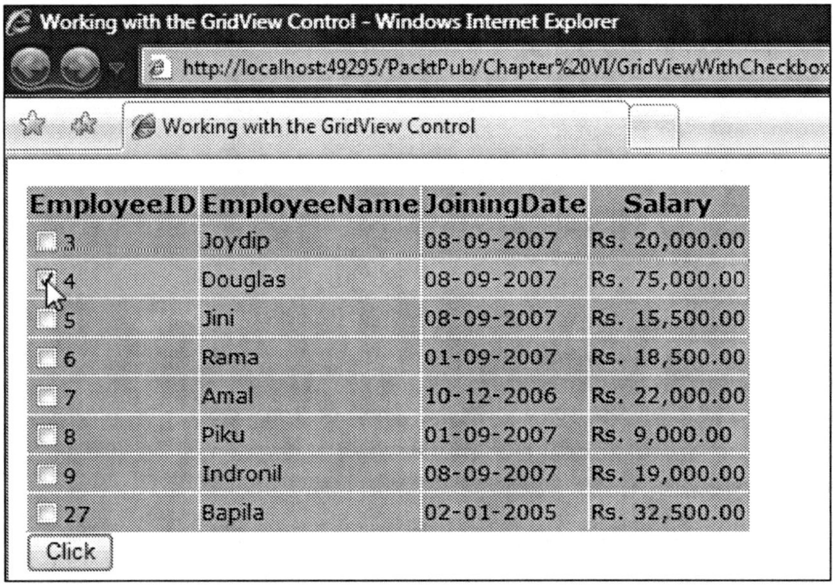

When the same row is clicked again, the original color is displayed for that row. Following is the output when you click on the same row for which the color has been changed on account of the **Click.**

EmployeeID	EmployeeName	JoiningDate	Salary
3	Joydip	08-09-2007	Rs. 20,000.00
4	Douglas	08-09-2007	Rs. 75,000.00
5	Jini	08-09-2007	Rs. 15,500.00
6	Rama	01-09-2007	Rs. 18,500.00
7	Amal	10-12-2006	Rs. 22,000.00
8	Piku	01-09-2007	Rs. 9,000.00
9	Indronil	08-09-2007	Rs. 19,000.00
27	Bapila	02-01-2005	Rs. 32,500.00

Click

To achieve this; it is simple. Use the following code in the `RowDataBound` event handler to set up the `JavaScript()` method to be called when any of the rows of the **GridView** control is clicked. The name of this method is `ChangeGridRowColor()`. Following is the complete source for the `RowDataBound` event handler.

```
protected void GridView1_RowDataBound(object sender,
    GridViewRowEventArgs e)
    {
        if (e.Row.RowType == DataControlRowType.DataRow)
           e.Row.Attributes["onclick"] =
               "javascript:ChangeGridRowColor(this);";
    }
```

The `JavaScript()` method `ChangeGridRow` is given as follows:

```
function ChangeGridRowColor(element)
{
  if(element.style.backgroundColor == 'cyan')
      element.style.backgroundColor='deepskyblue';
  else
      element.style.backgroundColor='cyan';
}
```

Changing row color of the GridView control using JavaScript when the mouse moves over the control's rows

We can also change the color of a row in the **GridView** as and when you move the mouse pointer from one row to the other. You need to write the following code in the RowDataBound event handler of the control.

```
protected void GridView1_RowDataBound(object sender,
    GridViewRowEventArgs e)
{
        if (e.Row.RowType == DataControlRowType.
DataRow)
        {
            e.Row.Attributes["onmouseover"] =
"javascript:ToggleRowColor(this);";
            e.Row.Attributes["onmouseout"] =
"javascript:ToggleRowColor(this);";
        }
}
```

Note that the `ToggleRowColor() JavaScript()` method is called on the `onmouseover` and the `onmouseout` events of the row of the **GridView** control. Following is the code for the `ToggleRowColor()` method.

```
function ToggleRowColor(element)
{
    if(element.style.backgroundColor == 'cyan')
    {
            element.style.backgroundColor='deepskyblue';
            element.style.cursor='hand';
            element.style.textDecoration='none';
    }
    else
    {
     element.style.backgroundColor='cyan';
     element.style.cursor='hand';
     element.style.textDecoration='underline';
    }
}
```

Displaying Tool Tip in a GridView Control

Let us now learn how we can display tool tip in a **GridView** control to display an employee's address. Following is the output when you execute the application.

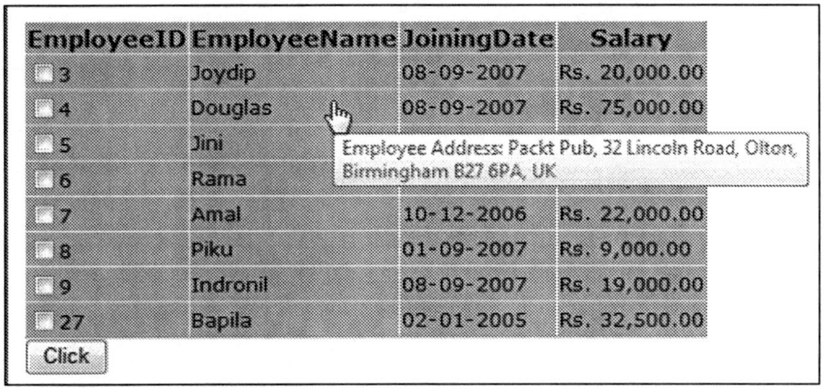

Refer to the screenshot above. Note that the employee **Douglas**'s address is displayed as a tool tip as and when you place the cursor on the record. To achieve this, you need to specify the following code in the `RowDataBound` event of the **GridView** control.

```
protected void GridView1_RowDataBound(object sender,
  GridViewRowEventArgs e)
{
        if (e.Row.RowType == DataControlRowType.DataRow)
        {
            e.Row.ToolTip = "Employee Address: " +
              Convert.ToString(DataBinder.Eval(e.Row.DataItem,
              "EmployeeAddress"));
            e.Row.Style.Add("Cursor", "Hand");
        }
}
```

Paging Using the GridView Control

Paging is a feature that displays a specified number of records from the entire result set. You need to set the page size appropriately to display a set of records of the entire result set. As we have seen, the data source that we have used so far displays all the records retrieved from the Employee table. This might look clumsy if there are hundreds or thousands of records in your resultset. With this in mind, we can use the paging feature with this control to ensure that the display is appealing. The user can then navigate to different pages of the result set simply by clicking the page numbers displayed with the control.

For this, we need to set the `AllowPaging` property of the control to `true` and set the `PageSize` property of the control to the required page size as appropriate. As our data source contains a few records only, let us set the `PageSize` property to `4`. The following code snippet illustrates this:

```
<asp:GridView ID="GridView1" runat="server" AllowPaging ="true"
  PageSize = "4" RowStyle-BackColor = "CadetBlue"
  AutoGenerateColumns= "False" DataKeyNames="EmployeeID"
  DataSourceID="SqlDataSource1">
```

Once this is set, execute the page to get a display, that is identical to what is shown in the following screenshot:

EmployeeID	EmployeeName	JoiningDate	DepartmentID	Salary
3	Joydip	08-09-2007	1	Rs. 20,000.00
4	Douglas	08-09-2007	1	Rs. 75,000.00
5	Jini	08-09-2007	2	Rs. 15,500.00
6	Rama	01-09-2007	3	Rs. 18,500.00

1 2

Note that you can navigate to the other pages simply by clicking the page index displayed at the bottom of the **GridView** control, as shown above.

You can also apply `PagerTemplate` to customize the paging behaviour. Here is how you specify the `PagerTemplate` in the **GridView** control's source:.

```
<PagerTemplate>
  Number of Pages: <%=GridView1.PageCount %>
  <asp:button ID="btnFirst" runat = "server" CommandName="Page"
    CommandArgument="First" Text="<<"/>
  <asp:button/>
  <asp:button ID="btnPrev" runat = "server" CommandName="Page"
    CommandArgument="Prev" Text="<"/>
  <asp:button/>
  <asp:button ID="btnNext" runat = "server" CommandName="Page"
    CommandArgument="Next" Text=">"/>
  <asp:button/>
  <asp:button ID="btnLast" runat = "server" CommandName="Page"
    CommandArgument="Last" Text=">>"/>
  <asp:button/>
</PagerTemplate>
```

Note that you have four buttons in the `PagerTemplate` of the `GridView` control's source code that corresponds to the `First`, `Previous`, `Next` and the `Last Page` of display. The following screenshot shows the output on execution:

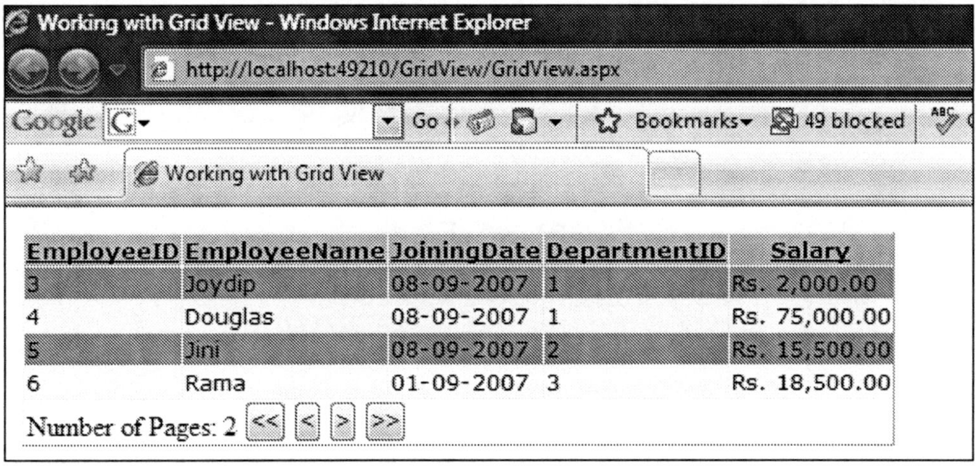

Implementing a Hierarchical GridView

The following section presents a **Hierarchical GridView** control, which is just a customized format of a **GridView** control. We'll just manipulate the markup code in the HTML source to make it hierarchical. This would display the employees grouped by each of the departments in the department table. Following is the output on execution of the sample application.

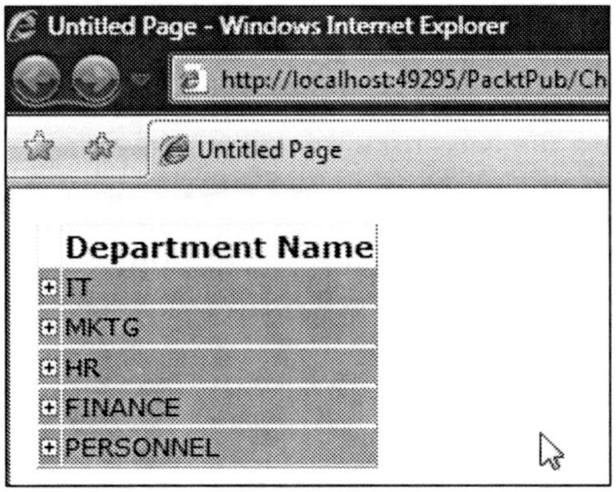

Note from the previous figure that the **GridView** is in the collapsed mode, that is, the department names are displayed with a plus sign preceding each of them. Once you click on the plus (**+**) signs of any of the department names, the employees belonging to the departments are displayed as shown in the following figure:

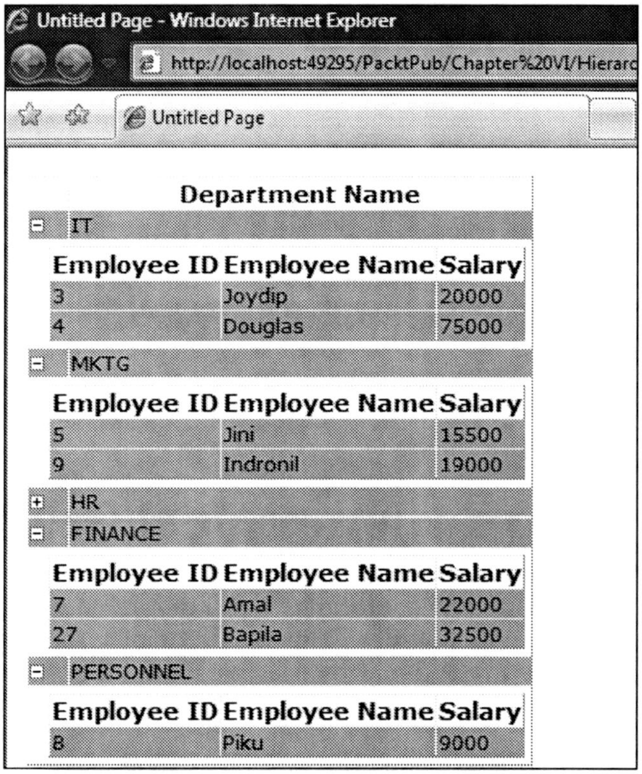

Let us now understand how we can implement this application. But, before we go into how this can be done, we just need to understand how a GridView control is rendered. The GridView control displays the data in rows and columns format. Therefore this control is rendered into a table tag. The headings would be rendered into in the first row which is a `<tr>` tag, and its heading names in a `<th>` tag. The actual row data is rendered in the successive `<tr>` tags with all the column data rendered into a `<td>` tag.

Following is a sample `GridView` markup code at design time, and its corresponding HTML code after rendering in the browser.

```
<asp:GridView ID="GridView1" runat="server" AutoGenerateColumns=
  "False" DataKeyNames="EmployeeID" DataSourceID="SqlDataSource1"
  HeaderStyle-Font-Names="Verdana"
  HeaderStyle-Font-Size="11pt"
  RowStyle-ForeColor ="Black"
  RowStyle-BackColor = "DeepSkyBlue"
  RowStyle-Font-Names="Verdana"
  RowStyle-Font-Size="10pt">
   <Columns>
     <asp:TemplateField Visible="False">
       <ItemTemplate>
         <asp:Label ID="lblDept" runat="server" Text='<%#
           Eval("DepartmentID") %>'/>
       </ItemTemplate>
     </asp:TemplateField>
     <asp:TemplateField Visible="True" ControlStyle-ForeColor="Black"
       HeaderStyle-BackColor = "DarkOrange" HeaderText="EmployeeID">
       <ItemTemplate>
         <asp:CheckBox ID="chkSelect" runat="server" Text='<%#
           Eval("EmployeeID") %>'/>
       </ItemTemplate>
     </asp:TemplateField>
     <asp:TemplateField ControlStyle-ForeColor="Black" HeaderStyle-
       BackColor = "DarkOrange" HeaderText="Department">
       <ItemTemplate>
         <asp:DropDownList ID="drpDept" ForeColor="Black"
           BackColor="Khaki" runat="server">
         </asp:DropDownList>
       </ItemTemplate>
     </asp:TemplateField>
     <asp:BoundField DataField="EmployeeName" HeaderStyle-BackColor =
       "DarkOrange" HeaderText="EmployeeName"/>
     <asp:BoundField DataField="Salary" HeaderStyle-BackColor =
       "DarkOrange" HeaderText="Salary" DataFormatString="{0:C}" />
   </Columns>
</asp:GridView>
```

The HTML code after the GridView is rendered in the web browser is shown as follows:

```
<table cellspacing="0" rules="all" border="1" id="GridView1"
  style="border-collapse:collapse;">
    <tr style="font-family:Verdana;font-size:11pt;">
      <th scope="col" style="background-color:DarkOrange;">
        EmployeeID
      </th>
      <th scope="col" style="background-color:DarkOrange;">
        Department
      </th>
      <th scope="col" style="background-color:DarkOrange;">
        EmployeeName
      </th>
      <th scope="col" style="background-color:DarkOrange;">
        Salary
      </th>
    </tr>
    <tr style="color:Black;background-color:DeepSkyBlue;font-
      family:Verdana;font-size:10pt;">
      <td>
        <span style="color:Black;"><input id=
          "GridView1_ctl02_chkSelect" type="checkbox"
          name="GridView1$ctl02$chkSelect" /><label
          for="GridView1_ctl02_chkSelect">3</label></span>
      </td>
      <td>
        <select name="GridView1$ctl02$drpDept"
          id="GridView1_ctl02_drpDept" style="color:Black;background-
          color:Khaki;">
          <option selected="selected" value="1">IT</option>
          <option value="2">MKTG</option>
          <option value="3">HR</option>
          <option value="4">FINANCE</option>
          <option value="5">PERSONNEL</option>
        </select>
      </td>
      <td>Joydip
      </td>
      <td>Rs. 20,000.00
      </td>
    </tr>
```

```
    <tr style="color:Black;background-color:DeepSkyBlue;font-
      family:Verdana;font-size:10pt;">
      <td>
        <span style="color:Black;"><input id=
          "GridView1_ctl03_chkSelect" type="checkbox"
          name="GridView1$ctl03$chkSelect" /><label
          for="GridView1_ctl03_chkSelect">4</label></span>
      </td>
      <td>
        <select name="GridView1$ctl03$drpDept"
          id="GridView1_ctl03_drpDept" style="color:Black;background-
          color:Khaki;">
          <option selected="selected" value="1">IT</option>
          <option value="2">MKTG</option>
          <option value="3">HR</option>
          <option value="4">FINANCE</option>
          <option value="5">PERSONNEL</option>
        </select>
      </td>
      <td>Douglas
      </td>
      <td>Rs. 75,000.00
      </td>
    </tr>
</table>
```

Observe code example, you can find that the data bound to the GridView control at runtime is rendered into the HTML code in the form of `<table>` tag. So, in essence, we can say that the `GridView` tag is converted to `<table>` tag; `<ItemTemplate>` and `<asp:BoundColumn>` tags in the `<asp:TemplateField>` tag are converted into `<th>` and `<td>` tags respectively. The `<th>` tag is for the first row which holds the header name for each of the column presented. The `<td>` tags are generated for data in each row. The `<tr>` tags are generated for each row bound to the `GridView` control dynamically.

Since we now understand how a GridView control is rendered, we'll look into the customization of this control to get the hierarchical behavior. This behavior is achieved by playing around with its rendering mechanism. Let us look at the HTML markup of the customized `GridView` control which can hold hierarchical data. Here is the HTML markup of hierarchical `GridView` control.

```
<asp:GridView ID="gvDepartment" runat="server"
  AutoGenerateColumns="False" OnRowDataBound=
  "gvDepartmentRowDataBound"
  HeaderStyle-Font-Names="Verdana" HeaderStyle-Font-Size="11pt"
```

```
RowStyle-ForeColor="Black"
RowStyle-BackColor="DeepSkyBlue" RowStyle-Font-Names="Verdana"
RowStyle-Font-Size="10pt">
<Columns>
  <asp:TemplateField>
    <ItemTemplate>
      <asp:ImageButton ImageUrl="~/Chapter V/Images/Plus.gif"
        CommandName="Expand" ID="btnExpandEmployee"
        runat="server"></asp:ImageButton>
    </ItemTemplate>
  </asp:TemplateField>
  <asp:TemplateField HeaderText="Department Name">
    <ItemTemplate>
      <asp:Label ID="lblDeptID" runat="server" Text='<%#
        Convert.ToString(DataBinder.Eval
        (Container.DataItem,"DeptName")) %>'>
      </asp:Label>
      <asp:TextBox ID="txtDeptID" Text='<%# Convert.ToString
        (DataBinder.Eval(Container.DataItem,"DeptCode")) %>'
        runat="server" Visible="false"></asp:TextBox>
            <asp:Table ID="TabEmp" runat="server"
              HorizontalAlign="Center" Style="display: none;">
            <asp:TableRow>
            <asp:TableCell Width="5"> </asp:TableCell>
            <asp:TableCell ColumnSpan="3">
            <asp:GridView ID="gvEmployee" runat="server"
              AutoGenerateColumns="false" HeaderStyle-Font-
              Names="Verdana" HeaderStyle-Font-Size="11pt"
              RowStyle-ForeColor="Black" RowStyle-
              BackColor="DeepSkyBlue"
              RowStyle-Font-Names="Verdana" RowStyle-Font-
              Size="10pt">
            <Columns>
              <asp:TemplateField HeaderText="Employee ID">
                <ItemTemplate>
                  <asp:Label ID="lblEmployeeID" runat="server"
                    Text='<%# Convert.ToString
                    (DataBinder.Eval(Container.DataItem,"EmpCode"))
                    %>'></asp:Label>
                </ItemTemplate>
              </asp:TemplateField>
              <asp:TemplateField HeaderText="Employee Name">
                <ItemTemplate>
```

```
                        <asp:Label ID="lblEmployeeName" runat="server"
                          Text='<%# Convert.ToString
                          (DataBinder.Eval(Container.DataItem,"EmpName"))
                          %>'>
                        </asp:Label>
                      </ItemTemplate>
                    </asp:TemplateField>
                    <asp:TemplateField HeaderText="Salary">
                      <ItemTemplate>
                        <asp:Label ID="lblSalary" runat="server"
                          Text='<%# Convert.ToString
                          (DataBinder.Eval(Container.DataItem,"Salary"))
                          %>'>
                        </asp:Label>
                      </ItemTemplate>
                    </asp:TemplateField>
                  </Columns>
                  </asp:GridView>
                  </asp:TableCell>
                  </asp:TableRow>
                  </asp:Table>
        </ItemTemplate>
      </asp:TemplateField>
    </Columns>
  </asp:GridView>
```

If you observe in this markup, we are trying to display all the `Department` information in the first `GridView` control, and under each department, we would display its employees in another `GridView` control. The first `<asp:TemplateField>` of the `GridView` `gvDepartment` holds an image indicating it is collapsed or not, in the form of plus (+) and minus (—) symbol. The minus symbol indicates, the employees GridView is seen on the browser, and plus symbol for a row indicates that it is collapsed and cannot be seen. The second `<asp:TemplateField>` holds the `Department Name` field. It also holds a textbox (which is hidden) that holds a `Department ID`, which is used to query the corresponding employees under it in the code behind. As soon as the `Department Name` template field is done, we are not closing the `<ItemTemplate>` and `<asp:TemplateField>` tag. We are just closing it with a `</td></tr>` and opening a new `<tr>` and `<td>` tag, which holds a `<asp:Table>` tag. At runtime, when this control is rendered, the first row after the heading is rendered as a `<tr>` and the data for `DepartmentName` is rendered into a `<td>` tag. Since the closing `</ItemTemplate>` tag is placed at the end of the internal `GridView` for employee data, its closing `</td>` would be generated after the employee `GridView` is rendered. So, what we've done by adding the manual closing `</td>` tag at design time is that we are forcing the completion of a `<td>` for the department name and opening a new `<tr>` under it to hold the employee data in a new GridView control. The `GridView` for the employee data is placed in a server side `<asp:Table>` tag so that this is accessible in the server side to bind data to it dynamically, and to also hide and show the table on a `Javascript` event when the plus (+) or minus (–) image is clicked. We are generating the event from the code behind in the `RowDataBound` event for every row dynamically.

Let us now look at the server code on how we are binding the hierarchical data. If you observe the attribute `OnRowDataBound` in the GridView's markup, we have a method being called `gvDepartmentRowDataBound`. This event is fired for every row when the `GridView gvDepartment` is bound. To be specific, this event is fired when `gvDepartment.DataBind()` method is invoked. The following is the code snippet for binding department information, which is called in the page load event.

```
private void BindData()
{
        DataSet dsDepartment = new DataSet();
        dsDepartment = dataManager.GetDepartmentList();
        gvDepartment.DataSource = dsDepartment;
        gvDepartment.DataBind();
}
```

Now when `gvDepartment.DataBind()` method is invoked, `gvDepartmentRowDataBound` event is fired. This method is fired for each department record that is bound to the `GridView-gvDepartment`. In this method, firstly, we render the JavaScript onclick for the control `btnExpandEmployee`, which represents the plus (+) or minus (–) for hiding or showing the employee `GridView`. Then, we pass the `DeptCode` required to retrieve the employees under this department and bind it to the internal GridView control-`gvEmployee`. Since this `GridView, gvEmployee` is inside the `<asp:Table>` tag, it is not recognized in the design time in your code behind file. So we are trying to find the control in this method, and then fetch data bind to this control. This happens for every department row bound to the `gvDepartment` control. So, all the hierarchical data is bound at once on the server side and the `GridView, gvDepartment` is displayed on the browser by hiding the `employee` information for every department. But remember, the employee information for every department is already bound with the internal `GridView-gvEmployee`. This is not displayed initially and is hidden. As we've generated the JavaScript event for every department row, just by clicking the image plus (+), the employee `GridView` is displayed. The `JavaScript` function `fnChangeImage()` is rendered for every department row which accepts the parameters the image client ID, and the table client ID of the corresponding Employee GridView.

```
protected void gvDepartmentRowDataBound(object sender,
  System.Web.UI.WebControls.GridViewRowEventArgs e)
{
        if (e.Row.RowType == DataControlRowType.DataRow)
        {
            ((ImageButton)e.Row.FindControl("btnExpandEmployee"))
            .Attributes["onClick"] = "return fnChangeImage('" +
            ((ImageButton)e.Row.FindControl("btnExpandEmployee"))
            .ClientID + "','" + ((Table)e.Row.
            FindControl("TabEmp")).ClientID + "')";
            string strDeptID =
            ((TextBox)e.Row.FindControl("txtDeptID")).Text;
            GridView gvEmp = (GridView)e.Row.
            Cells[gvDepartment.Columns.Count -
            1].FindControl("gvEmployee");
            ArrayList employeeList =
            dataManager.GetEmployeeByDept(strDeptID);
            if (employeeList != null)
            {
                gvEmp.DataSource = employeeList;
                gvEmp.DataBind();
                if (employeeList.Count < 1)
                {
                     ((ImageButton)e.Row.Cells[0].FindControl
                     ("btnExpandEmployee")).Visible = false;
                }
            }
        }
}
```

The JavaScript function fnChangeImage code snippet is as follows:

```
<script language="javascript" type="text/javascript">
  function fnChangeImage(ClientId,TableId)
  {
    if (document.getElementById(ClientId).getAttribute
       ("src").indexOf("Plus.gif") !=-1)
    {
          document.getElementById(ClientId).setAttribute
          ("src","Images/Minus.gif");
    }
    else
    {
          document.getElementById(ClientId).setAttribute
          ("src","Images/Plus.gif");
    }
    var aa = document.getElementById(TableId).style;
```

```
        if(aa.display=="none") aa.display="block";
        else aa.display="none";
        return false;
    }
</script>
```

The `JavaScript` function shown in the code example above gets the attribute for the image ID and employee table ID to hide or show it. We are done! We have implemented a hierarchical GridView control.

Sorting Data Using the GridView Control

You can also enable sorting in the GridView control with minimal effort. When you enable sorting in the GridView control, the field headers in the GridView control will show a link; when you click on this link, the ASP.NET page will be posted back. After a postback, the GridView control will be populated with data from its data source control and the appropriate sort command will be invoked to sort the data being displayed. When you click on the field header links, the data for that column will be sorted once again, but, this time in the reverse order.

> Note that when you click on the field header links the first time, the data in that column will be sorted in the ascending order.

To enable sorting for the `GridView` control, simply set the `AllowSorting` property of the control to `true` as depicted in the following code snippet:

```
<asp:GridView ID="GridView1" runat="server" AllowSorting="true"
  AllowPaging ="true" PageSize = "4" RowStyle-BackColor =
  "CadetBlue" AutoGenerateColumns= "False" DataKeyNames="EmployeeID"
  DataSourceID="SqlDataSource1">
```

Now when you execute the page, you get an output similar to the following.

EmployeeID	EmployeeName	JoiningDate	DepartmentID	Salary
3	Joydip	08-09-2007	1	Rs. 20,000.00
4	Douglas	08-09-2007	1	Rs. 75,000.00
5	Jini	08-09-2007	2	Rs. 15,500.00
6	Rama	01-09-2007	3	Rs. 18,500.00
1 2				

As you can see from the above figure, both paging and sorting for our **GridView** control is enabled.

You can sort any of the columns simply by clicking the column header link. The following screenshot illustrates how the output looks once you click on the **EmployeeName** column in the **GridView** control.

EmployeeID	EmployeeName	JoiningDate	DepartmentID	Salary
7	Amal	10-12-2006	4	Rs. 22,000.00
27	Bapila	02-01-2005	4	Rs. 32,500.00
4	Douglas	08-09-2007	1	Rs. 75,000.00
9	Indronil	08-09-2007	2	Rs. 19,000.00
1 2				

Note how the employee names are sorted once you click on the **EmployeeName** column in the **GridView** control.

You can customize the sorting functionality of the **GridView** control. You can also specify the columns that you don't want to be sortable, that is, disable sorting at the column level, even if you enable sorting at the control level. To do this, you need to go to the design view of the **GridView** control and then click on the **EditColumns** option from the control's **Smart Tag** option. Then you need to specify the columns that you do not want to be sorted on.

You have two events associated with the sorting functionality of the **GridView** control, namely, **Sorting** and **Sorted.**

While the former is invoked prior to sorting of data within the control, the latter is fired after the data in the control has been sorted. You can override the respective event handlers and write your custom logic there.

Inserting, Updating and Deleting Data Using the GridView Control

The GridView control can also be used to insert, update and delete data. Moreover, we need not write even a single line of code for these operations. Let us understand how we can use the GridView control to insert data.

To insert, update or delete data using the GridView control we need to first configure the data source. The steps for configuring the data source are simple. Go to the design view of your web page and drag-and-drop the **SqlDataSource** control. Configure the data source by following the same steps that we discussed in Chapter 1 of the book. Now, after the appropriate database and the connection string are specified, select the **Employee** table from the list of the tables displayed in the dropdown and select the fields that you want to be displayed. Now we need to set up the **SqlDataSource** to support the insert, update, and delete operations. For this, click the **Advanced** button which will open up the **Advanced SQL Generation Options** dialog box. Refer to the following snapshot that illustrates this.

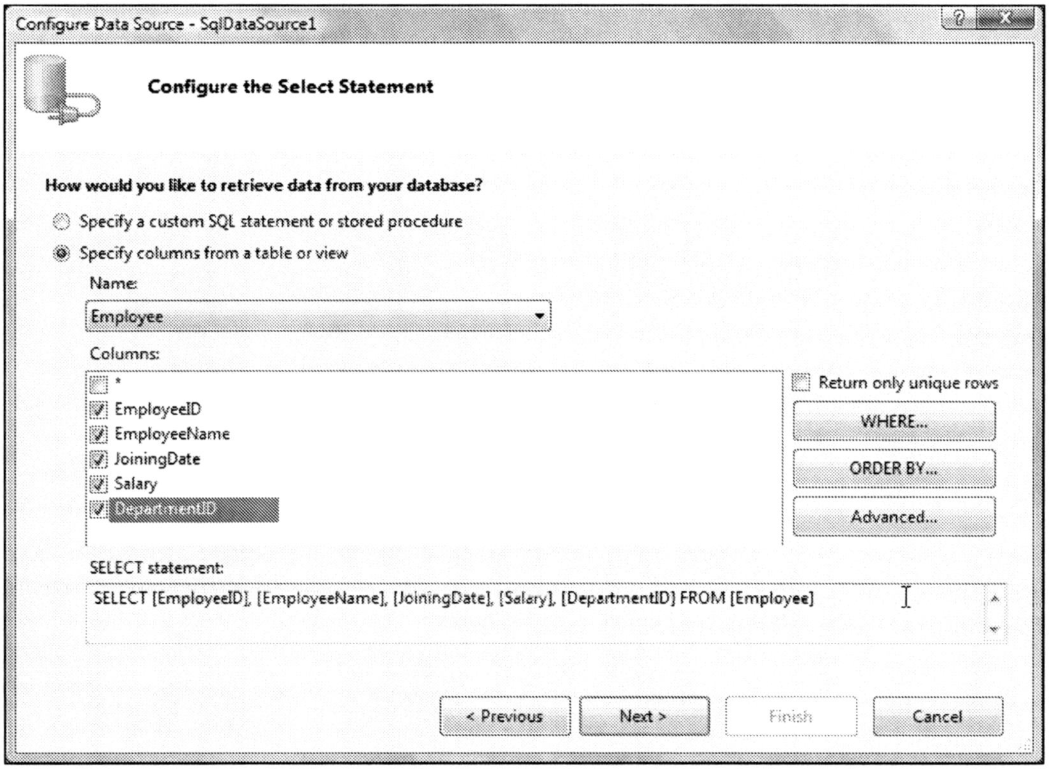

The next screenshot shows a dialog box that opens up, displays two check boxes, that is, Generate **INSERT**, **UPDATE**, and **DELETE** statements and **Use optimistic concurrency**. Fine, but what is optimistic currency? optimistic concurrency is a database concurrency handling technique that handles concurrency without the need to lock the particular database in use. In this methodology, concurrency is controlled using logic in the code such that the database need not be locked. The record being updated by a user is not accessible to another user for an update operation unless the updated operation is done. In this regard, MSDN states, "When a user wants to update a row, the application must determine whether another user has changed the row since it was read. Optimistic concurrency is generally used in environments with a low contention for data. This improves performance as no locking of records is required, and locking of records requires additional server resources. Also, in order to maintain record locks, a persistent connection to the database server is required. Since, this is not the case in an optimistic concurrency model; connections to the server are free to serve a larger number of clients in less time."

When you click on the first checkbox, as shown in the following figure, **INSERT**, **UPDATE** and **DELETE** statements are generated automatically.

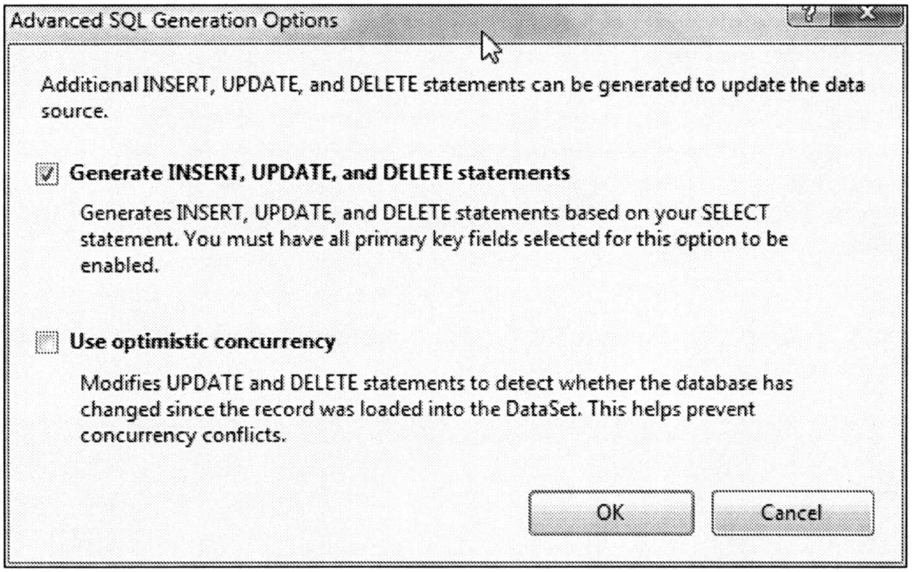

You need to check the second check box if you require optimistic concurrency. Once this is checked, the control will allow updates and deletes to data, if the data has not changed since the data was last accessed. Let us select the first check box and then click on the **OK** button. The declarative mark up that is generated now looks as shown in the following code snippet:

```
<asp:SqlDataSource ID="SqlDataSource1" runat="server"
  ConnectionString="Data Source=.;Initial Catalog=Test;User ID=sa"
  DeleteCommand="DELETE FROM [Employee] WHERE [EmployeeID] =
  @EmployeeID" InsertCommand="INSERT INTO [Employee] ([EmployeeName],
  [JoiningDate], [Salary], [DepartmentID]) VALUES (@EmployeeName,
  @JoiningDate, @Salary, @DepartmentID)"
  ProviderName="System.Data.SqlClient" SelectCommand="SELECT
  [EmployeeID], [EmployeeName], [JoiningDate], [Salary],
  [DepartmentID] FROM [Employee]"
```

```
    UpdateCommand="UPDATE [Employee] SET [EmployeeName] =
    @EmployeeName, [JoiningDate] = @JoiningDate, [Salary] = @Salary,
    [DepartmentID] = @DepartmentID WHERE [EmployeeID] = @EmployeeID">
    <DeleteParameters>
      <asp:Parameter Name="EmployeeID" Type="Int32" />
    </DeleteParameters>
    <UpdateParameters>
      <asp:Parameter Name="EmployeeName" Type="String" />
      <asp:Parameter Name="JoiningDate" Type="DateTime" />
      <asp:Parameter Name="Salary" Type="Decimal" />
      <asp:Parameter Name="DepartmentID" Type="Int32" />
      <asp:Parameter Name="EmployeeID" Type="Int32" />
    </UpdateParameters>
    <InsertParameters>
      <asp:Parameter Name="EmployeeName" Type="String" />
      <asp:Parameter Name="JoiningDate" Type="DateTime" />
      <asp:Parameter Name="Salary" Type="Decimal" />
      <asp:Parameter Name="DepartmentID" Type="Int32" />
    </InsertParameters>
  </asp:SqlDataSource>
```

Once you execute the application, the output is similar to what is shown in the following screenshot:

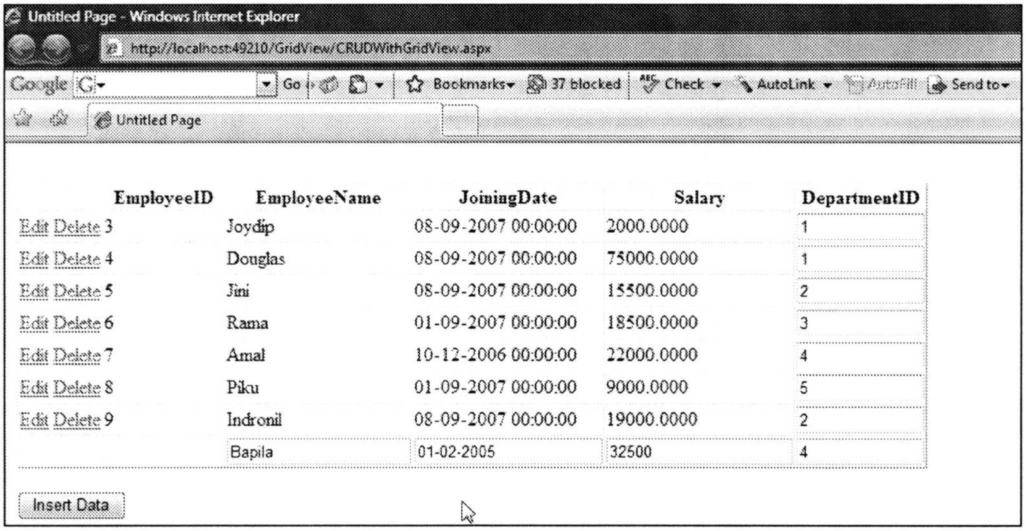

Note the footer row in the **GridView** control shown in the previous screenshot. Also note that data for a new record is being entered. After you have finished entering data for a new record, click on the **InsertData** button to add a new record to the Employee table.

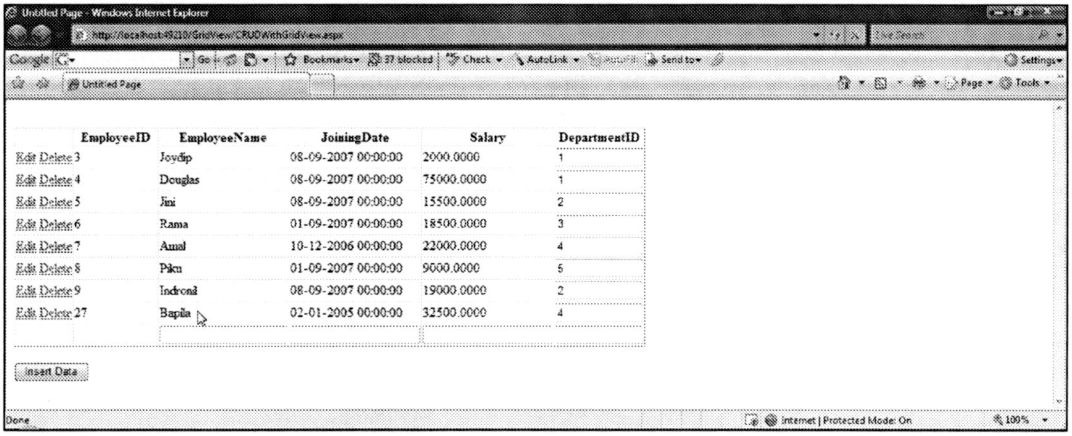

Editing and deleting data with the **GridView** control is very simple. You simply have to check the **EnableEditing** or the **EnableDeleting** checkboxes, as shown in the following figure:

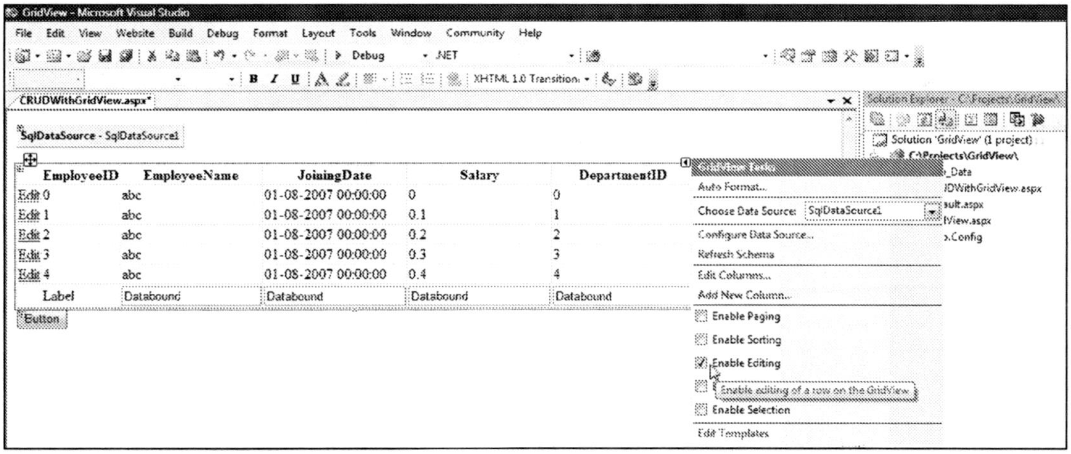

Once you select these checkboxes, a corresponding link is displayed with the respective captions that indicate the action to be performed. When you click on the **Edit** button, the fields become editable. Moreover, you have the **Update** and **Cancel** links displayed in place of the **Edit** link in the **GridView** control, as displayed in the following screenshot:

Refer to the previous screenshot. Now you can make your changes and click on the **Update** button to update the data or **Cancel** to cancel the changes made. Similarly, you can enable the **EnableDeleting** property so that you can make the **GridView** support deletion of data. Note that you can enable both the **EnableEditing** and **EnableDeleting** properties so as to make the **GridView** both editable and also make it support deletion of data. The best part here is that you can do all this without writing even a single line of code! The following screenshot illustrates the **GridView** control in design view with both **Editing** and **Deleting** enabled.

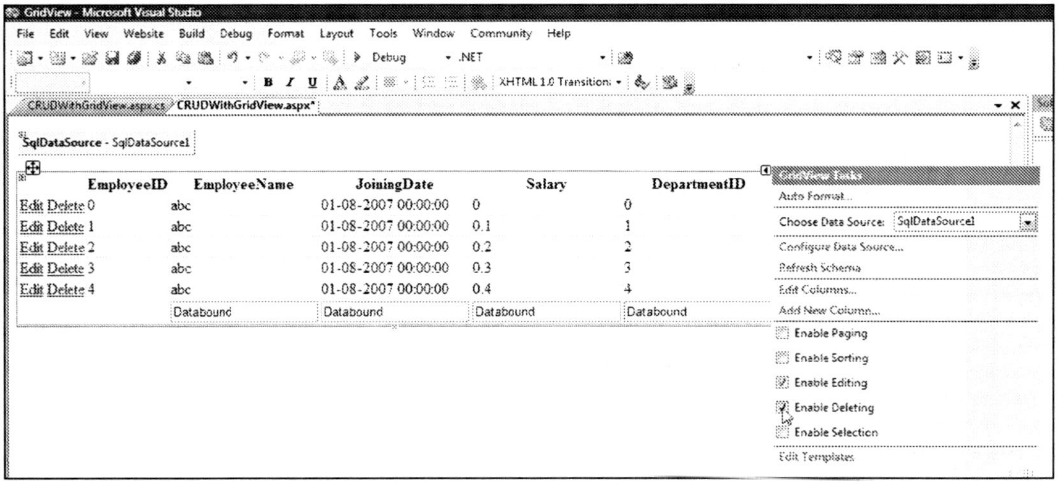

Exporting the GridView Data

In this section we will explore how we can export the data displayed in a **GridView** control to MS Excel and MS Word.

In order to export data from a **GridView** control, ensure that the `AllowSorting` and `AllowPaging` properties are turned off. I will add two buttons in the user interface that correspond to the export format types, that is, I will show you how to export data to MS Excel and MS Word. Refer to the following screenshot which illustrates the application in execution with two buttons that can be used to export the data in the **GridView** control to MS Excel and MS Word respectively.

Note the two buttons with their respective captions beneath the **GridView** control populated with data.

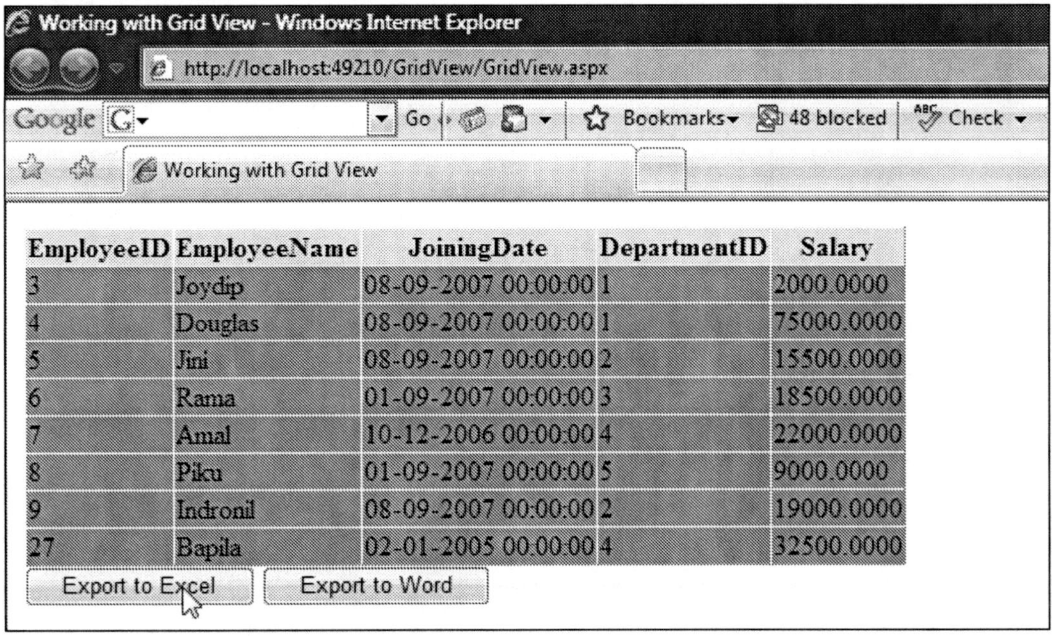

Now once you click on the **Export to Excel** button, a window pops up, as shown in the following screenshot:

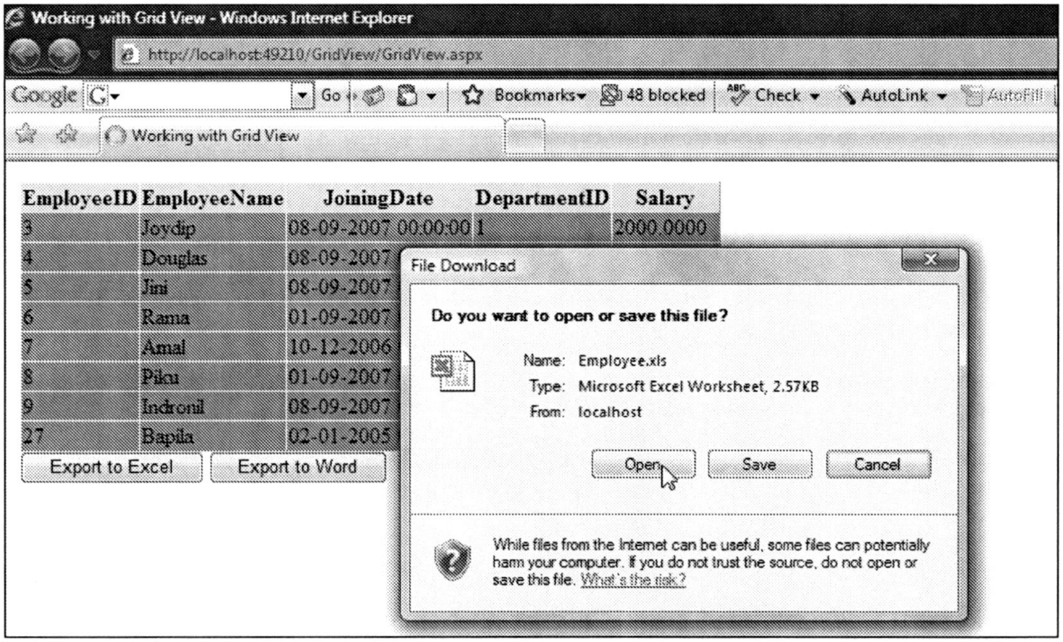

Once you click on the **Open** button, the data from the **GridView** control is exported to Excel and displayed in an **Excel Worksheet**, as shown in the following screenshot:

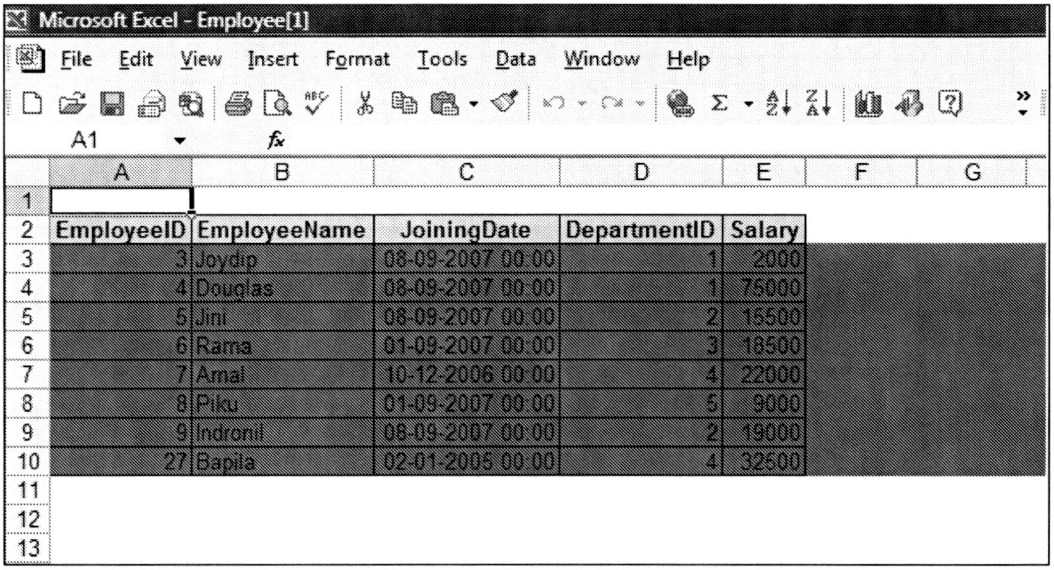

Let us now understand how we achieved this. In the click event of these buttons, you need to write the necessary code to export the data. Following is the code for the `Click` events of these buttons:

```
protected void btnExportGridViewToExcel_Click(object sender,
    EventArgs e)
{
        ExportToExcel();
}
protected void btnExportGridViewToWord_Click(
                    object sender, EventArgs e)
{
        ExportToWord();
}
```

Note that we have invoked the `ExportToExcel()` and the `ExportToWord()` methods respectively in the `Click` events of these buttons. Following is the source code for these two methods:

```
private void ExportToExcel()
{
  Response.ClearContent();
  Response.AddHeader("content-disposition", "attachment;
   filename=Employee.xls");
  Response.ContentType = "application/ms-excel";
  StringWriter stringWriter = new StringWriter();
  HtmlTextWriter htmlTextWriter = new HtmlTextWriter(stringWriter);
  HtmlForm htmlForm = new HtmlForm();
  GridView1.Parent.Controls.Add(htmlForm);
  htmlForm.Attributes["runat"] = "server";
  htmlForm.Controls.Add(GridView1);
  htmlForm.RenderControl(htmlTextWriter);
  Response.Write(stringWriter.ToString());
  Response.End();
}
private void ExportToWord()
{
  Response.ClearContent();
  Response.AddHeader("content-disposition", "attachment;
   filename=Employee.doc");
  Response.ContentType = "application/ms-word";
  StringWriter stringWriter = new StringWriter();
  HtmlTextWriter htmlTextWriter = new HtmlTextWriter(stringWriter);
  HtmlForm htmlForm = new HtmlForm();
```

```
    GridView1.Parent.Controls.Add(htmlForm);
    htmlForm.Attributes["runat"] = "server";
    htmlForm.Controls.Add(GridView1);
    htmlForm.RenderControl(htmlTextWriter);
    Response.Write(stringWriter.ToString());
    Response.End();
}
```

Refer to the code snippets above. The `Response.ClearContent()` method is used to erase the content in the Response object. The `AddHeader()` method of the Response object is used to add a header and its corresponding value or the content to the response being rendered. The `Response.AddHeader()` method accepts two parameters, that is, the name of the header of the response being rendered, and, its corresponding value. While the first argument is used to specify the name of the header to be added to the response, the second is used to specify the corresponding value of the header, or, its content. Note that we have created an `HtmlForm` object to store the `GridView` object inside it.

Adding Bound Fields to a GridView at Runtime

To add a bound field to a GridView control at runtime, use the following code.

```
BoundField boundField = new BoundField();
boundField.DataField = "JoiningDate";
boundField.HeaderText = "Joining Date";
boundField.DataFormatString = "{0:d}";
GridView1.Columns.Add(boundField);
```

Formatting the GridView Control

You can format the GridView rows as per your requirements. You can use the `AlternatingRowStyle` property by specifying the style for each alternate row. Here is how you can specify this property at design time in the `.aspx` file.

```
AlternatingRowStyle-BackColor ="AliceBlue"
```

Once you execute the application, the **GridView** displays the data from the Employee table with its alternate rows in `AliceBlue`. Following is a screenshot of the output:

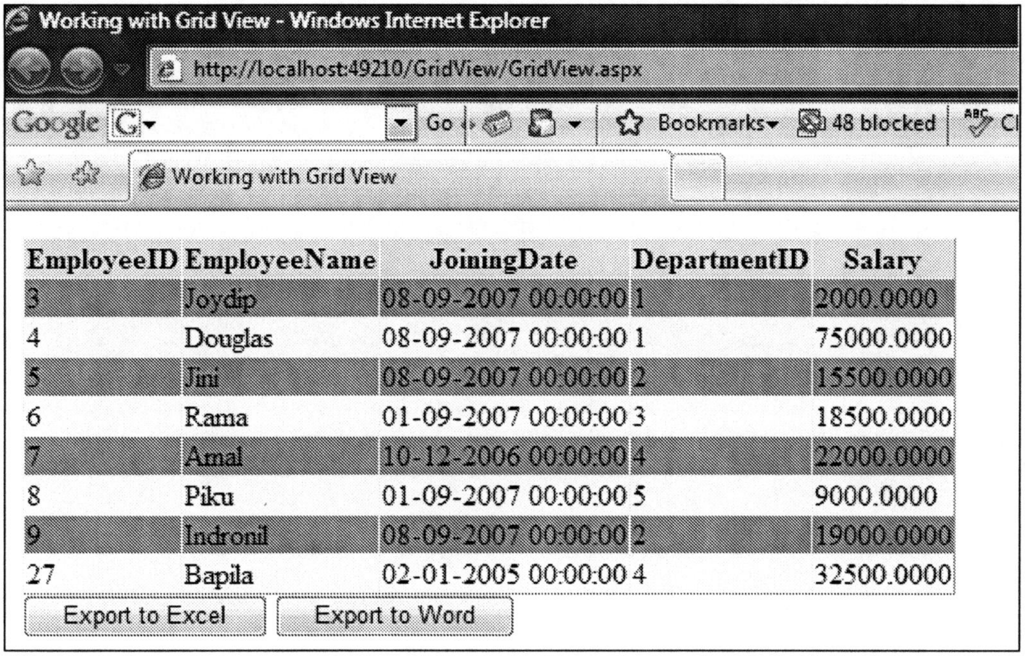

You can also specify the same at runtime using the `OnRowCreated` event of the **GridView** control. Here is how you specify the event handler for this event in the `.aspx` file.

```
OnRowCreated="OnRowCreated"
```

The source code for the event handler is shown as follows:

```
protected void OnRowCreated(object sender, GridViewRowEventArgs e)
{
        if (e.Row.RowType == DataControlRowType.DataRow)
        {
            if (((e.Row.RowIndex + 1) % 3) == 0)
            {
                e.Row.BackColor = System.Drawing.Color.AliceBlue;
            }
        }
}
```

Refer to the code snippet shown. Note how the background color for every third row of the **GridView** control has been set using the `BackColor` property of the `Row` object. The following is the output on execution.

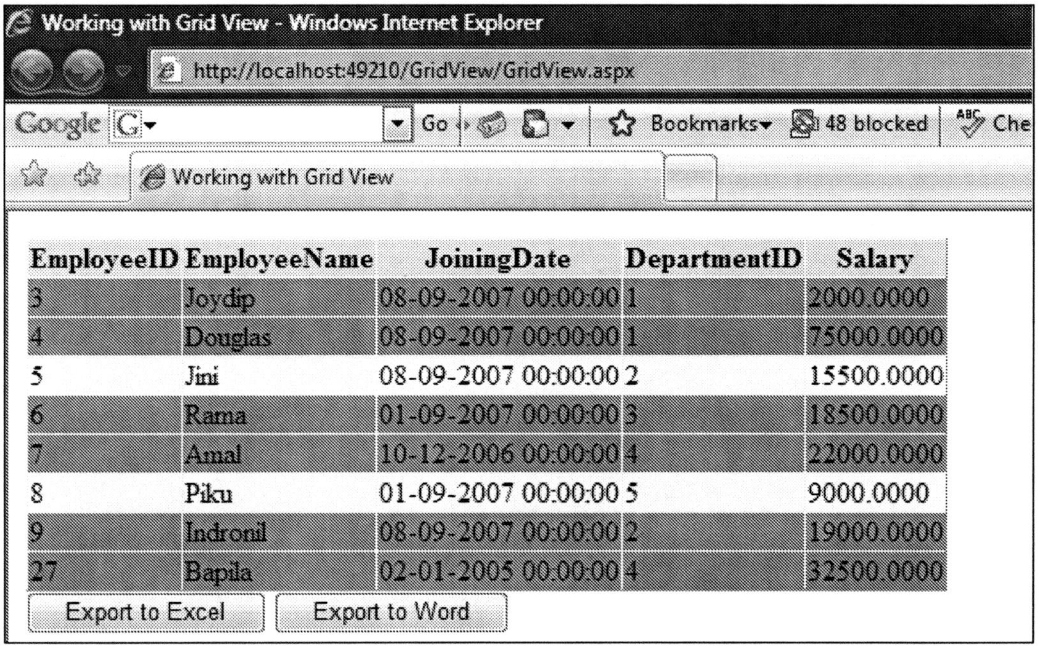

Let us now understand how we can set attributes to the rows of the **GridView** control using client side scripts, such that it highlights the row it is pointed to, with a specified color. Here is the code that illustrates how you can highlight and unhighlight the rows using the `OnRowCreated` event when the mouse pointer is being moved across the rows of the **GridView** control.

```
protected void OnRowCreated(object sender, GridViewRowEventArgs e)
{
        if (e.Row.RowType == DataControlRowType.DataRow)
        {
            e.Row.Attributes.Add("onmouseover",
            "this.style.backgroundColor='AliceBlue'");
            e.Row.Attributes.Add("onmouseout",
            "this.style.backgroundColor='CadetBlue'");
        }
}
```

The following screenshot shows the output on execution:

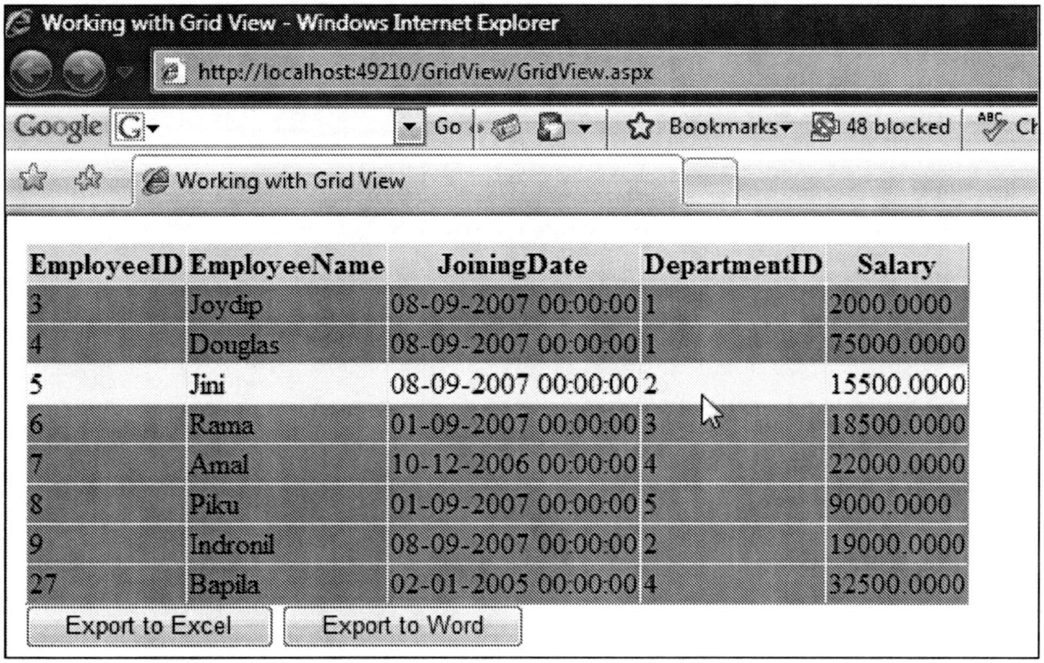

The background color of the row of the **GridView** control, on which the mouse pointer hovers, is set to `AliceBlue` color.

You can also use client side scripting to retrieve the row index in the **GridView** control that has been clicked. You only need to add the script to the `Attributes` collection of the `Row` object of the `GridViewEventArgs` instance, as shown in the following code snippet:

```
protected void OnRowCreated(object sender, GridViewRowEventArgs e)
{
   if (e.Row.RowType == DataControlRowType.DataRow)
    {
       int rowIndex = e.Row.DataItemIndex;
       rowIndex += 1;
       e.Row.Attributes.Add("onClick", "alert('You have clicked row :
       " + rowIndex.ToString()+ "')");
    }
}
```

Execute the application and click on any row of the **GridView** control to see an alert message box displayed. The output is similar to the following.

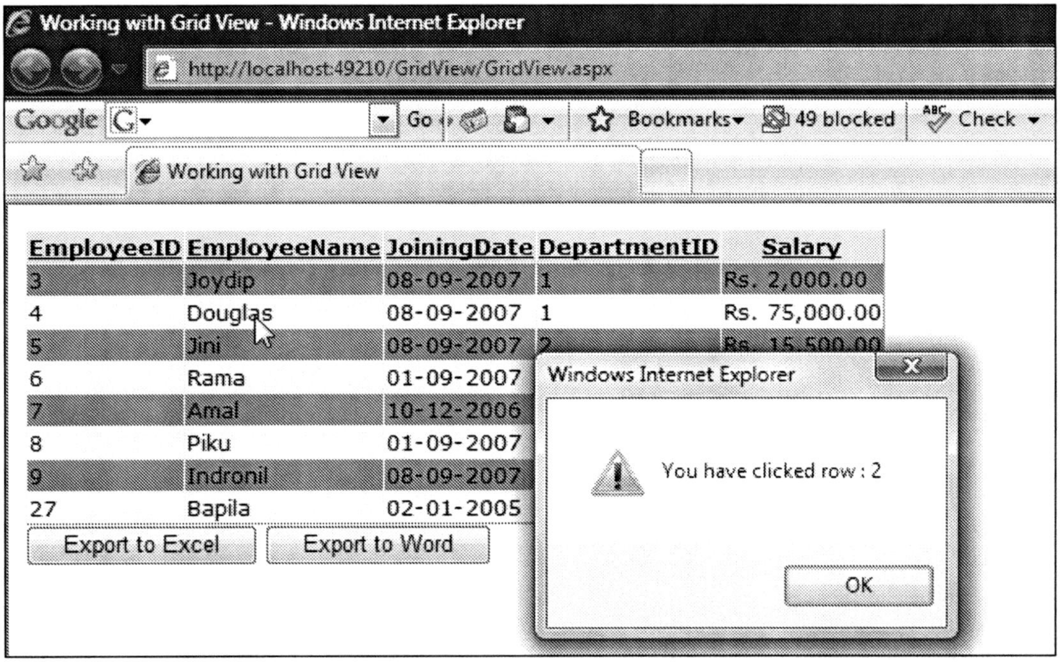

You can also retrieve the value of a specific cell using client side scripting. Following is the output:

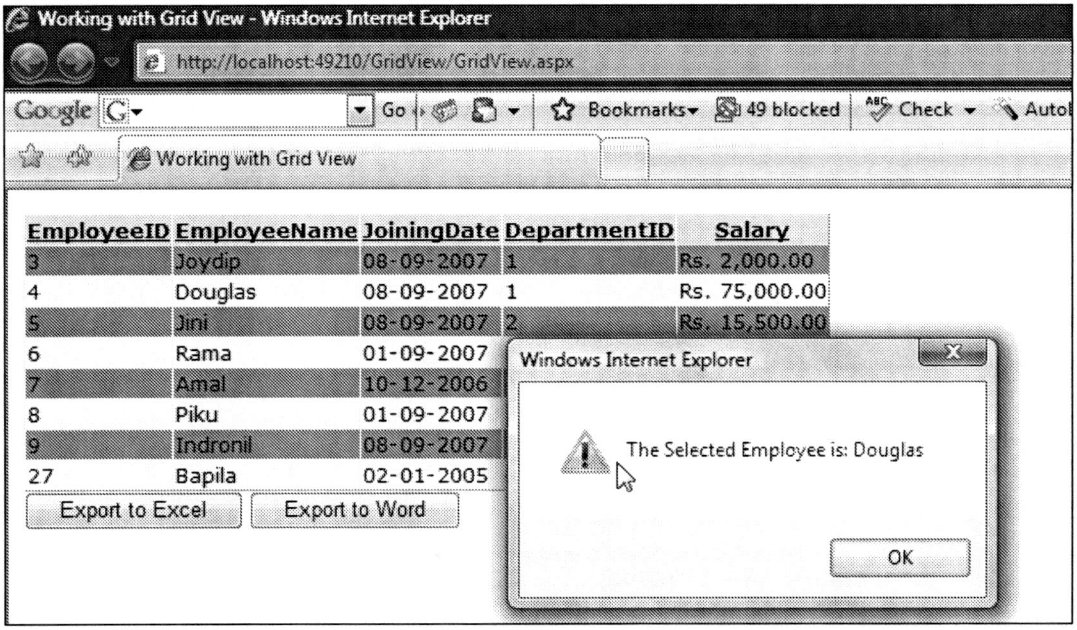

I will now show you how this can be accomplished. The following is the code snippet that illustrates how you can use the `OnRowDataBound` event handler to retrieve the name of the employee that corresponds to the row of the **GridView** control that is clicked by the user:

```
protected void OnRowDataBound(object sender, GridViewRowEventArgs e)
{
        if (null != e.Row.Cells)
        {
            e.Row.Attributes.Add("onClick", "alert('The Selected
            Employee is: " + e.Row.Cells[1].Text + "')");
        }
}
```

The GridView control that we have used so far does not have a proper `Font` applied to it. Let us format the display by specifying `Font` styles and sizes to the GridView control's header and rows. For this, you need to specify the following at the GridView control level in the `.aspx` file.

```
HeaderStyle-BackColor="Cyan"
HeaderStyle-ForeColor="Black"
HeaderStyle-Font-Names="Verdana"
HeaderStyle-Font-Size="10pt"
RowStyle-BackColor = "CadetBlue"
RowStyle-Font-Names="Verdana"
RowStyle-Font-Size=»10pt»
```

Following is the screenshot of the output on execution of the application.

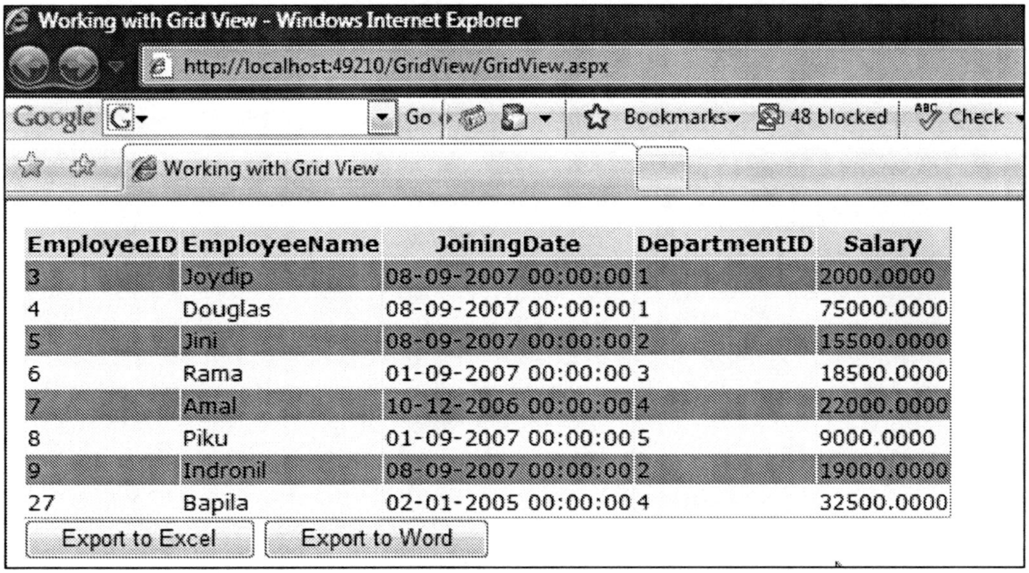

Refer to the screenshot shown previously. The output is much better with font style and size applied to the **GridView** header and also the rows of the **GridView** control.

If you look at the **GridView** displayed in the previous screenshot, you'll find that the **JoiningDate** and the **Salary** columns are not properly formatted. The output still looks awkward, doesn't it? Following, is how you can apply proper formatting to these columns using the `DataFormatString` property of the **GridView** control at design time in your `.aspx` file.

```
<asp:BoundField DataField="JoiningDate" HeaderStyle-BackColor =
  "Aqua" HeaderText="JoiningDate" SortExpression="JoiningDate"
  HtmlEncode="False" DataFormatString="{0:d}"/>
<asp:BoundField DataField="Salary" HeaderStyle-BackColor = "Aqua"
  HeaderText="Salary" SortExpression="Salary"
  HtmlEncode="False" DataFormatString="{0:C}"/>
```

When you execute the application, the output will look like this:

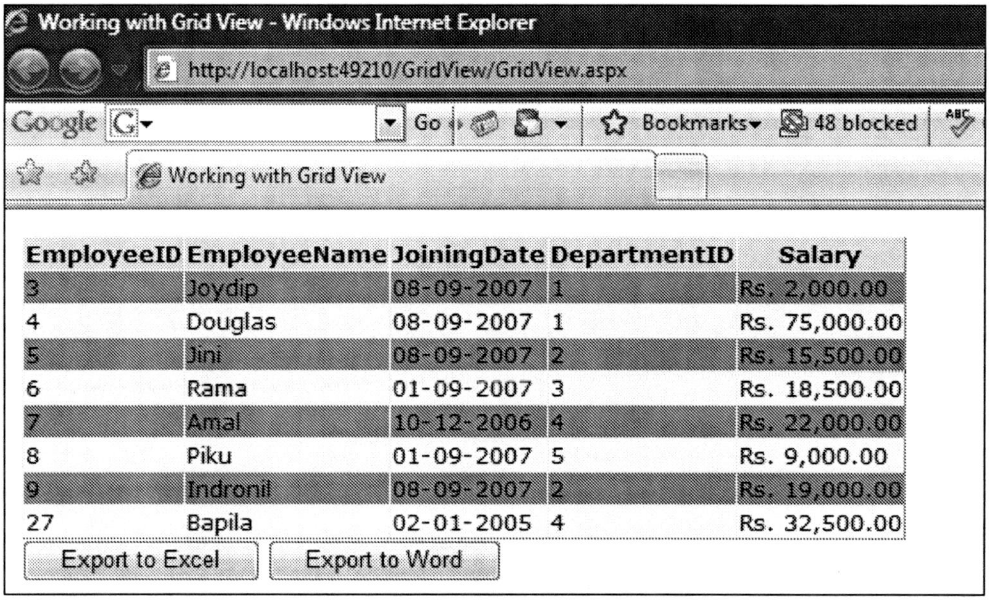

This looks like a much more polished output with the header, the rows, the columns and the data displayed in **GridView** control properly formatted. In this section, we have seen how we can have our custom look and feel of the **GridView** control by using its various attributes, and also format the data rendered by it. Note that you can even use custom format strings for formatting data displayed in the **GridView** control.

Let us now learn how we can apply images to the column headers of the GridView control. We will see how to apply images that correspond to the ascending and descending operations while we sort a column of the GridView control. Note that you should enable sorting in the control as usual by setting the `AllowSorting` property to `true` in your `.aspx` file, shown as follows:

```
AllowSorting ="true"
```

Further, you need to use the `OnRowCreated` event and write the necessary code there to apply images to the column headers of the GridView control. Following is the code for the `OnRowCreated` event, that is, the source code for the `OnRowCreated` event handler.

```
protected void OnRowCreated(object sender, GridViewRowEventArgs e)
{
        if (e.Row.RowType == DataControlRowType.DataRow)
        {
            if (((e.Row.RowIndex + 1) % 2) == 0)
            {
                e.Row.BackColor = System.Drawing.Color.AliceBlue;
            }
        }
   SetGridViewImageForSort(e, "lamp.gif", "up.gif", "down.gif");
}
```

Note that the `SetGridImageForSort()` method is called in the above method with the `GridViewRowEventArgs` instance and the respective images as parameters. Following is the source code for the `SetGridImageForSort()` method:

```
private void SetGridViewImageForSort(GridViewRowEventArgs e, String
   defaultImageFileName, String upArrowImageFileName, String
   downArrowImageFileName)
{
        if (e.Row != null && e.Row.RowType ==
          DataControlRowType.Header)
        {
            foreach (TableCell cell in e.Row.Cells)
            {
                LinkButton linkButton = (LinkButton)cell.Controls[0];
                if (null != linkButton)
                {
                    Image image = new Image();
                    if (GridView1.SortExpression ==
                       linkButton.CommandArgument)
```

```
                        image.ImageUrl = (GridView1.SortDirection ==
                        SortDirection.Ascending) ?
                        downArrowImageFileName : upArrowImageFileName;
                    else
                        image.ImageUrl = defaultImageFileName;
                        cell.Controls.Add(image);
                }
            }
        }
    }
```

The logic is simple; you set the respective images after checking whether the value of `SortDirection` is `Ascending` or `Descending`. After you execute the application, the output will look like this:

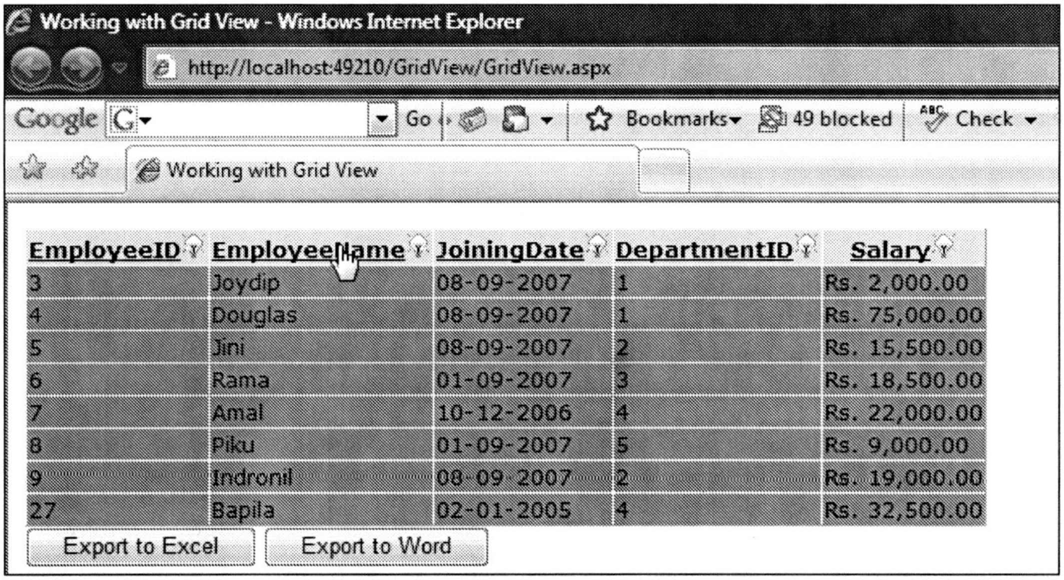

Initially the data in the **GridView** displayed above is unsorted. The default image is displayed in the column headers of all columns. Once you click on the **EmployeeName** column header, the rows in the control are sorted in ascending order of employee names. The sorted employee records now resemble the following:

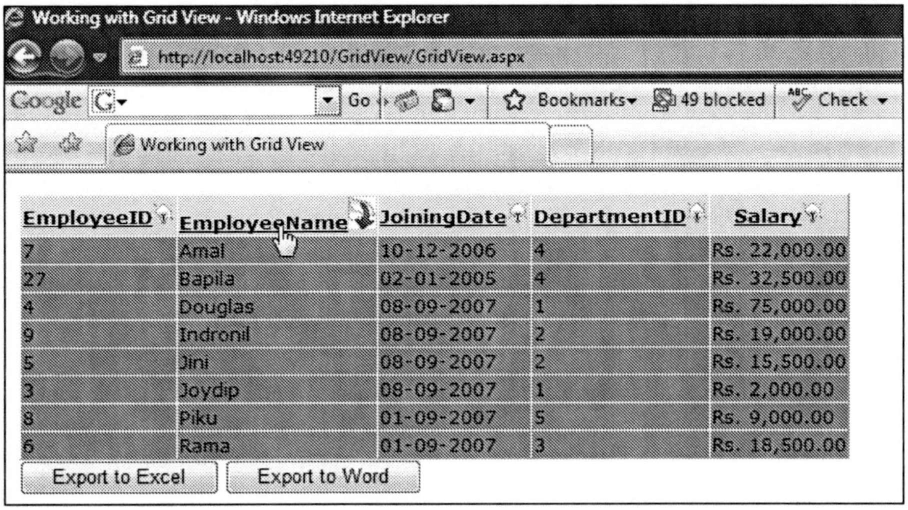

The image associated with the **EmployeeName** column header illustrates that the records have been sorted in ascending order of the employee names. When you click on the column header once again, the records are now sorted in the reverse order, that is, descending order of employee names and the corresponding image is displayed in the column header of the column on which the records have been sorted. The output is captured in the following screenshot:

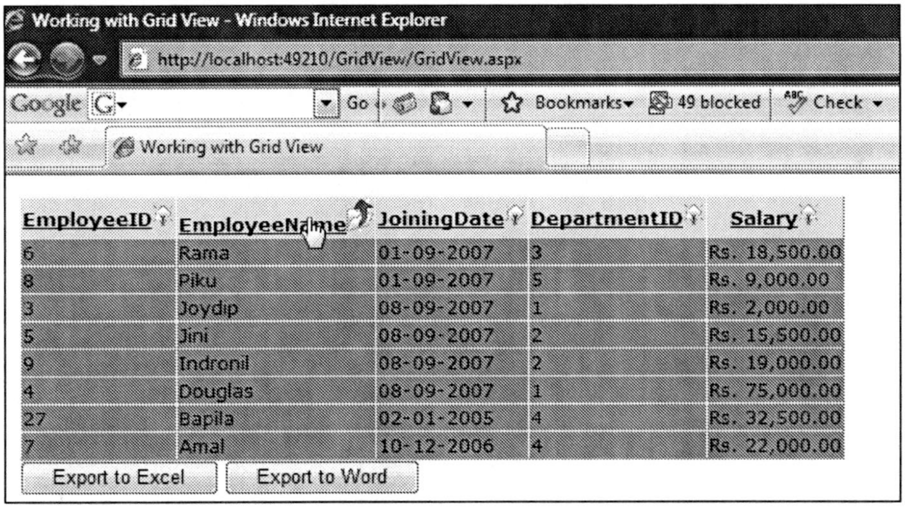

Summary

In this chapter, we've seen the working of **GridView** control and how we can use it to perform CRUD (Create, Update, Read and Delete) operations, and export data without writing even a single line of code. This control makes use of the data source controls available with ASP.NET 2.0 to bind data to it and perform various CRUD operations. In this chapter, we've used SqlDataSource control to bind data and perform data modification operations; however you can also use other data source controls too, for binding data to the **GridView** control. We have learnt how we can format the data rendered by this control, use CheckBox and DropDownList controls inside **GridView** and even export the **GridView** control to MS Excel and MS Word. We will learn the other view controls in the next chapter.

7
Displaying Views of Data (Part II)

In Chapter 6, we discussed how we can work with the GridView control in ASP. NET. This is the last part in the series of two chapters on how we can use the view controls to display different views of data in ASP.NET. In this chapter, I will present the DetailsView and the FormView control and show how we can use these controls to bind data to them and perform various CRUD operations.

In this chapter, we will learn about:

- Working with the DetailsView Control
- Working with the FormView Control
- Working with the TreeView Control
- Implementing a Directory Structure as a TreeView

Working with the ASP.NET DetailsView Control

The **DetailsView** control available in ASP.NET 2.0 is actually complementary to the **GridView** control with its added ability to display data in a Master—Detail relationship—a feature not provided by the **GridView** control by default. Unlike the **GridView** control, you can use the **DetailsView** control to insert data into the database. However, you can bind data to this control much the same as what you did with the **GridView.** It should be noted that the default view type of the **DetailsView** control is vertical; you would find that each column of the associated record is displayed actually as a separate column. To use the **DetailsView** control, you can drag and drop it from the toolbox as shown in the screenshot on the next page:

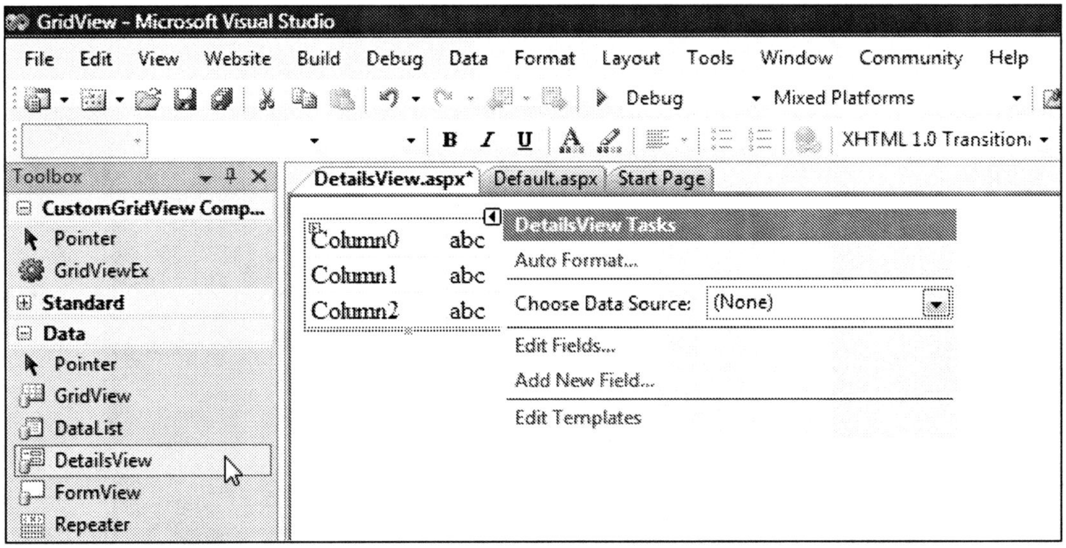

You can also create the **DetailsView** control programmatically in your `.aspx` file. Here is the corresponding source code for the `DetailsView` control in your `.aspx` file once you drag and drop a **DetailsView** control from the toolbox onto your web page in the design mode.

```
<asp:DetailsView ID="DetailsView1" runat="server">
</asp:DetailsView>
```

You can bind data to this web control using any of the data source controls available with ASP.NET 2.0. We will use the SQL datasource control in this chapter.

Using the DetailsView Control

I will now show you how you can implement a Master—Details relationship of data using the **DetailsView** control. Consider our **Employee** table that we discussed in Chapter 1 of this book. We will take a DropDownList control that will display the names of all the employees in the database table. On selection of a particular employee, the corresponding record will be displayed in the **DetailsView** control. When you execute the application, the output will be similar to what is shown as follows:

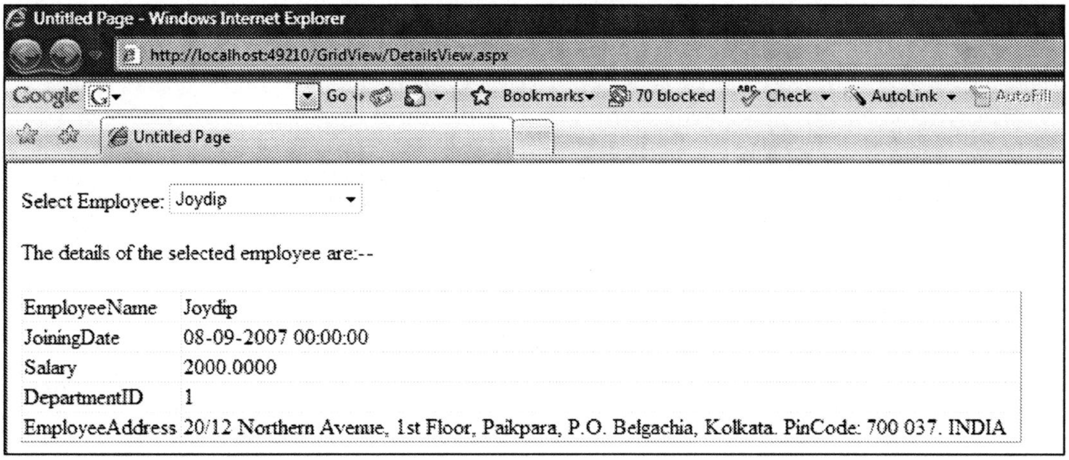

Note that the details pertaining to the employee called **Joydip** have been displayed in the **DetailsView** control just beneath the **DropDownList** control. Now, select a different employee and see how the corresponding details in the **DetailsView** control changes.

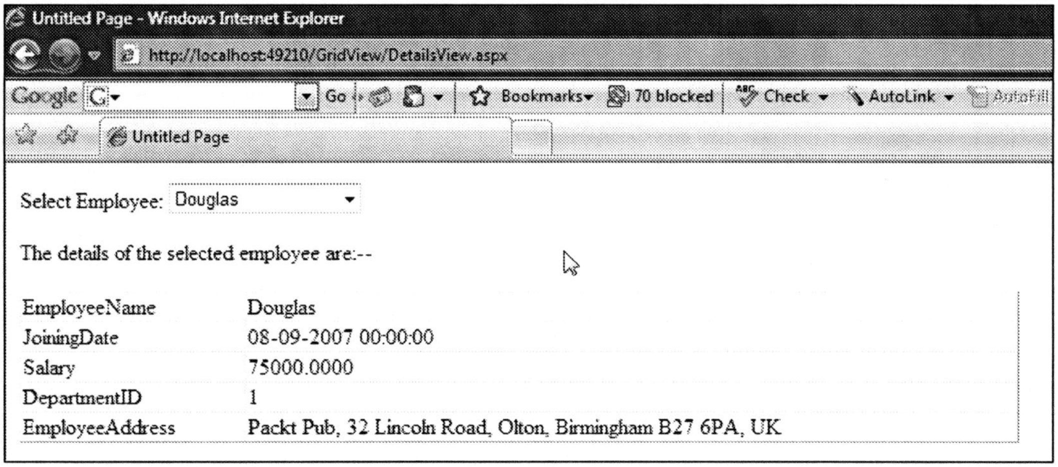

Let us now understand how we can accomplish the above. In the design view of your web page, drag and drop two SqlDataSource controls and configure them accordingly. While one of these controls would be used to bind data to the DropDownList control, the other would be used to bind data to the DetailsView control based on the employee selected by the user. We have discussed how we can use the data source controls of ASP.NET in Chapter 1 of this book. Therefore, I will skip some steps while discussing on the configuration of these SqlDataSource controls that we will use in this section:

Configuring the select statement for the first **SqlDataSource** control is simple, just specify two fields from the list of the fields displayed shown as follows:

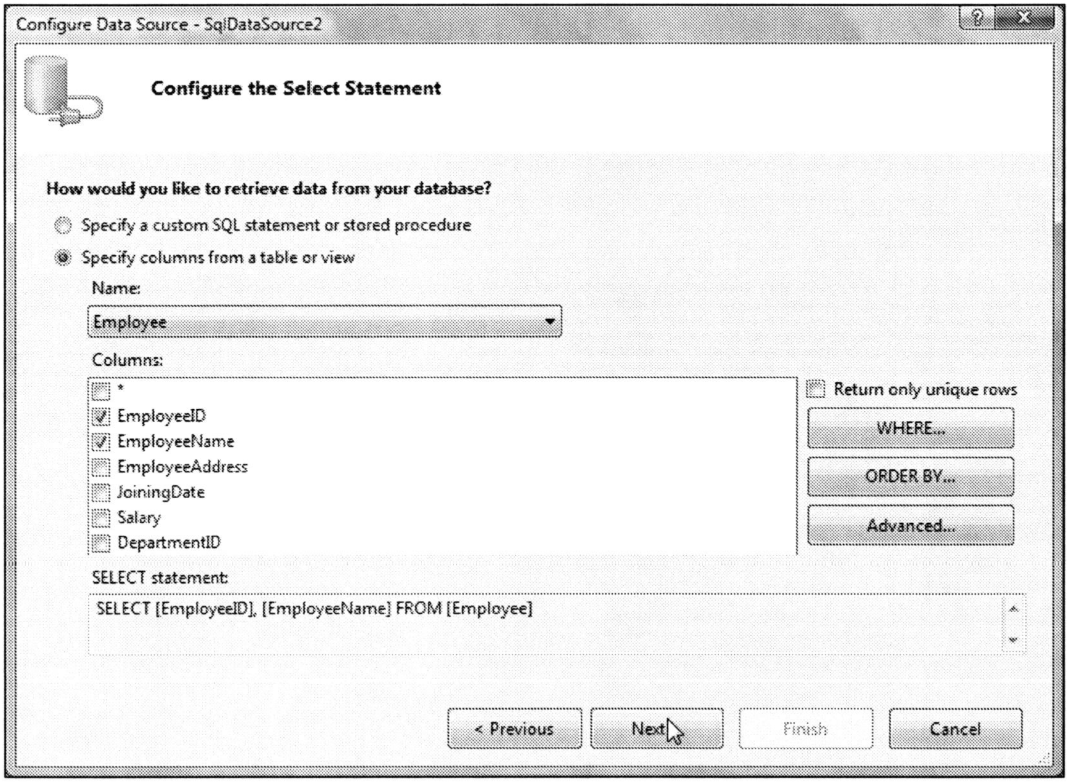

Now click on **Next** and make sure that you test the query to check whether it is fine. Following is the output once you test your query by clicking on the **Test Query** button:

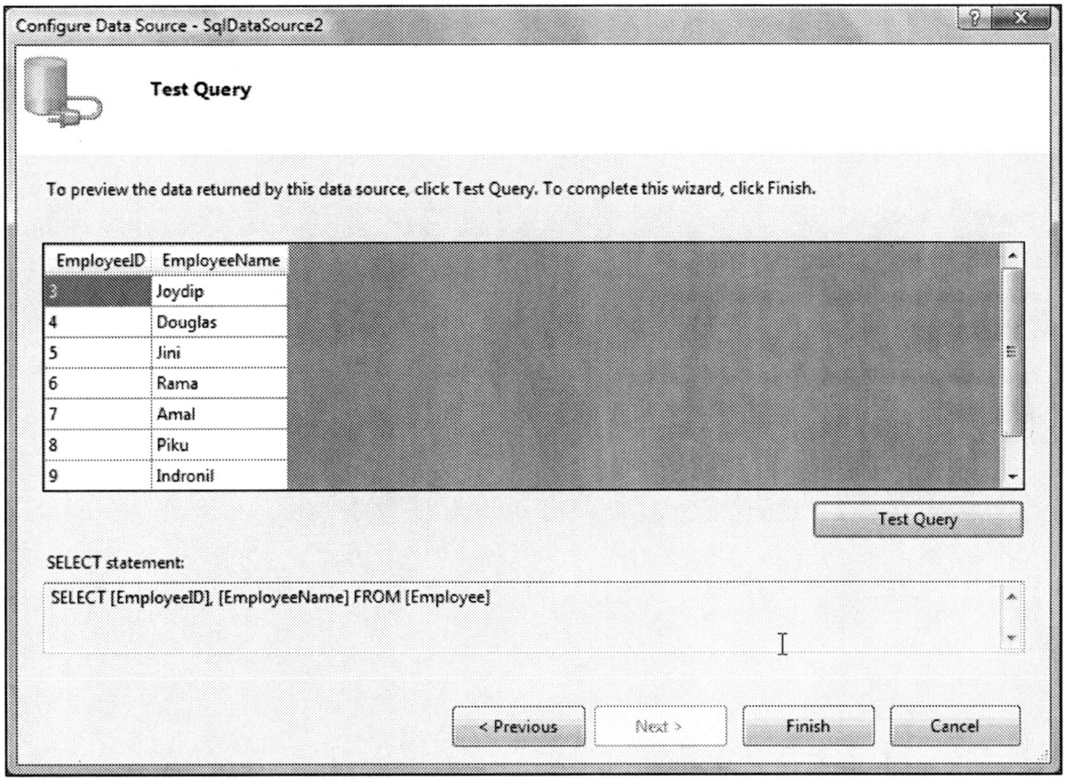

The next step is to drag and drop a **DropDownList** control from the tool box and associate the control with the **SqlDataSource** control that we just configured. The following screenshot illustrates how you can associate this control to the data source control and specify its display and the value fields.

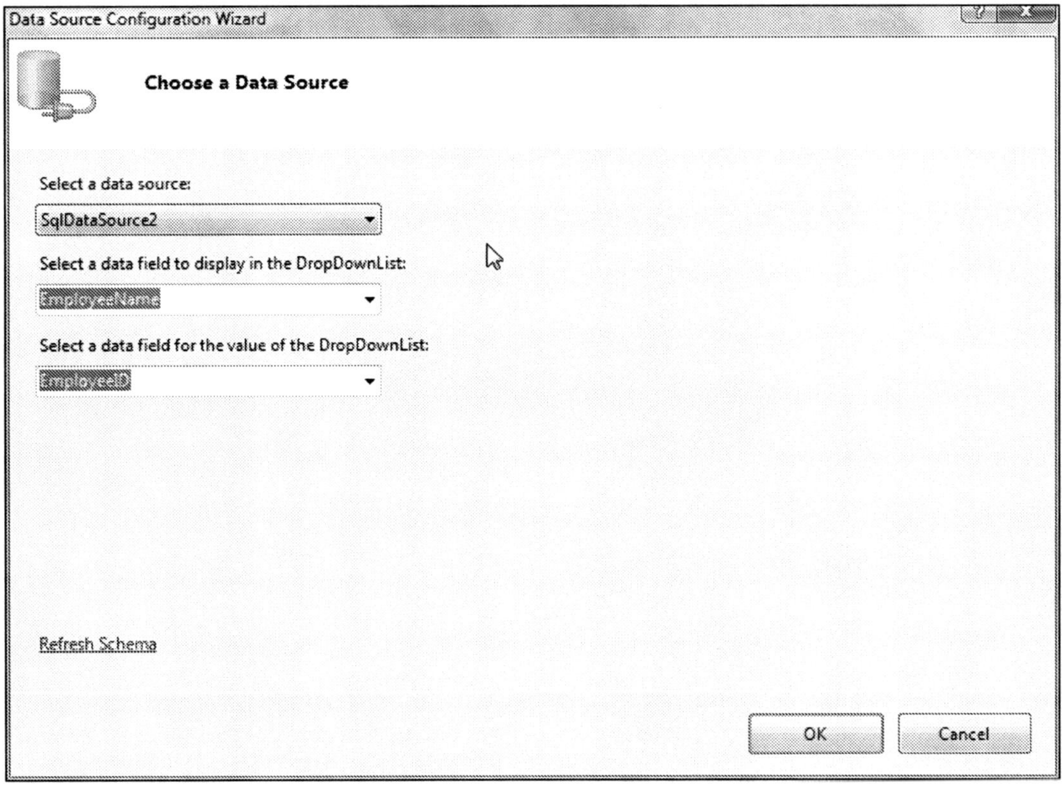

Now, click on the **OK** button to complete the process. Next, drag and drop another **SqlDataSource** control from the tool box and configure the **Select statement** for the control as shown in the following screenshot:

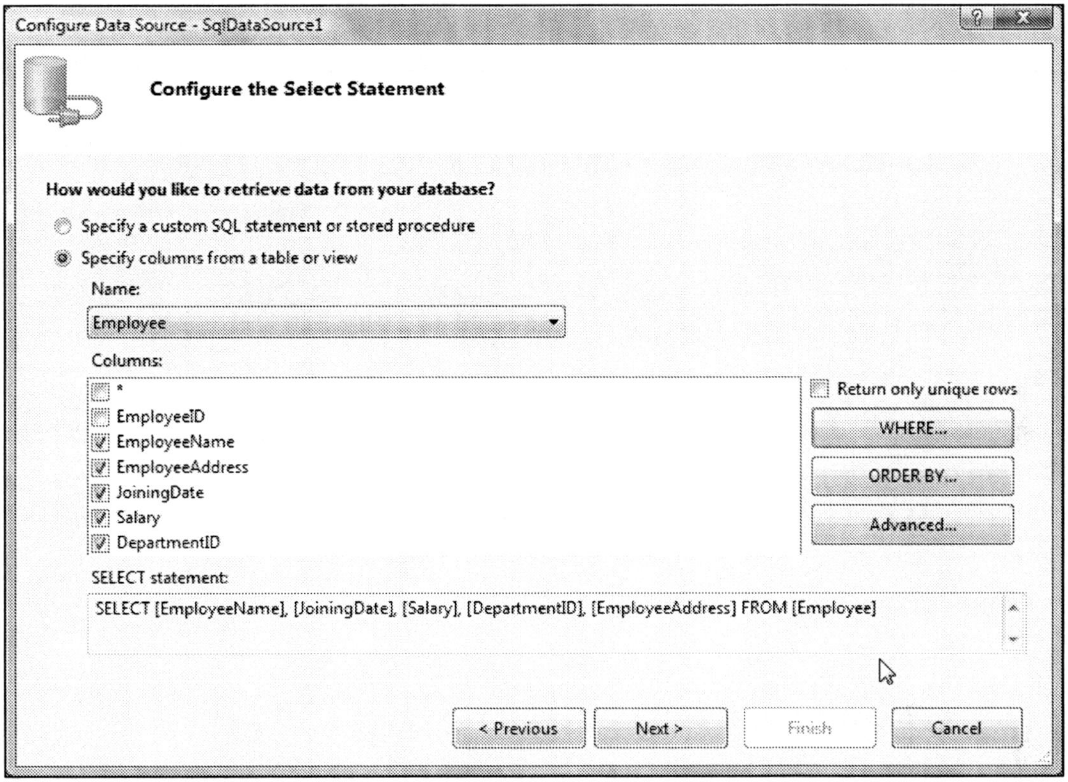

Note that we have specified the fields we want to display using the **DetailsView** control. Now, we have to display the details of the employee selected by the user. Hence, we need to specify the *where* clause in this query to restrict the output. When you click on the **WHERE** button, a window pops up where you can specify the same. This is shown as follows:

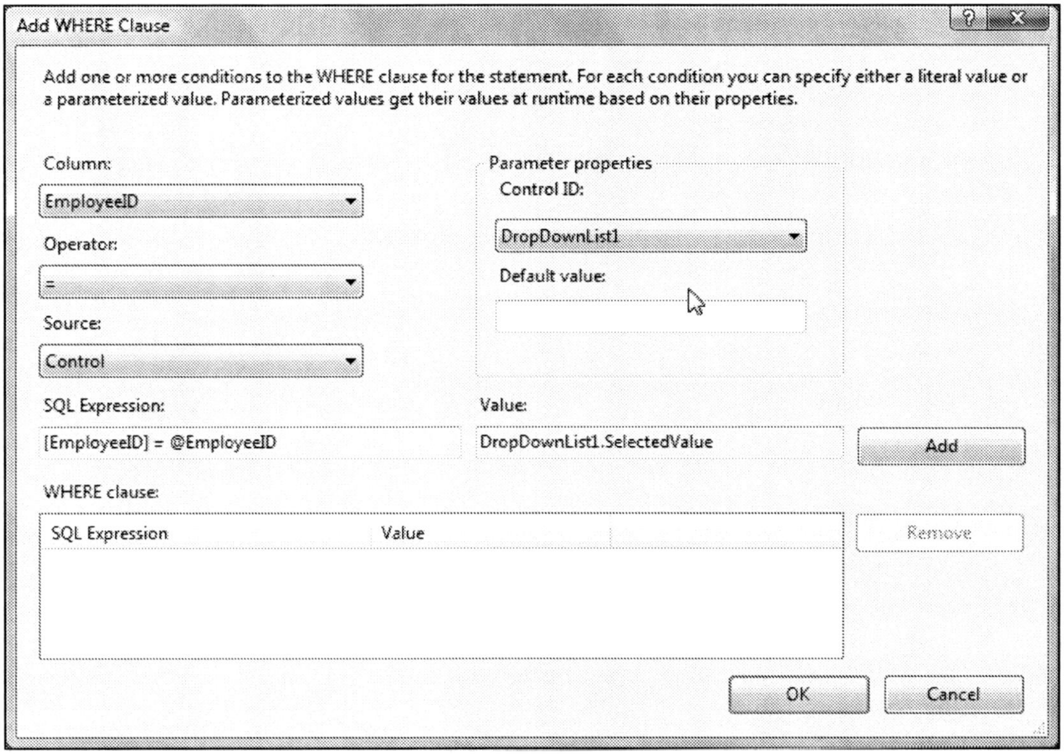

Note how the **Column**, **Source** and **Control ID** properties have been specified. Now, click on the **Add** button to finish off this process. What we are left with now is the **DetailsView** control that we would use to display the details for the selected employee.

Drag-and-drop a **DetailsView** control onto the web form in its design view mode and associate its data source with the data source control that we just configured. Refer to the following screenshot:

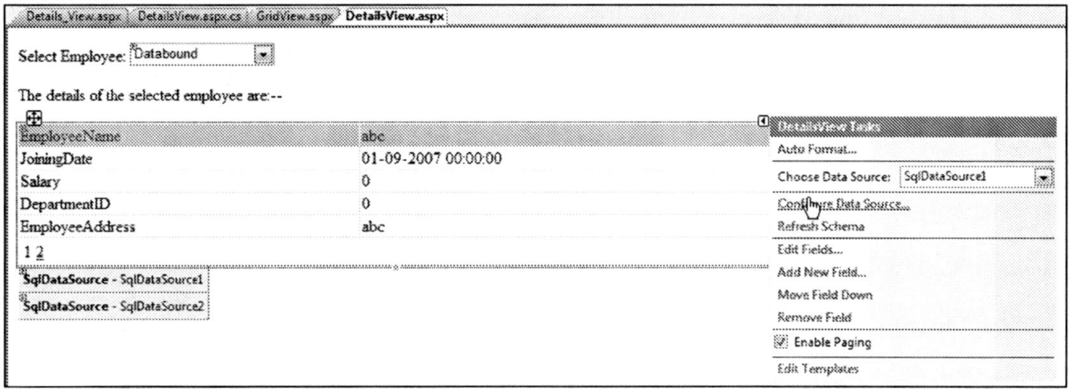

You are done! When you execute the application, the output is similar to what is shown in the following screenshot:

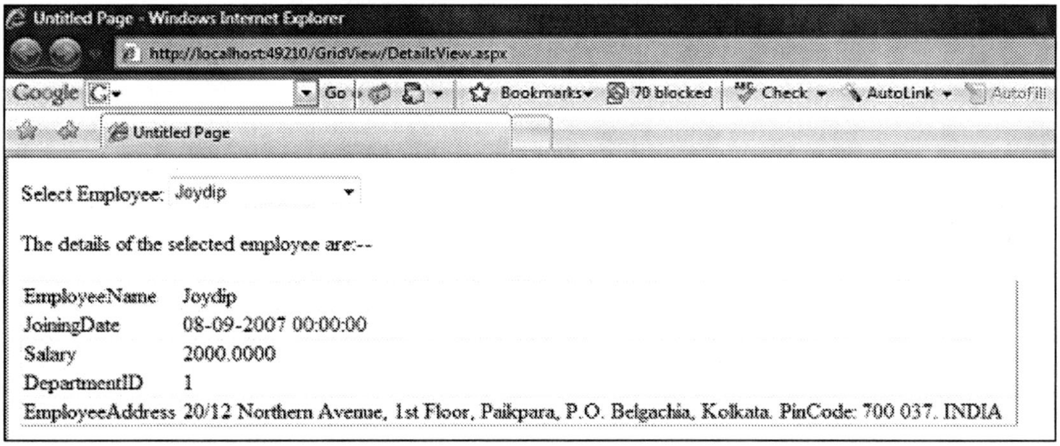

The output shown above is not well formatted. Similar to the **GridView** control, you can use the style properties of the **DetailsView** control and its templates to customize the display. I will not discuss much on how these styles and templates work as we have had a detailed discussion on this in the Chapter 6 on the **GridView** control.

Displaying a DropDownList inside the DetailsView control

You can display a DropDownList control inside a DetailsView and bind data to it at design time using the `<asp:TemplateField>` tag in the markup as shown in the code snippet below.

```
<asp:TemplateField HeaderText = "Department Name">
            <ItemTemplate>
            <asp:DropDownList
            ID="DeptDropDown" runat="server"
                 DataSourceID="SqlDataSource1"
                 DataTextField="DepartmentName"
                    DataValueField="DepartmentID"
                   SelectedValue=
                   '<%# Eval("DepartmentID") %>' />
            </ItemTemplate>
</asp:TemplateField>
```

The above markup code will display a `DropDownList` control named `DeptDropDown` containing all the department names.

Changing the DetailsView mode

Suppose you want to change the DetailsView mode to **Insert** if there are no records in the control. You can do this in the code behind by using the `ChangeMode()` method of the control. Here is the code snippet that illustrates how you can achieve this:

```
if (DetailsView1.Rows.Count == 0)
  DetailsView1.ChangeMode(DetailsViewMode.Insert);
else
  DetailsView1.ChangeMode(DetailsViewMode.ReadOnly);
```

Note that we have changed the mode to `Insert` if there are no records in the control and to `ReadOnly` if there are records within it.

The following code snippet illustrates that the source code for the control looks like after formatting, using the style properties and the templates of the control:

```
<asp:DetailsView ID="DetailsView1" runat="server" Height="50px"
  Width="727px" BorderStyle="None" BorderColor="Black"
  BorderWidth="1px" AutoGenerateRows="False"
  DataSourceID="SqlDataSource1" AllowPaging="True">
    <FooterStyle ForeColor="Blue" BackColor="White"></FooterStyle>
    <RowStyle ForeColor="Teal"></RowStyle>
    <PagerStyle ForeColor="Blue" HorizontalAlign="Left"
       BackColor="White"></PagerStyle>
     <Fields>
```

```
        <asp:BoundField DataField="EmployeeName"
          HeaderText="EmployeeName" SortExpression="EmployeeName" />
        <asp:BoundField DataField="JoiningDate"
          HeaderText="JoiningDate"
          SortExpression="JoiningDate" HtmlEncode="False"
          DataFormatString="{0:d}"/>
        <asp:BoundField DataField="Salary" HeaderText="Salary"
          SortExpression="Salary" HtmlEncode="False"
          DataFormatString="{0:C}"/>
        <asp:BoundField DataField="DepartmentID"
          HeaderText="DepartmentID"
          SortExpression="DepartmentID" />
        <asp:BoundField DataField="EmployeeAddress"
          HeaderText="EmployeeAddress"
          SortExpression="EmployeeAddress" />
      </Fields>
          <HeaderStyle ForeColor="White" Font-Bold="True"
              BackColor="#336699"></HeaderStyle>
  </asp:DetailsView>
```

When you execute the application now, the output is similar to the one shown in the following screenshot:

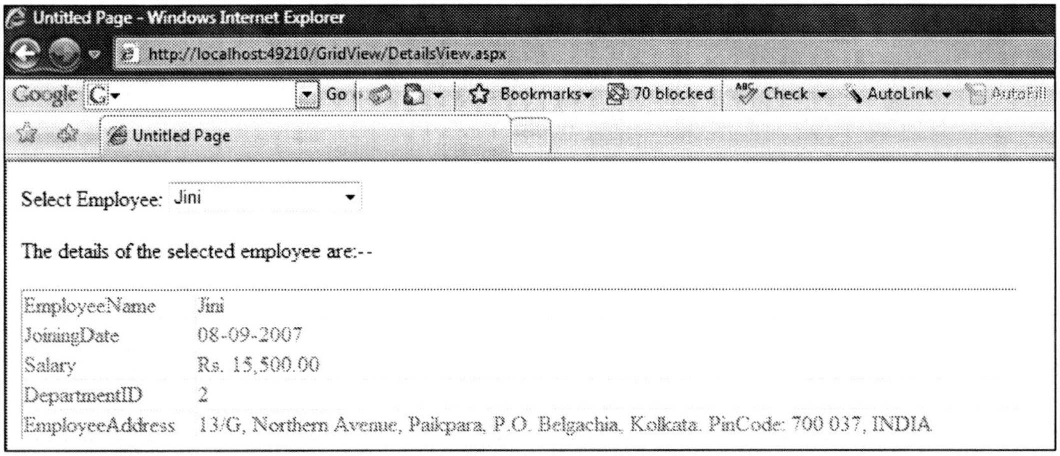

As you can see from the figure, the output looks much better. The following is the complete source code in the `.aspx` file for the simple application that we have designed.

```
<form id="form1" runat="server">
    <div>
        Select Employee: 
         <asp:DropDownList ID="DropDownList1" runat="server"
           AutoPostBack="True" DataSourceID="SqlDataSource2"
           DataTextField="EmployeeName" DataValueField="EmployeeID"
           Width="140px">
        </asp:DropDownList>
         
        <br />
        <br />
        The details of the selected employee are:--<br />
        <br />
        <asp:DetailsView ID="DetailsView1" runat="server"
          Height="50px" Width="727px" BorderStyle="None"
          BorderColor="Black" BorderWidth="1px
          AutoGenerateRows="False" DataSourceID="SqlDataSource1"
          AllowPaging="True">
        <FooterStyle ForeColor="Blue"
           BackColor="White"></FooterStyle>
        <RowStyle ForeColor="Teal"></RowStyle>
        <PagerStyle ForeColor="Blue" HorizontalAlign="Left"
           BackColor="White"></PagerStyle>
        <Fields>
        <asp:BoundField DataField="EmployeeName"
          HeaderText="EmployeeName" SortExpression="EmployeeName" />
        <asp:BoundField DataField="JoiningDate"
          HeaderText="JoiningDate" SortExpression="JoiningDate"
          HtmlEncode="False" DataFormatString="{0:d}"/>
        <asp:BoundField DataField="Salary" HeaderText="Salary"
          SortExpression="Salary" HtmlEncode="False"
          DataFormatString="{0:C}"/>
        <asp:BoundField DataField="DepartmentID"
          HeaderText="DepartmentID" SortExpression="DepartmentID" />
        <asp:BoundField DataField="EmployeeAddress"
          HeaderText="EmployeeAddress"
          SortExpression="EmployeeAddress" />
        </Fields>
        <HeaderStyle ForeColor="White" Font-Bold="True"
           BackColor="#336699"></HeaderStyle>
        </asp:DetailsView>
    </div>
         <asp:SqlDataSource ID="SqlDataSource1" runat="server"
           ConnectionString="Data Source=.;
           Initial Catalog=Test;User ID=sa;Password=sa"
```

```
            ProviderName="System.Data.SqlClient"
            SelectCommand="SELECT [EmployeeName], [JoiningDate],
            [Salary], [DepartmentID], [EmployeeAddress] FROM
            [Employee] WHERE ([EmployeeID] = @EmployeeID)">
            <SelectParameters>
        <asp:ControlParameter ControlID="DropDownList1"
          Name="EmployeeID" PropertyName="SelectedValue"
              Type="Int32" />
            </SelectParameters>
        </asp:SqlDataSource>
        <asp:SqlDataSource ID="SqlDataSource2" runat="server"
          ConnectionString="<%$
          ConnectionStrings:TestConnectionString %>"
          SelectCommand="SELECT [EmployeeID], [EmployeeName] FROM
          [Employee]">
        </asp:SqlDataSource>
       <br />
</form>
```

The best part as we have seen so far is that we didn't write even a single line of code. Awesome, isn't it?

Finding Controls inside a DetailsView control

You can find a control nested within a DetailsView control using the `FindControl()` method in the `DataBound` event of the control as shown in the following code snippet:

```
protected void DetailsView1_DataBound(object sender,
EventArgs e)
    {
        if (((DetailsView)sender).
               CurrentMode == DetailsViewMode.Edit)
        {
             TextBox txtBox = (TextBox)((DetailsView)
                sender).FindControl("txtEmployeeName");
             if (myTextBox != null)
             {
                 //Write your custom code here
             }
        }
    }
```

Accessing bound fields of a DetailsView control in the code behind

To access the bound fields of a DetailsView control from the code behind, you can write the following code in the DataBound event of the control.

```
protected void DetailsView1_DataBound(object sender,
EventArgs e)
    {
        foreach (DetailsViewRow dvr in
                 DetailsView1.Rows)
        {
            Response.Write("<br> " +
                           dvr.Cells[1].Text);
        }
    }
```

Using a CheckBox inside a DetailsView control

You can use a CheckBox control inside the DetailsView control using the `<asp:TemplateField>` tag and then creating the control inside the `<ItemTemplate>` and binding data using the `Bind()` method. Here is the markup code for the control:

```
<asp:TemplateField HeaderText = "Employee Name">
   <ItemTemplate>
     <asp:Checkbox ID="ChkSelect" Runat="Server"
       Text='<%# Bind("EmployeeName") %>'
             Checked ="false"/>
   </ItemTemplate>
</asp:TemplateField>
```

Working with the ASP.NET FormView Control

The ASP.NET FormView control is a data-bound control that renders a single record at a time from its associated data source. It is quite similar to the DetailsView control except that while the DetailsView renders itself into a tabular format, the FormView control requires user-defined templates for rendering. According to the MSDN, "When using the FormView control, you specify templates to display and edit bound values. The templates contain formatting, controls, and binding expressions to create the form. The FormView control is often used in combination with a GridView control for master or detail scenarios."

To use the FormView control, simply drag and drop it from the tool box and then associate the control with a data source. In our example we will take the SqlDataSource control to bind data to the FormView control. You can use an existing data source or create a fresh new one using the smart tag of the control.

As we have seen in Chapter 1, the SqlDataSource is a data source control with simple configuration needs and can be used to bind data to a databound control without the need to write even a single line of code. It merely involves the steps of creating the connection string, generating or writing SQL query or Stored Procedure, and generating an optional insert, update and delete statements. Once this configuration is done, it can be bound to a data bound control seamlessly. The following screenshot illustrates the **FormView** control and the **SqlDataSource** control that it is bound to in design view mode:

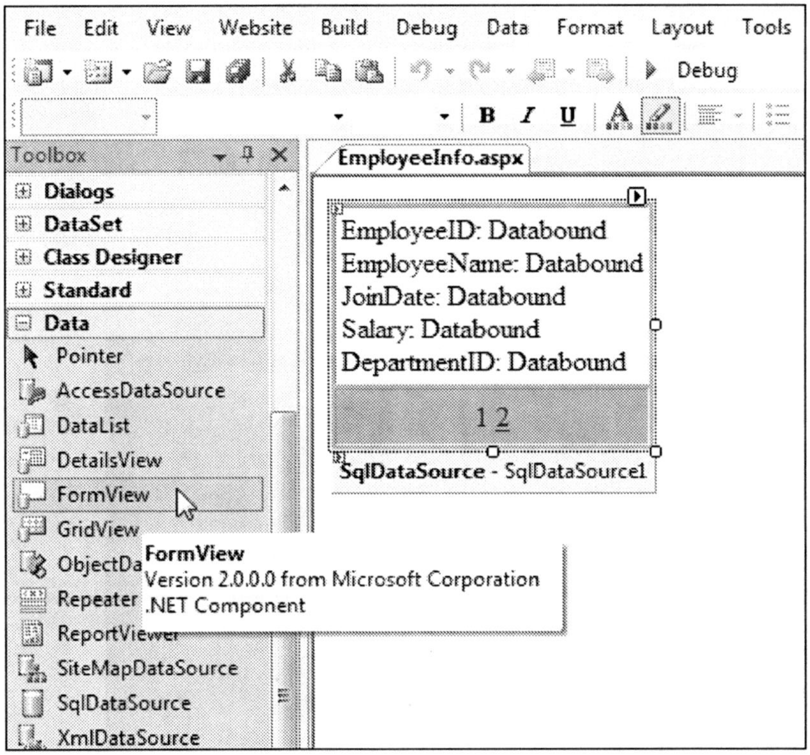

You can also apply templates and styles just as you did with the other data bound controls in the previous chapters. We will also enable **paging** for this control so that it can display multiple records with one record per page. Here is the display once you execute the application.

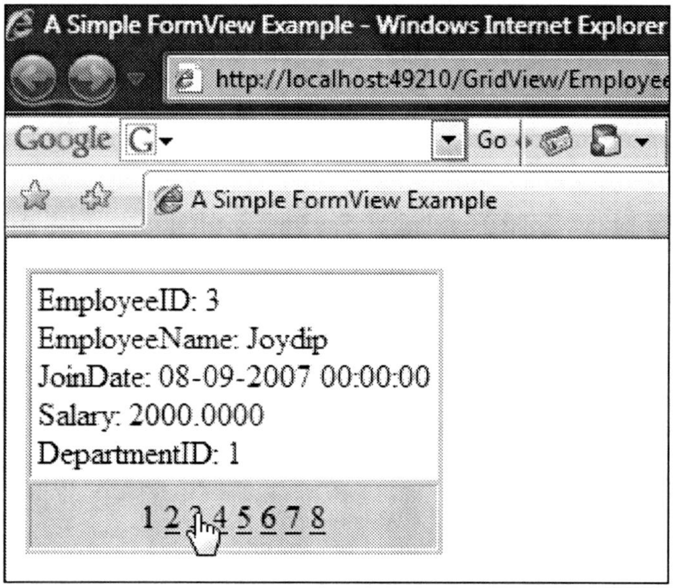

Specifying the PrimaryKey of the DataSource using the DataKeyNames property

The purpose of the `DataKeyNames` property for the data controls we have used so far is to specify the PrimaryKey(in this case `EmployeeID`) field from the DataSource that is used to bind data to these controls. You can use this property in the markup code in the `.aspx` file as shown as follows:

```
DataKeyNames="EmployeeID"
```

Finding controls within a FormView control

Similar to the DetailsView control, you can use the `FindControl()` method to find nested controls within a FormView control. The following code snippet illustrates how this can be achieved.

```
if (FormView1.CurrentMode == FormViewMode.Edit ||
FormView1.CurrentMode == FormViewMode.Insert)
        {
            //Write your custom code here
        }
```

Note that the **FormView** control shown in the screenshot above has paging enabled and it displays the details of the employees, one in each page. The following code snippet shows the source code that gets generated in your `.aspx` file.

```
<asp:FormView ID="FormView1" runat="server" AllowPaging="True"
  BackColor="White" BorderColor="Red" BorderStyle="None"
  BorderWidth="1px" CellPadding="3" CellSpacing="2"
  DataKeyNames="EmployeeID" DataSourceID="SqlDataSource1"
  GridLines="Both">
    <FooterStyle BackColor="#F7DFB5" ForeColor="#8C4510" />
       <EditRowStyle BackColor="#738A9C" Font-Bold="True"
         ForeColor="White" />
    <RowStyle BackColor="White" ForeColor="Black" />
    <PagerStyle ForeColor="Blue" HorizontalAlign="Center" />
       <ItemTemplate>
         EmployeeID:<asp:Label ID="EmployeeIDLabel" runat="server"
          Text='<%# Eval("EmployeeID") %>'>
           </asp:Label><br />
         EmployeeName:<asp:Label ID="EmployeeNameLabel"
          runat="server" Text='<%# Bind("EmployeeName") %>'>
           </asp:Label><br />
         JoinDate:<asp:Label ID="JoiningDateLabel" runat="server"
           Text='<%# Bind("JoiningDate") %>'></asp:Label><br />
         Salary:<asp:Label ID="SalaryLabel" runat="server" Text='<%#
           Bind("Salary") %>'></asp:Label><br />
         DepartmentID:<asp:Label ID="DepartmentIDLabel"
           runat="server" Text='<%# Bind("DepartmentID") %>'>
            </asp:Label><br />
       </ItemTemplate>
 <HeaderStyle BackColor="Black" Font-Bold="True" ForeColor="White" />
</asp:FormView>
```

And here is the markup code for the SqlDataSource control that we have used to bind data to the FormView control.

```
<asp:SqlDataSource ID="SqlDataSource1" runat="server"
  ConnectionString="Data Source=.;
  Initial Catalog=Test;UserID=sa;Password=sa"
   SelectCommand="SELECT [EmployeeID], [EmployeeName],
   [JoiningDate], [Salary], [DepartmentID] FROM [Employee]">
</asp:SqlDataSource>
```

Formatting Data Using the FormView Control

As you can see from the figure given earlier, the employee data displayed in the FormView control is not properly formatted. In this section we will learn how we can use custom formatting to display data in the FormView control in a properly formatted manner.

To ensure that the FormView control displays a custom text when there are no records in the control, we will use the property called `EmptyDataText` shown as follows:

```
EmptyDataText="No Records"
```

Now, to test whether the above message is displayed, let us bind an empty data source to the FormView control. We will make the data source empty by changing its Select statement shown as follows:

```
<asp:SqlDataSource ID="SqlDataSource1" runat="server"
  ConnectionString="Data Source=.;
  Initial Catalog=Test;UserID=sa;Password=sa"
   SelectCommand="SELECT [EmployeeID], [EmployeeName],
   [JoiningDate], [Salary], [DepartmentID] FROM [Employee] where
   1=0">
</asp:SqlDataSource>
```

The above data source is empty as the condition specified 1=0 is always false. When you bind such a data source to the **FormView** control with its `EmptyDataText` property set, the text gets displayed in place of the records which would otherwise have been displayed if the data source contained data. Here is the output on execution:

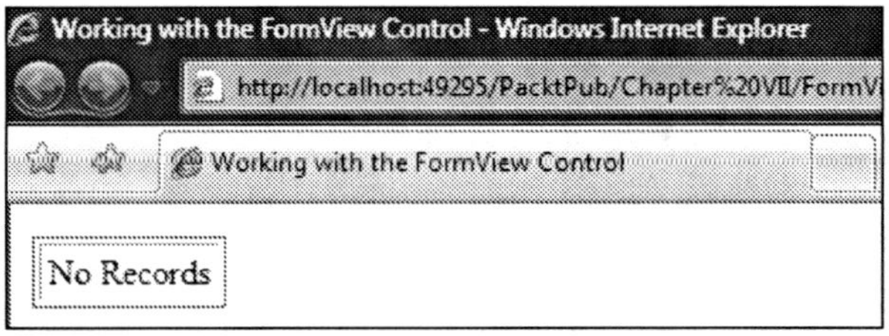

The `JoiningDate` and the `Salary` fields displayed in the **FormView** control shown in the earlier section were not properly formatted. Here is how you can use the `Bind()` method in the markup code in the `.aspx` file to format the display of these fields in the control.

```
</asp:Label><br />
      Joining Date:<asp:Label ID="lblJoiningDate" runat="server"
      Text='<%# Bind("JoiningDate","{0:d}") %>'></asp:Label><br/>
      Salary:<asp:Label ID="lblSalary" runat="server" Text='<%#
      Bind("Salary","{0:c}") %>'>
</asp:Label><br />
```

Note how we have used the data format string in the second parameter to the `Bind()` method.

We can also use a DropDownList control within the FormView control to display the department names with the department to which the specific employee belongs as the selected department in the DropDownList. The markup code follows:

```
<asp:DropDownList ID="DeptDropDownList" runat="server"
      DataSourceID="SqlDataSource2" DataTextField="DepartmentName"
      DataValueField="DepartmentID" SelectedValue='<%#
      Eval("DepartmentID") %>'/>
```

To customize paging, we can use the `PagerTemplate` of the FormView control with LinkButtons and appropriate texts on them. Here is the markup code in the `.aspx` file that illustrates how you can use the `PagerTemplate` of the FormView control to display a customized pager. Note that the AllowPaging property should be set to true to enable paging for the control.

```
<PagerTemplate>
     <table>
       <tr>
         <td>
           <asp:LinkButton ID="FirstButton" CommandName="Page"
             CommandArgument="First" Text="First" RunAt="server"/>
         </td>
         <td>
           <asp:LinkButton ID="PrevButton"  CommandName="Page"
             CommandArgument="Prev"  Text="Prev" RunAt="server"/>
         </td>
         <td>
           <asp:LinkButton ID="NextButton"  CommandName="Page"
             CommandArgument="Next"  Text="Next" RunAt="server"/>
         </td>
         <td>
           <asp:LinkButton ID="LastButton"  CommandName="Page"
             CommandArgument="Last"  Text="Last" RunAt="server"/>
         </td>
       </tr>
     </table>
</PagerTemplate>
```

Here is the complete source code for the `FormView` control with the customized formatting we have just discussed.

```
<asp:FormView ID="FormView1" runat="server" AllowPaging="True"
  BackColor="White" DefaultMode="ReadOnly"
  BorderColor="Red" BorderStyle="Solid" EmptyDataText="No Records"
  BorderWidth="1px" CellPadding="3" CellSpacing="2"
     DataKeyNames="EmployeeID" DataSourceID="SqlDataSource1"
     GridLines="Both">
      <FooterStyle BackColor="#F7DFB5" ForeColor="#8C4510" />
      <EditRowStyle BackColor="#738A9C" Font-Bold="True"
         ForeColor="White" />
      <RowStyle BackColor="White" ForeColor="Black" />
      <PagerStyle ForeColor="Blue" HorizontalAlign="Center" />
      <ItemTemplate>
         Employee ID:<asp:Label ID="lblEmpID" runat="server"
           Text='<%# Eval("EmployeeID") %>'>
           </asp:Label><br />
         Employee Name:<asp:Label ID="lblEmpName" runat="server"
           Text='<%# Bind("EmployeeName") %>'>
           </asp:Label><br />
         Joining Date:
           <asp:Label ID="lblJoiningDate" runat="server" Text='<%#
             Bind("JoiningDate","{0:d}") %>'></asp:Label><br />
             Salary:<asp:Label ID="lblSalary" runat="server"
             Text='<%# Bind("Salary","{0:c}") %>'>
           </asp:Label><br />
         Department Name:
           <asp:DropDownList ID="DeptDropDownList"
             runat="server" DataSourceID="SqlDataSource2"
             DataTextField="DepartmentName"DataValueField=
             "DepartmentI D"
             SelectedValue='<%# Eval("DepartmentID") %>' />
              <br />
      </ItemTemplate>
      <PagerTemplate>
         <table>
            <tr>
             <td><asp:LinkButton ID=»FirstButton» CommandName=»Page»
                   CommandArgument=»First» Text=»First»
                   RunAt=»server»/></td>
             <td><asp:LinkButton ID=»PrevButton»  CommandName=»Page»
                   CommandArgument=»Prev» Text=»Prev»
                   RunAt=»server»/></td>
```

```
                <td><asp:LinkButton ID=»NextButton»  CommandName=»Page»
                      CommandArgument=»Next» Text=»Next»
                      RunAt=»server»/></td>
                <td><asp:LinkButton ID=»LastButton»  CommandName=»Page»
                      CommandArgument=»Last» Text=»Last»
                      RunAt=»server»/></td>
              </tr>
            </table>
        </PagerTemplate>
        <HeaderStyle BackColor=»Black» Font-Bold=»True»
          ForeColor=»White» />
</asp:FormView>
```

The markup code for the data source controls used for binding data to the FormView control and the DropDownList control contained within it is shown as follows:

```
<asp:SqlDataSource ID="SqlDataSource1" runat="server"
  ConnectionString="Data Source=.;
  Initial Catalog=Test;UserID=sa;Password=sa"
  SelectCommand="SELECT [EmployeeID], [EmployeeName],
  [JoiningDate], [Salary], [DepartmentID] FROM [Employee]">
</asp:SqlDataSource>
<asp:SqlDataSource ID="SqlDataSource2" runat="server"
  ConnectionString="<%$ ConnectionStrings:TestConnectionString %>"
  SelectCommand="SELECT [DepartmentID], [DepartmentName] FROM
  [Department]">
</asp:SqlDataSource>
```

When you execute the application, the output is similar to what is shown in the following screenshot:

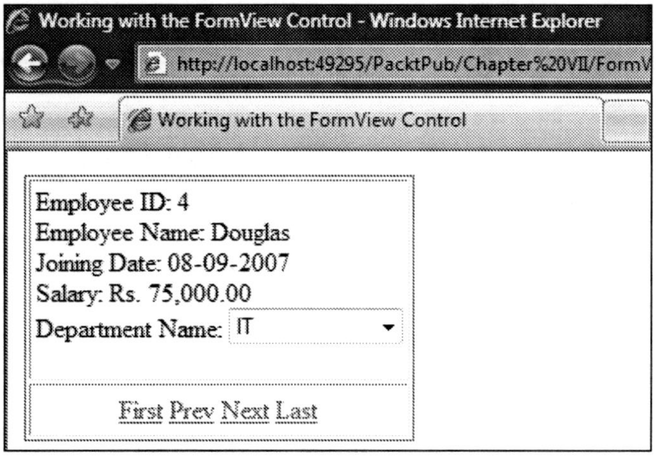

> **Data binding using the `DataSource` and `DataSourceID` properties**
>
> The ASP.NET data controls facilitate binding data to it using either of the two properties. `DataSource` and `DataSourceID`. While you can use the `DataSource` property to bind the control to `DataSet` and `DataReader` instances, the `DatasourceID` property is typically used to bind data to the `DataSource` controls such as the SqlDataSource or ObjectDataSource controls. The latter is the recommended approach since you can exploit the built-in capabilities of the control to perform the CRUD (Create, Update, Read and Delete) operations without having to write much code in
> your applications.

I will now quickly run you through some of the most important properties of the FormView control. You can find similar properties for the other ASP.NET data controls as well. You can refer to MSDN for more information in this regard.

- **DefaultMode**: You can set the default behavior of the control using this property. It can accept one of the three possible values. ReadOnly, Edit and Insert.
- **EmptyDataText**: You can use this property to display text in the control if there are no records, that is, the data source is empty.
- **AllowPaging**: This is a boolean property that, if set to true, will enable paging and if set to false, paging will be disabled for the control. The page numbers will also be displayed at the bottom; you can, however, change those using custom styles.
- **DataKeyNames**: This is the PrimaryKey of the data source.
- **DataSourceID**: This typically will be the ID of the data source control that is used to bind data to the FormView control.

In the section that follows, we will explore the ASP.NET TreeView control and learn how we can work with it to display hierarchical data.

Working with the ASP.NET TreeView Control

The ASP.NET 2.0 **TreeView** control can be used to display hierarchical data from a data source. You can create a `TreeView` control programmatically in the `.aspx` file as shown in the following code snippet:

```
<asp:TreeView ID="TreeView1" runat="server"></asp:TreeView>
```

When you switch over to the design view of the web form, the control looks as shown in the following screenshot:

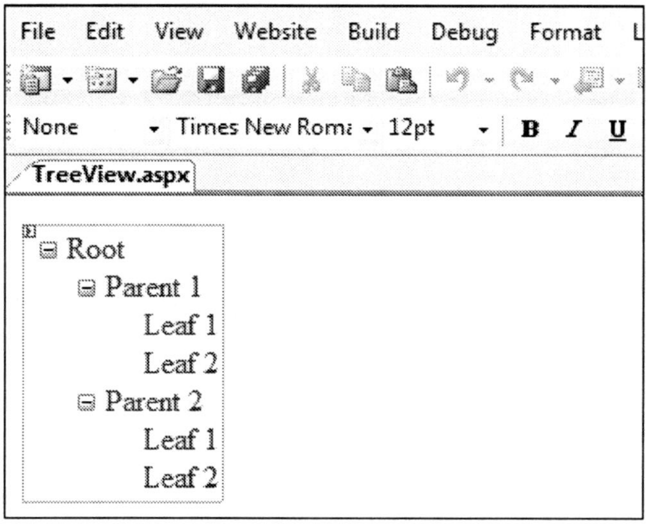

You can easily add nodes to the **TreeView** control programmatically. You need to remember how to associate one node with another. Refer to the following code snippet that shows how we can create a simple `TreeView` control with two child nodes:

```
TreeNode root = new TreeNode();
root.Text = "Root Node";
this.TreeView1.Nodes.Add(root);
TreeNode child1 = new TreeNode();
child1.Text = "Child 1";
root.ChildNodes.Add(child1);
TreeNode child2 = new TreeNode();
child2.Text = "Child 2";
root.ChildNodes.Add(child2);
this.TreeView1.ExpandAll();
```

Notice how we have created new nodes using the `TreeNode` class and associated the child nodes to the parent node using the `ChildNodes` property of the `TreeNode` instance. When you execute the sample application, the output is similar to the following.

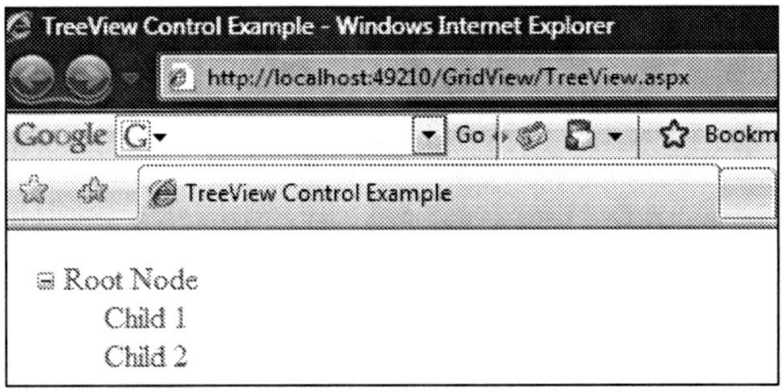

Fine, let us now examine how we can bind data to the **TreeView** data control without writing even a single line of code. We haven't used the **XMLDataSource** control so far, right? Let us now discuss how we can use the **XMLDataSource** control to bind data to the **TreeView Control**.

First, drag and drop an XMLDataSource control onto your web form in design view mode. Then associate this control to the **Employee_Addresses.xml** file that contains the addresses of all the employees in the Employee table as shown in the following screenshot:

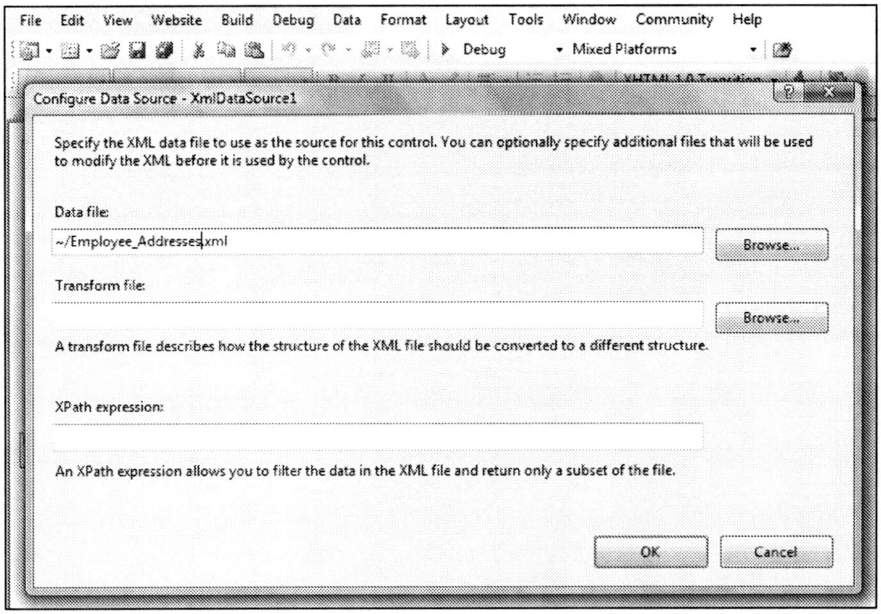

Here is what the **Employee_Addresses.xml** file looks like.

```
<?xml version="1.0" encoding="utf-8" ?>
<Employee_Addresses>
  <Employee Name="Joydip">
    <Address Value="20/12 Northern Avenue, Paikpara, P.O. Belgachia,
       Kolkata. PinCode: 700 037. INDIA.">
    </Address>
  </Employee>
  <Employee Name="Douglas">
    <Address Value="Packt Pub, United Kingdom">
    </Address>
  </Employee>
  <Employee Name="Jini">
    <Address Value="25/1 Anath Nath Deb Lane, Paikpara, Kolkata.
       PinCode:700 037.INDIA.">
    </Address>
  </Employee>
  <Employee Name="Rama">
    <Address Value="13/G Northern Avenue, Paikpara, Kolkata.
       PinCode:700 037.INDIA.">
    </Address>
  </Employee>
  <Employee Name="Amal">
    <Address Value="25/1 Rani Branch Road, Paikpara, Kolkata.
       PinCode: 700 002. INDIA.">
    </Address>
  </Employee>
</Employee_Addresses>
```

Next use the **DataBindings Editor** as shown below to specify the bindings for the nodes of the **TreeView** control.

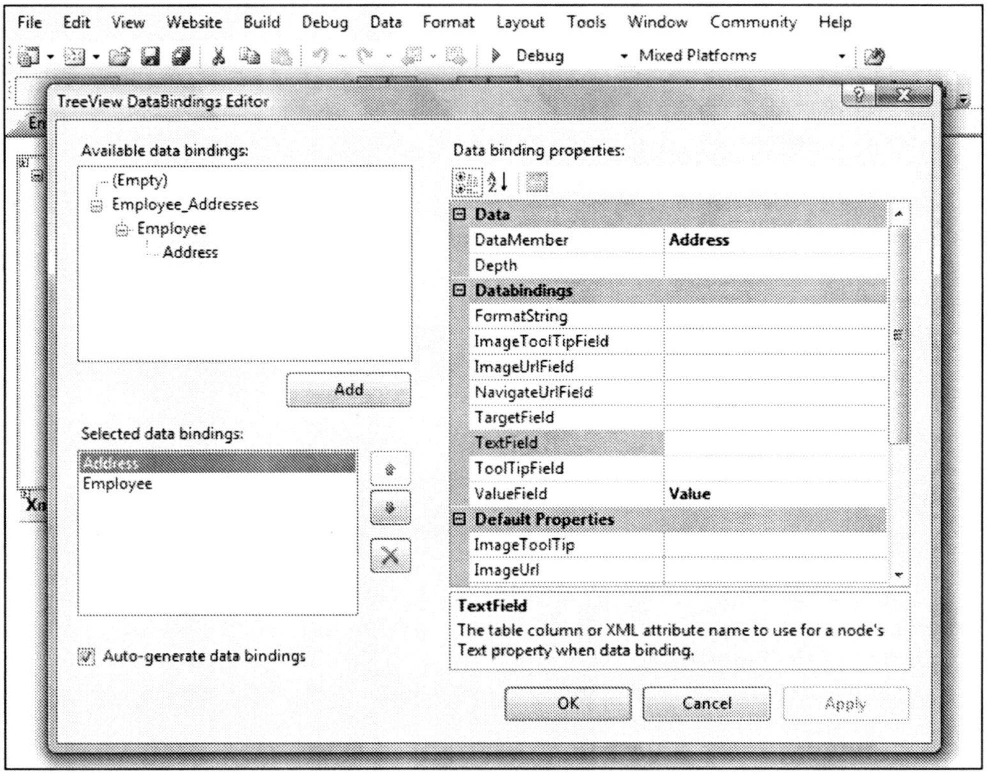

You can customize the display by specifying the color, font and node styles of your choice using the `ParentNodeStyle`, `SelectedNodeStyle` and the `NodeStyle` properties of the `TreeView` control. The source code for the `TreeView` control now looks like:

```
<asp:TreeView ID="TreeView1" runat="server"
  DataSourceID="XmlDataSource1" BackColor="White" Font
  Bold="True" Font-Italic="True" ForeColor="Black">
    <ParentNodeStyle Font-Bold="True" ForeColor="Black"
                           BackColor="SkyBlue" />
    <SelectedNodeStyle Font-Underline="True" HorizontalPadding="0px"
                     VerticalPadding="0px" BackColor="#C04000" />
    <NodeStyle Font-Names="Verdana" Font-Size="8pt" ForeColor="Black"
                        HorizontalPadding="5px" NodeSpacing="0px"
```

```
                                VerticalPadding="0px" BackColor="#00C0C0" />
      <DataBindings>
        <asp:TreeNodeBinding DataMember="Address" ValueField="Value"/>
        <asp:TreeNodeBinding DataMember="Employee" ValueField="Name"/>
      </DataBindings>
      <LeafNodeStyle BackColor="#FFE0C0" />
    </asp:TreeView>
```

You are done! When you execute the application, the output is similar to the following:

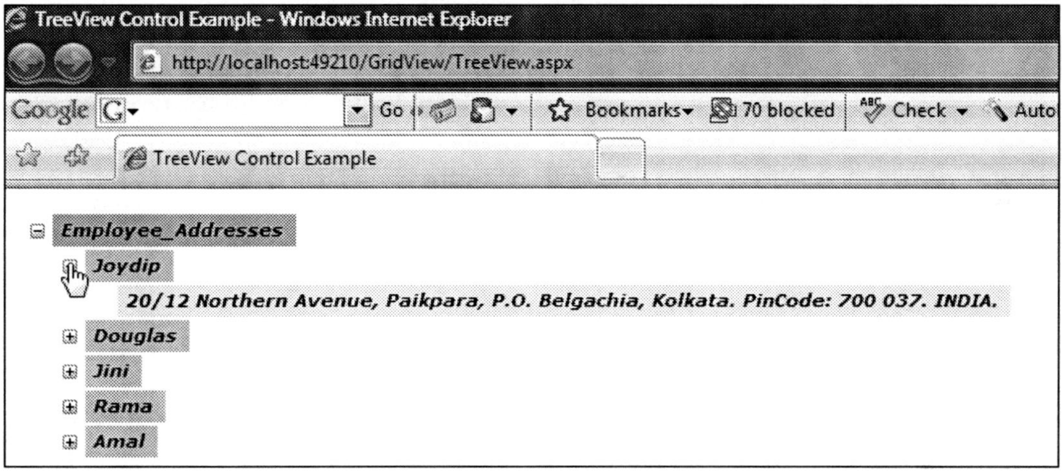

Note how the node with the caption as **Joydip** expands once you click on it. The corresponding address for the employee **Joydip** is then displayed as text.

> **`SelectedNodeChanged` event of the `TreeView` control**
>
> The `SelectedNodeChanged` event of the TreeView control is used to detect whether a selection has changed. This event gets fired when the user selects a particular node of the `TreeView` control. However, this event will not be fired if the `SelectedNodeChanged` property is changed programmatically.

Creating the nodes of TreeView control programmatically

You can create the nodes of a `TreeView` control programmatically. The following code snippet illustrates how this can be achieved.

```
private void CreateTreeView()
  {
       for (int i = 0; i < 10; i++)
       {
          TreeNode treeNode = new TreeNode();
          treeNode.Text = "Node Item: " + i.ToString();
          treeNode.Value = "Node Item: " + i.ToString();
          treeNode.ShowCheckBox = true;
          treeNode.ToolTip =
                   "This is Node Item: " + i.ToString();
           TreeView1.Nodes.Add(treeNode);
       }
       this.Panel1.Controls.Add(TreeView1);
  }
```

In this code snippet, the `TreeView` control is placed inside a `Panel control`.

Implementing a Directory Structure as a TreeView

In this section I will demonstrate how we can make use of the **TreeView** control to display the list of directories and files in your system. The directories will be displayed as parent nodes with the child nodes displaying the files under those directories. When you execute the sample application, the output is similar to what is shown in the following screenshot:

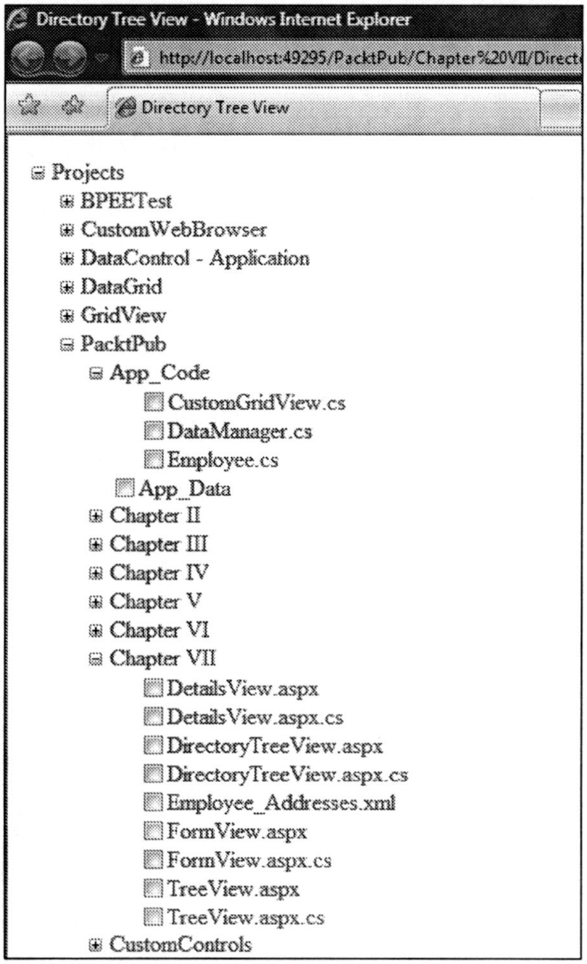

Note that the directories are displayed as parent nodes with the files under those directories displayed as child nodes and are marked with check boxes. Let us now see how we can implement such an application.

Simply create a **TreeView** control with the following markup code in your `.aspx` file:

```
<asp:TreeView ID="TreeView1" runat="server" SelectedNodeStyle
  ForeColor="Green" SelectedNodeStyle-VerticalPadding="0
      ShowCheckBoxes="Leaf" BackColor="White" Font-Size="Medium"
      ForeColor="Blue">
</asp:TreeView>
```

From the code behind, we will invoke a method called `CreateDirectoryTreeView()` in the `Page_Load` event of the web page as shown as follows:

```
if (!IsPostBack)
{
        String directoryPath = "C:\\Projects";
        DirectoryInfo directoryInfo = new
          System.IO.DirectoryInfo(directoryPath);
         if (directoryInfo != null)
         {
               TreeNode rootDirectoryNode =
                  CreateDirectoryTreeView(directoryInfo, null);
                   if (rootDirectoryNode != null)
                       TreeView1.Nodes.Add(rootDirectoryNode);
         }
}
```

Note that we have set the base directory path as `"C:\\Projects"`. You can change this path depending on your requirements. The `CreateDirectoryTreeView()` method is a recursive method that accepts two arguments, one is an instance of `DirectoryInfo` that points to the base directory and the other is the parent node. We will pass the second parameter as null.

Inside the `CreateDirectoryTreeView()` method the base node is created using the `TreeNode` instance. The sub-directories and the files contained under a specific directory are retrieved using the `DirectoryInfo` and the `FileInfo` classes as shown in the following code snippet:

```
TreeNode baseNode = new TreeNode(directoryInfo.Name);
DirectoryInfo[] subDirectories = directoryInfo.GetDirectories();
FileInfo[] filesInDirectory = directoryInfo.GetFiles();
```

Now, the sub-directories inside the base directory are iteratively retrieved inside a loop and the `CreateDirectoryTreeView()` method is recursively called. Then the child nodes under a particular parent node are added. Refer to the following code snippet:

```
for (int i = 0, n = subDirectories.Length; i < n; i++)
    CreateDirectoryTreeView(subDirectories[i], baseNode);
```

Note how the `CreateDirectoryTreeView()` method is recursively called with the sub-directory and the base node as parameters. The sub-directories collection contains a collection of all directories under a particular directory.

```
for (int ctr = 0, cnt = filesInDirectory.Length; ctr < cnt; ctr++)
{
       TreeNode childNode = new TreeNode(filesInDirectory[ctr].Name);
       baseNode.ChildNodes.Add(childNode);
}
```

Refer to the code snippet above. The `filesInDirectory` collection contains a collection of the list of files under a particular directory. Next, the base node (if the parent node is null) or the parent node itself is returned. Here is the complete source code for the `CreateDirectoryTreeView()` method:

```
TreeNode CreateDirectoryTreeView(DirectoryInfo directoryInfo,
 TreeNode parentNode)
   {
        TreeNode baseNode = new TreeNode(directoryInfo.Name);
        DirectoryInfo[] subDirectories =
          directoryInfo.GetDirectories();
        FileInfo[] filesInDirectory = directoryInfo.GetFiles();
        for (int i = 0, n = subDirectories.Length; i < n; i++)
            CreateDirectoryTreeView(subDirectories[i], baseNode);
        for (int ctr = 0, cnt = filesInDirectory.Length; ctr < cnt;
            ctr++)
        {
            TreeNode childNode = new
              TreeNode(filesInDirectory[ctr].Name);
            baseNode.ChildNodes.Add(childNode);
        }
    if (parentNode == null)
        return baseNode;
        parentNode.ChildNodes.Add(baseNode);
        return parentNode;
   }
```

Using the TreeView SelectedNodeChanged event handler

You can use the `SelectedNodeChanged` event handler of the TreeView control to perform any custom operations such as, collasping the nodes. You can also check the depth of the selected nodes using the `Depth` property. Here is the code snippet that illustrates this:

```
protected void TreeView1_SelectedNodeChanged
    (object sender, EventArgs e)
    {
        if (TreeView1.SelectedNode.Depth == 0)
        {
            TreeView1.CollapseAll();
        }
        else if (TreeView1.SelectedNode.Depth == 1)
        {
            Response.Write(TreeView1.SelectedNode.Text);
        }
    }
```

Summary

In this chapter, we saw some of the data view controls like the DetailsView, FormView and the TreeView controls and how we can use them in our ASP.NET applications. In the following and the concluding chapter of this book we will have a look at LINQ and how we can use it to bind data to the new data controls available in Orcas.

8
Working with LINQ

This is the last chapter in our journey. I will show you how to work with the new data source controls using LINQ and how we can use LINQ to bind data to these controls and perform various other operations. LINQ is a part of the new versions of the C# and VB.NET compilers and it comes with a powerful set of operators to ease the task of querying different data sources, like, SQL Server, XML and so on.

In this chapter, we will learn about the following:

- Introducing LINQ; its benefits and features
- The architecture of LINQ
- Querying data using LINQ
- Using the ListView Control
- Using the DataPager Control
- Data binding using LINQ

Introducing LINQ

In this section we will explore how we can use LINQ with the new data source controls that have been shipped as part of Orcas. Fine, but, what is LINQ anyway? LINQ or Language Integrated Query is a query translation pipeline that has been introduced as part of the C# 3.0 library. Microsoft states, "The LINQ Project is a codename for a set of extensions to the .NET Framework that encompasses language-integrated query, set, and transform operations. It extends C# and Visual Basic with native language syntax for queries and provides class libraries to take advantage of these capabilities." It is Microsoft's offering for an Object Relational Mapping between your business objects and the underlying data sources. These data sources can be databases or even XML document files. As of now, C# 3.0, F# and VB 9 have support for LINQ. You can get more information from the LINQ FAQ at the MSDN forums.

LINQ comprises of a standard set of operators to facilitate query operations. We will learn more on LINQ query operators later in this chapter.

Why LINQ?

LINQ is an awesome, new feature available as part of C# 3.0 and allows you to integrate queries right into your programs. It is an extension to the C# language and provides a simplified framework for accessing relational data in an Object Oriented manner. Here is how you can search for an employee from our employee table using LINQ:

```
var result =
    from  emp in Employee
    where  emp.EmpName == "Jini"
    select c.EmpCode;
```

So, how do you benefit? Well, in using LINQ, the complexities are much reduced and you can easily debug your queries.

Understanding the LINQ Architecture

In this section we will discuss the basic components of the architecture of LINQ. I will now familiarize you with what LINQ is all about, the components involved in its architecture, and so on. The following figure illustrates the LINQ architecture:

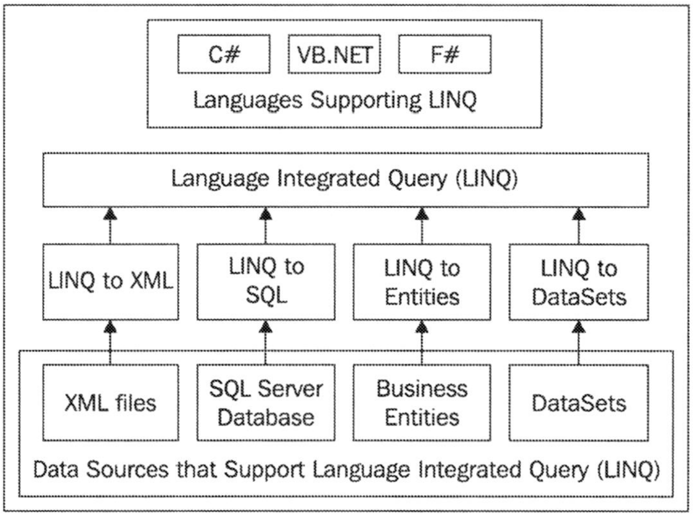

LINQ to XML maps your LINQ queries or LINQ statements to the corresponding XML data sources. It helps you to use the LINQ standard query operators to retrieve XML data. LINQ to XML is commonly known as **XLINQ**. You can also use LINQ to query your in-memory collections and business entities (objects that contain data related to a particular entity) seamlessly.

Similar to XLINQ (for querying your XML documents), you also have **DLINQ** which is an implementation of LINQ that allow you to query your databases. LINQ to SQL is or DLINQ as it is called is actually an **ORM** (Object relational Mapping) tool. When using LINQ to SQL, the **DataContext** class in the `System.Data.Linq` namespace is used to create your data contexts. All your data context classes will derive from the base DataContext class. DataContexts are responsible for generating the corresponding SQL statements when using LINQ to SQL. In other words, the DataContext accepts the LINQ statements as input, processes them, and produces the corresponding **T-SQL** statements as output. We will learn more on DataContexts later in this chapter.

> **Creating Business Entities that are mapped to database tables**
>
> You can use either the Designer included in **VS.NET** or the **SqlMetal.exe** tool for creating business entities that are mapped to database tables.

Before we start using LINQ to bind data to the data controls, let us have a look at the new data controls introduced in Orcas. We will then use LINQ to bind data to those controls. We will discuss these new data controls later in this chapter.

Operators in LINQ

Powered by a rich set of query operators and expressions, you can use LINQ with absolutely any data source! You can use LINQ with any supported data sources like relational databases, XML files. Moreover, LINQ is type safe and extensible.

LINQ offers you a collection of some powerful operators that make your task of querying data much easier.

The following is the list of some commonly used operators in LINQ:

- Select
- SelectAll
- Where
- OrderBy
- Skip
- SkipWhile

I recommend taking a look at the LINQ specification documents to have a more detailed reference to these operators and how they are used.

> **Required namespaces**
>
> You should include the `System.Data.DLinq` namespace if you want to use LINQ for SQL. For LINQ to XML or XLINQ, include the `System.Xml.Linq` namespace. If you want LINQ to Business entities, include the `System.Linq` in your applications. For using Lamda expressions, you should include the `System.Linq.Expressions` namespace.

Querying Data Using LINQ

Let us take a look at how we can use LINQ to query data in our applications. The following code snippet illustrates how you can use LINQ to display the contents of an array:

```
String[] employees = {"Joydip", "Douglas", "Jini", "Piku", "Amal",
                      "Rama", "Indronil"};
var employeeNames = from employee in employees select employee;
foreach (var empName in employeeNames)
    Response.Write(empName);
```

Let us now understand how we can use LINQ to query a generic list. Consider the `Generic Employee List` given as follows:

```
private static List<String> GenericEmployeeList = new List<String>()
{
  "Joydip", "Douglas", "Jini", "Piku",
  "Rama", "Amal", "Indronil"
};
```

Now you can use LINQ to query this list as shown in the following code snippet:

```
IEnumerable<String> employees = from emp in GenericEmployeeList
                                select emp;
  foreach (string employee in employees)
  {
    Response.Write(employee);
  }
```

You can use conditions with your LINQ query too. The following example shows how.

```
IEnumerable<String> employees = from emp in GenericEmployeeList where
emp.Length > 4 select emp;
  foreach (string employee in employees)
```

```
{
  Response.Write(employee);
}
```

In this code snippet, we used LINQ to display the employee names that are more than 4 characters in length. The above query displays the following output:

```
Joydip
Douglas
Indronil
```

Here is another example of how you can use conditional queries with LINQ. To display the names of the employees whose names start with the letter "J", you can use the following:

```
IEnumerable<String> employees = from emp in GenericEmployeeList where
                                emp.StartsWith("J")
                                select emp;
foreach (String employee in employees)
{
  Response.Write(employee);
}
```

This code snippet will result in the following employee names being displayed.

```
Joydip
Jini
```

As you can see from the above output, only those employees whose names start with the letter "J" are displayed.

Alternatively, you can use LINQ with any other collections too. As an example, the following code illustrates how you can use LINQ to retrieve the details of selective employees from a `DataTable` instance that contains a collection of employees:

```
DataTable empDataTable = new DataTable();
empDataTable.Columns.Add("EmpCode", typeof(String));
empDataTable.Columns.Add("EmpName", typeof(String));
empDataTable.Columns.Add("DeptCode", typeof(String));
empDataTable.Columns.Add("Salary", typeof(Decimal));
empDataTable.Rows.Add("E0001", "Joydip", "D0001",23000);
empDataTable.Rows.Add("E0002", "Douglas", "D0002", 45000);
empDataTable.Rows.Add("E0003", "Jini", "D0001", 12000);
empDataTable.Rows.Add("E0004", "Piku", "D0003", 13000);
empDataTable.Rows.Add("E0005", "Rama", "D0003", 27500);
empDataTable.Rows.Add("E0006", "Amal", "D0002", 19500);
```

```
var empRecords = from row in empDataTable.AsEnumerable()
  where row.Field<decimal>("Salary") > 15000
        select row;
foreach (var emp in empRecords)
Response.Write("<BR>"+emp["EmpCode"].ToString() + "\t" +
emp["EmpName"].ToString() + "\t" + emp["Salary"].ToString());
```

I will now show you how you can use LINQ to query data from a generic list. Here is the code that illustrates this.

```
List<Employee> empList = new List<Employee>()
{
         new Employee
         {
              EmpCode = "E0001", EmpName = "Joydip", DeptCode =
                        "D0001", Salary = 23000
         },
         new Employee
         {
             EmpCode = "E0002", EmpName = "Douglas", DeptCode =
                       "D0003", Salary = 45000
         },
         new Employee
         {
             EmpCode = "E0003", EmpName = "Jini", DeptCode = "D0002",
                        Salary = 15000
         }
};
var empRecords = from row in empList.AsEnumerable()
  where row.Salary > 15000
        select row;
foreach (var emp in empRecords)
    Response.Write("<BR>" + emp.EmpCode.ToString() + "\t" +
      emp.EmpName.ToString() + "\t" + emp.Salary.ToString());
```

Here is the code for our `Employee` class.

```
public class Employee
{
    public string EmpCode { get; set;}
    public string EmpName { get; set;}
    public string DeptCode { get; set;}
    public DateTime JoiningDate { get; set;}
    public decimal Salary { get; set;}
}
```

The New Data Controls in VS.NET 2008 (Orcas)

Orcas, as it is called, is the next release of Microsoft's Visual Studio .NET (VS.NET 2008) and is compliant with the Microsoft's Vista Operating System. The new data controls added with Orcas include the DataPager control and the ListView control. In this section we will discuss how we can use LINQ to bind data to these controls seamlessly. We will use the `DataManager` class as we did in the earlier chapters to retrieve data from the database and bind the data retrieved to the data controls.

Using the ListView Control

Using the **ListView** control you have complete control over the generated HTML code. Moreover, you can use the ListView control for CRUD (Create, Update, Read and Delete) operations and data paging too. To use the **ListView** control, switch to the design view mode of your web page and then simply drag and drop the control from the toolbox as shown in the following screenshot:

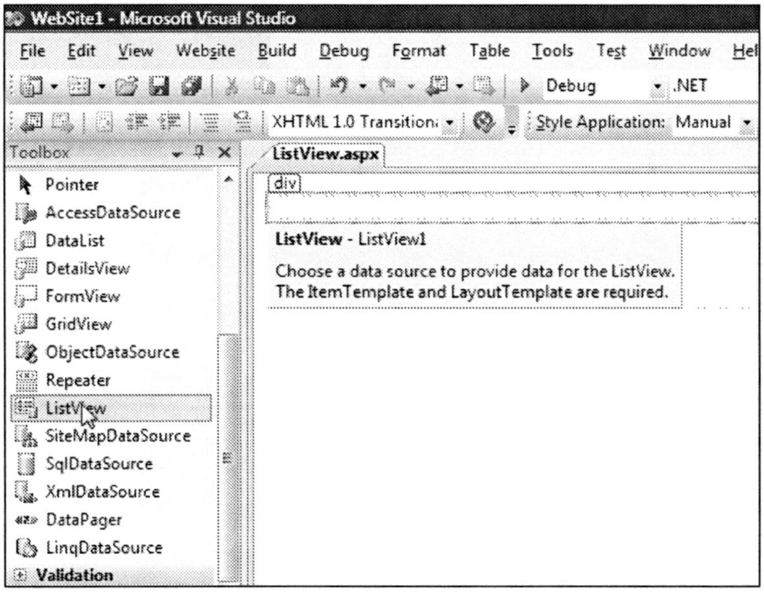

The corresponding code that gets generated in the `.aspx` file is as follows.

```
<asp:ListView ID="ListView1" runat="server"></ asp:ListView>
```

The **ListView** control in **ASP.NET** supports the following templates for customization.

- ItemTemplate
- LayoutTemplate
- EmptyItemTemplate
- EmptyDataTemplate
- SelectedItemTemplate
- EditItemTemplate
- AlternatingItemTemplate
- InsertItemTemplate
- ItemSeparatorTemplate
- GroupTemplate
- GroupSeparatorTemplate

I will now show you how to use the **ListView** control to display data without writing even a single line of code. Configure the **DataSource** property of the **ListView** control to a valid **DataSource**. Refer to the following screenshot:

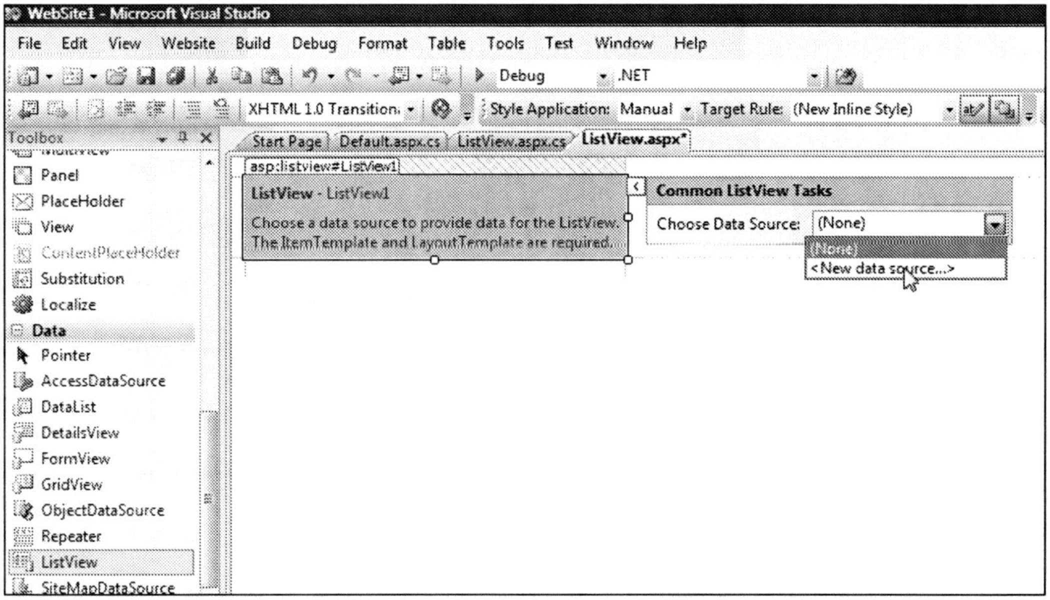

We will skip this section on configuring the **DataSource** as we have already discussed it with other controls in Chapter 1 of this book. Once you have configured the **DataSource**, you can configure the **ListView** control using the **ConfigureListView** option of the **ListView** control in the design view mode of the web page. When you select the above option, the window shown in the following screenshot pops up:

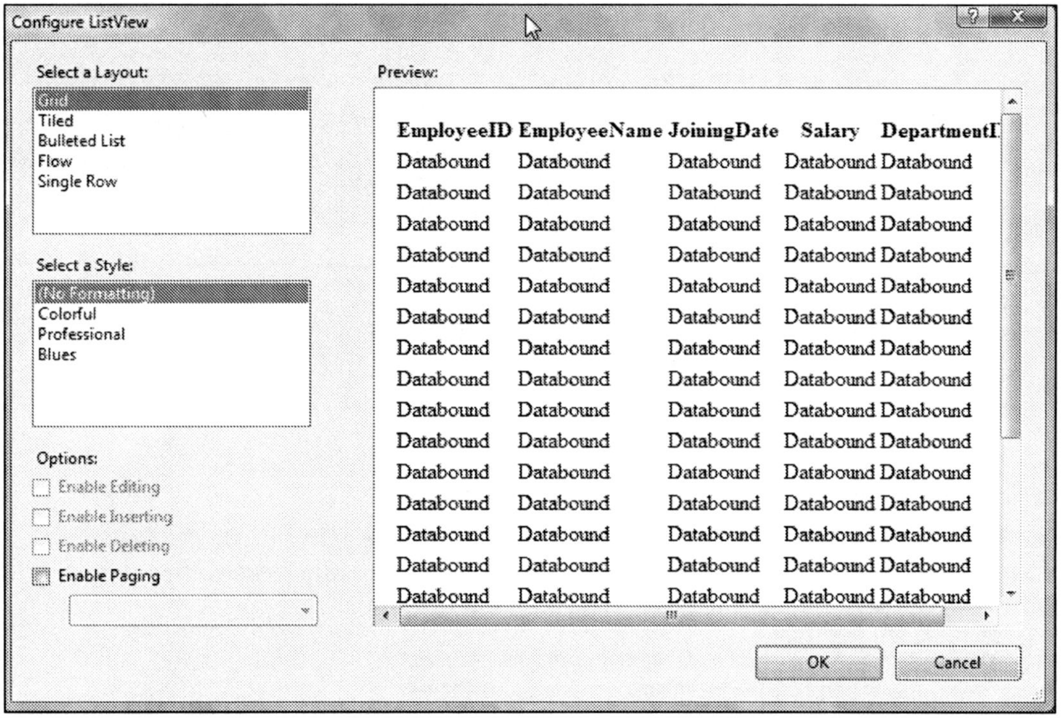

Select **Professional** in the **Select a Style** option and then click on the **OK** button. When you execute the application, the output is similar to what is shown in the following screenshot:

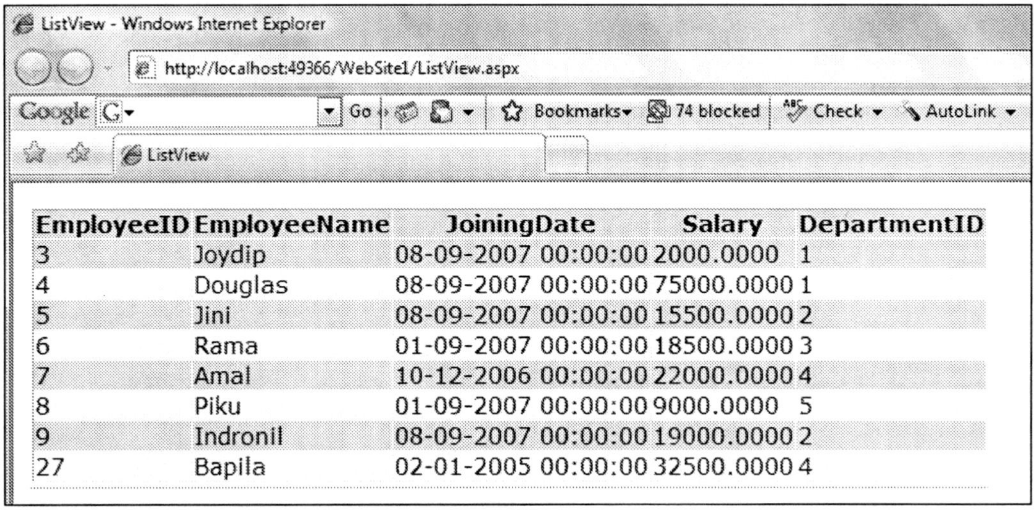

Using the DataPager Control

The DataPager control in Orcas can be used for custom paging using the ListView control. Here is the code that you can write in your `.aspx` file to use a `DataPager` control.

```
<asp:DataPager ID="dataPager" runat="server"
  PagedControlID="GridView1" PageSize="4">
     <Fields>
     <asp:NumericPagerField NextPageText="Next Page"
       PreviousPageText="Previous Page"/>
     </Fields>
</asp:DataPager>
```

Note that you can specify the list control with which you want to enable paging using the `PagedControlID` and you can set the page size of your choice using the `PageSize` property. I will now illustrate how easily you can achieve customized paging with the `ListView` control using a `DataPager`. Here is the code that you need to write in your `.aspx` file.

```
<asp:ListView ID="ListView1" runat="server"
  DataSourceID="SqlDataSource1"
        DataKeyNames="EmployeeID" ItemContainerID="SqlDataSource1">
        <layouttemplate>
```

```
                <table id="employeeTable" runat="server" border="1">
                    <tr>
                      <th>EmployeeID</th>
                      <th>EmployeeName</th>
                      <th>JoiningDate</th>
                      <th>Salary</th>
                      <th>DepartmentID</th>
                   </tr>
                              <tbody id="SqlDataSource1"
                                     runat="server">
                              </tbody>
                </table>
<asp:Panel ID="itemContainer" runat="server">
                  <asp:DataPager ID="dataPager" runat="server"
                    PageSize="4" PagedControlID="ListView1">
                     <Fields>
                         <asp:NumericPagerField/>
                     </Fields>
                 </asp:DataPager>
</asp:Panel>
        </layouttemplate>
    <ItemTemplate>
        <tr>
            <td>
                <asp:Label ID="EmployeeIDLabel" runat="server"
                    Text='<%# Eval("EmployeeID") %>'/>
            </td>
            <td>
                <asp:Label ID="EmployeeNameLabel" runat="server"
                    Text='<%# Eval("EmployeeName") %>'/>
            </td>
            <td>
                <asp:Label ID="JoiningDateLabel" runat="server"
                    Text='<%# Eval("JoiningDate") %>'/>
            </td>
            <td>
                <asp:Label ID="SalaryLabel" runat="server" Text='<%#
                  Eval("Salary") %>'/>
            </td>
            <td>
                <asp:Label ID="DepartmentIDLabel" runat="server"
                    Text='<%# Eval("DepartmentID") %>'/>
            </td>
        </tr>
```

```
        </ItemTemplate>
    </asp:ListView>
    <asp:SqlDataSource ID="SqlDataSource1" runat="server"
            ConnectionString="<%$
            ConnectionStrings:joydipConnectionString %>"
            SelectCommand="SELECT [EmployeeID], [EmployeeName],
            [JoiningDate], [Salary], [DepartmentID] FROM [Employee]">
    </asp:SqlDataSource>
```

And, here is the output when you execute the sample application.

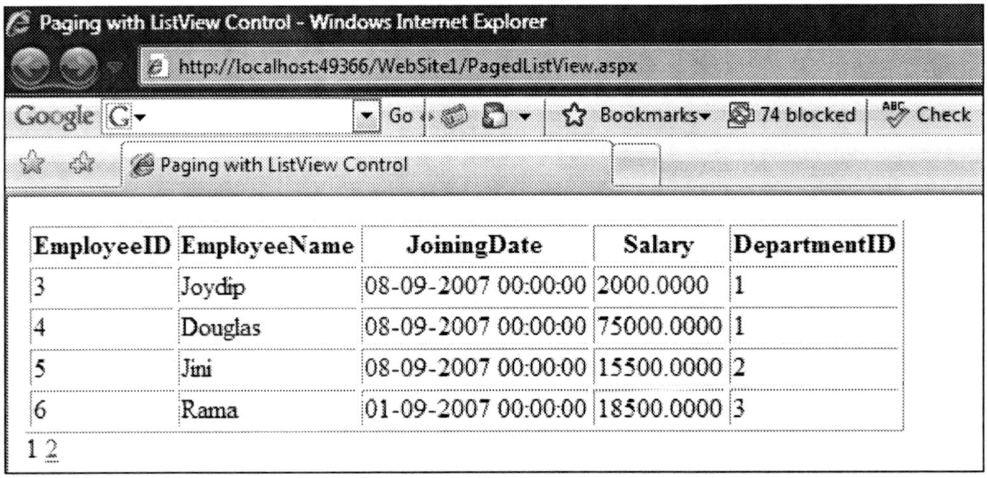

The next section discusses how you can use LINQ to bind data to ASP.NET data controls. We will learn how we can use LINQ to bind data to GridView and the newly introduced ListView control of Orcas.

Data Binding Using LINQ

In this section we will explore how we can use LINQ to bind data to the new data controls introduced in Orcas, ListView and use the DataPager control for paging through the records of the ListView control. The DataPager control is used for providing paging features to the ListView control as the latter does not support this feature by default. I will first show you how you can use LINQ to bind data to the GridView control.

Drag and drop a **GridView** control onto your web form from the toolbox. Now, we will create an Employee Collection class and name it as Employees. This class will hold a collection of Employee instances.

We will add the following method to our existing `DataManager` class:

```
public Employees GetAllEmployees()
{
        SqlConnection conn = null;
        Employees employeeList = null;
        try
        {
            conn = new SqlConnection(connectionString);
            conn.Open();
            string sql = "select EmployeeID as EmpCode, EmployeeName
              as EmpName, Salary as Salary, e.DepartmentID as
              DeptCode, d.DepartmentName as DeptName from employee e,
              Department d where e.DepartmentID = d.DepartmentID";
            SqlCommand cmd = new SqlCommand(sql, conn);
            SqlDataReader dr = cmd.ExecuteReader();
            employeeList = new Employees();
            while (dr.Read())
            {
                Employee emp = new Employee();
                if (dr["EmpCode"] != DBNull.Value)
                    emp.EmpCode = dr["EmpCode"].ToString();
                if (dr["EmpName"] != DBNull.Value)
                    emp.EmpName = dr["EmpName"].ToString();
                if (dr["Salary"] != DBNull.Value)
                    emp.Basic =
                  Convert.ToDouble(dr["Salary"].ToString());
                if (dr["DeptCode"] != DBNull.Value)
                    emp.DeptCode = dr["DeptCode"].ToString();
                if (dr[«DeptName»] != DBNull.Value)
                    emp.DeptName = dr[«DeptName»].ToString();
                employeeList.Add(emp);
                emp = null;
            }
        }
        catch
        {
            throw;
        }
        finally
        {
            conn.Close();
        }
        return employeeList;
}
```

Note that the `GetAllEmployees()` method returns an instance of `Employees` class. The `Employees` class is actually List type and comprises of a collection of Employee instances. In the Page_Load event of the web form, write the following code:

```
DataManager dataManager = new DataManager();
GridView1.DataSource = from emp in dataManager.GetAllEmployees()
                       where emp.Basic > 10000
                              select new
                              {
                                   emp.EmpCode,
                                   emp.EmpName,
                                   emp.Basic
                              };
GridView1.DataBind();
```

Note that we have used the `Where` clause to restrict the display. Only those employees whose Basic is greater then 10000 will be retrieved by the LINQ statement and the result set bound to the GridView control.

Let us now take a look at how we can use LINQ with the ListView control. We will use the same ListView control that we used earlier. We will however need to change the DataSourceID and the ItemContainerID of the ListView control to point to the LINQ DataSource that we will create. Here is the source code for the LINQ data source control that we will use.

```
<asp:LinqDataSource ID="linkDataSource" runat="server"
  ContextTypeName="DataClassesDataContext"
  TableName="Employee" Select="new (EmployeeID as EmployeeID,
  EmployeeName as EmployeeName, JoiningDate as JoiningDate, Salary
  as Salary, DepartmentID as DepartmentID)"
  OrderBy="EmployeeName" />
```

Note that we have used the `OrderBy` clause to sort the result set in ascending order of employee names.

As you can see in this code snippet, we have used a `DataContext`. You use a `DataContext` to convert your requests in LINQ for objects into corresponding queries in Sql. Data contexts are supported using the `System.Data.Linq.DataContext` class. Note that we specified our `DataContext` using the `ContextTypeName` clause in the above code snippet. Let us now understand how we can create our own `DataContext`.

Create a new data class and name it **DataClasses.dbml** as shown in the following screenshot:

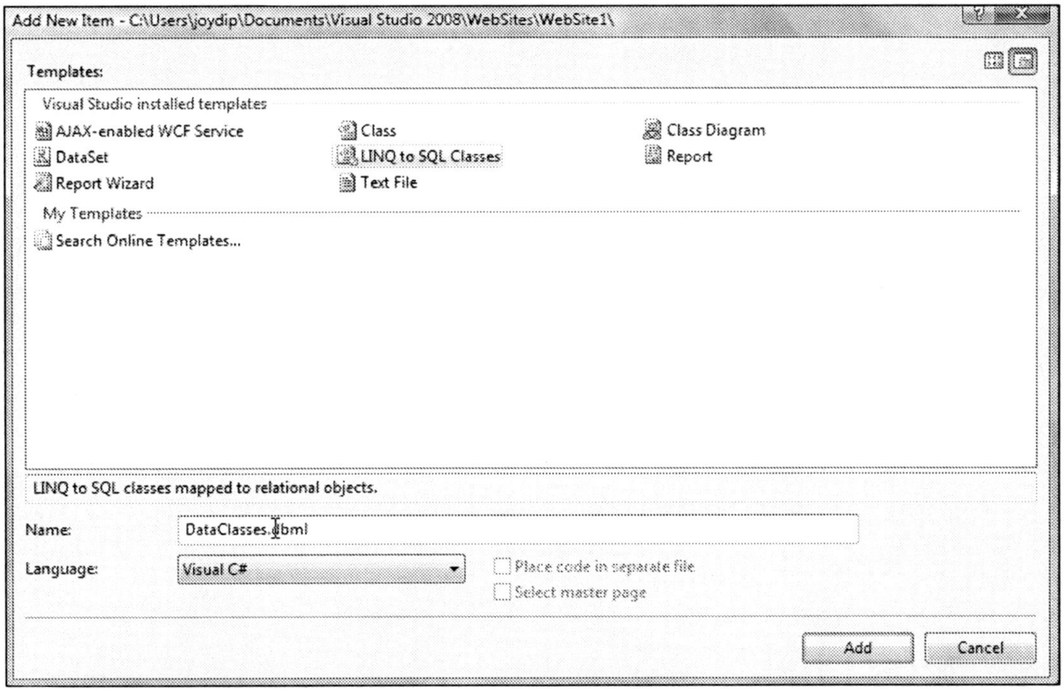

Switch to the designer view of the newly created file and create a DataContext by dragging and dropping the employee table from the **ServerExplorer** as shown in the following screenshot:

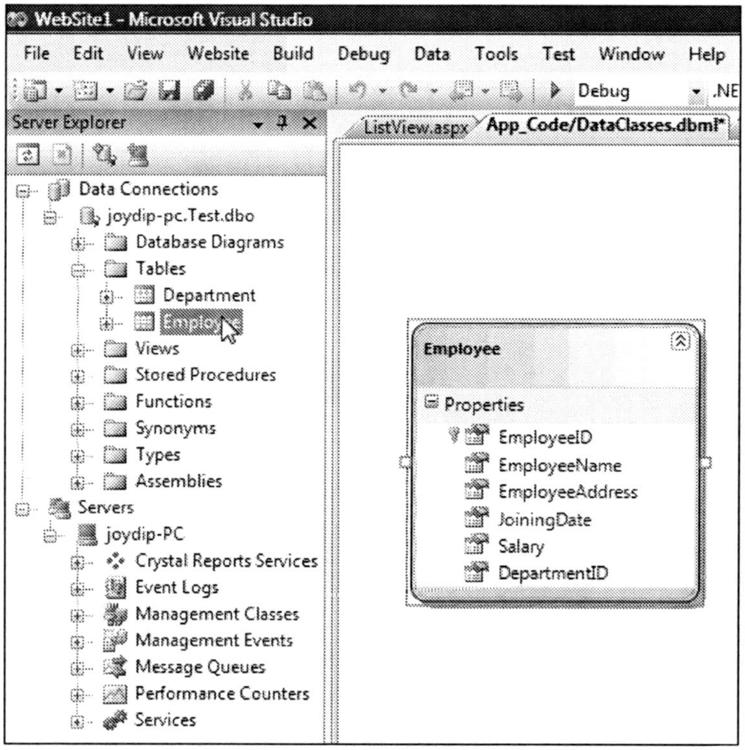

Save and you are done! Your `DataContext` class is created.

To put it simply, the DataContext accepts LINQ statements, processes them and generates corresponding T-SQL code. You can generate a DataContext either using the Designer as we have seen or even using a tool called SqlMetal. Note that all `DataContext` classes actually derive from the `DataContext` class that belongs to the `System.Data.Linq` namespace.

Here is the compiler generated code for the DataContext we just created.

```
using System;
using System.Collections.Generic;
using System.ComponentModel;
using System.Data;
using System.Data.Linq;
using System.Data.Linq.Mapping;
using System.Linq;
```

```
using System.Linq.Expressions;
using System.Reflection;
[System.Data.Linq.Mapping.DatabaseAttribute(Name="Test")]
public partial class DataClassesDataContext:
   System.Data.Linq.DataContext
{
    private static System.Data.Linq.Mapping.MappingSource
        mappingSource = new AttributeMappingSource();
  #region Extensibility Method Definitions
  partial void OnCreated();
  partial void InsertEmployee(Employee instance);
  partial void UpdateEmployee(Employee instance);
  partial void DeleteEmployee(Employee instance);
  #endregion
    static DataClassesDataContext()
    {
    }
    public DataClassesDataContext(string connection):
       base(connection, mappingSource)
    {
           OnCreated();
    }
    public DataClassesDataContext(System.Data.IDbConnection
    connection): base(connection, mappingSource)
    {
           OnCreated();
    }
    public DataClassesDataContext(string connection,
    System.Data.Linq.Mapping.MappingSource mappingSource):
    base(connection, mappingSource)
    {
           OnCreated();
    }
    public DataClassesDataContext(System.Data.IDbConnection
    connection, System.Data.Linq.Mapping.MappingSource
    mappingSource): base(connection, mappingSource)
   {
           OnCreated();
   }
    public DataClassesDataContext():
    base(global::System.Configuration.ConfigurationManager.Connection
    Strings["TestConnectionString"].ConnectionString, mappingSource)
    {
           OnCreated();
```

```
        }
        public System.Data.Linq.Table<Employee> Employees
        {
               get
               {
                    return this.GetTable<Employee>();
               }
        }
    }
    [Table(Name="dbo.Employee")]
    public partial class Employee:INotifyPropertyChanging,
       INotifyPropertyChanged
    {
        private static PropertyChangingEventArgs emptyChangingEventArgs =
         new PropertyChangingEventArgs(String.Empty);
        private int _EmployeeID;
        private string _EmployeeName;
        private string _EmployeeAddress;
        private System.Nullable<System.DateTime> _JoiningDate;
        private decimal _Salary;
        private int _DepartmentID;
        #region Extensibility Method Definitions
        partial void OnLoaded();
        partial void OnValidate();
        partial void OnCreated();
        partial void OnEmployeeIDChanging(int value);
        partial void OnEmployeeIDChanged();
        partial void OnEmployeeNameChanging(string value);
        partial void OnEmployeeNameChanged();
        partial void OnEmployeeAddressChanging(string value);
        partial void OnEmployeeAddressChanged();
        partial void OnJoiningDateChanging(System.Nullable
                     <System.DateTime> value);
        partial void OnJoiningDateChanged();
        partial void OnSalaryChanging(decimal value);
        partial void OnSalaryChanged();
        partial void OnDepartmentIDChanging(int value);
        partial void OnDepartmentIDChanged();
        #endregion
        public Employee()
        {
               OnCreated();
        }
         [Column(Storage="_EmployeeID", AutoSync=AutoSync.OnInsert,
```

```
  DbType="Int NOT NULL IDENTITY", IsPrimaryKey=true,
  IsDbGenerated=true)]
public int EmployeeID
{
      get
      {
            return this._EmployeeID;
      }
      set
      {
            if ((this._EmployeeID != value))
            {
                  this.OnEmployeeIDChanging(value);
                  this.SendPropertyChanging();
                  this._EmployeeID = value;
                  this.SendPropertyChanged("EmployeeID");
                  this.OnEmployeeIDChanged();
            }
      }
}
[Column(Storage="_EmployeeName", DbType="VarChar(50) NOT NULL",
CanBeNull=false)]
public string EmployeeName
{
      get
      {
             return this._EmployeeName;
      }
      set
      {
            if ((this._EmployeeName != value))
            {
                  this.OnEmployeeNameChanging(value);
                  this.SendPropertyChanging();
                  this._EmployeeName = value;
                  this.SendPropertyChanged("EmployeeName");
                  this.OnEmployeeNameChanged();
            }
      }
}
[Column(Storage="_EmployeeAddress", DbType="VarChar(MAX)")]
public string EmployeeAddress
{
      get
```

```
        {
                return this._EmployeeAddress;
        }
        set
        {
                if ((this._EmployeeAddress != value))
                {
                        this.OnEmployeeAddressChanging(value);
                        this.SendPropertyChanging();
                        this._EmployeeAddress = value;
                        this.SendPropertyChanged("EmployeeAddress");
                        this.OnEmployeeAddressChanged();
                }
        }
}
[Column(Storage="_JoiningDate", DbType="DateTime")]
public System.Nullable<System.DateTime> JoiningDate
{
        get
        {
                return this._JoiningDate;
        }
        set
        {
                if ((this._JoiningDate != value))
                {
                        this.OnJoiningDateChanging(value);
                        this.SendPropertyChanging();
                        this._JoiningDate = value;
                        this.SendPropertyChanged("JoiningDate");
                        this.OnJoiningDateChanged();
                }
        }
}
[Column(Storage="_Salary", DbType="Money NOT NULL")]
public decimal Salary
{
        get
        {
                return this._Salary;
        }
        set
        {
                if ((this._Salary != value))
                {
```

```
                        this.OnSalaryChanging(value);
                        this.SendPropertyChanging();
                        this._Salary = value;
                        this.SendPropertyChanged("Salary");
                        this.OnSalaryChanged();
                    }
}
    }
    [Column(Storage="_DepartmentID", DbType="Int NOT NULL")]
    public int DepartmentID
    {
          get
          {
                 return this._DepartmentID;
          }
          set
          {
                 if ((this._DepartmentID != value))
                 {
                        this.OnDepartmentIDChanging(value);
                        this.SendPropertyChanging();
                        this._DepartmentID = value;
                        this.SendPropertyChanged("DepartmentID");
                        this.OnDepartmentIDChanged();
                 }
          }
    }
    public event PropertyChangingEventHandler PropertyChanging;
    public event PropertyChangedEventHandler PropertyChanged;
    protected virtual void SendPropertyChanging()
    {
          if ((this.PropertyChanging != null))
          {
                this.PropertyChanging(this, emptyChangingEventArgs);
          }
    }
    protected virtual void SendPropertyChanged(String propertyName)
    {
          if ((this.PropertyChanged != null))
          {
                this.PropertyChanged(this, new
                 PropertyChangedEventArgs(propertyName));
          }
    }
}
```

You can even use your `DataContext` in more ways than one. The following code illustrates how you can play with the `DataContext` to retrieve the `EmployeeID` of the employee whose name is "Jini".

```
using (DataClassesDataContext context = new DataClassesDataContext())
        {
            Employee emp = context.Employees.Single<Employee>
                                (e => e.EmployeeName.Equals("Jini"));
            Response.Write(emp.EmployeeID);
        }
```

Next we need the ListView control in our web form which will be used to display the employee records. This ListView control will make use of the LINQ data source that we just created to retrieve data from the employee table.

The following is the source code for the ListView control in our `.aspx` file.

```
<asp:ListView ID="ListView1" runat="server"
      DataSourceID="linkDataSource"
      DataKeyNames="EmployeeID" ItemContainerID="linkDataSource">
<layouttemplate>
            <table id="employeeTable" runat="server" border="1">
                              <tr>
                                 <th>EmployeeID</th>
                                 <th>EmployeeName</th>
                                 <th>JoiningDate</th>
                                 <th>Salary</th>
                                 <th>DepartmentID</th>
                              </tr>
                            <tbody id="linkDataSource"
                                       runat="server">
                            </tbody>
                     </table>
<asp:Panel ID="itemContainer" runat="server">
                 <asp:DataPager ID="dataPager" runat="server"
PageSize="4" PagedControlID="ListView1">
                   <Fields>
                       <asp:NumericPagerField/>
                   </Fields>
                </asp:DataPager>
                </asp:Panel>
        </layouttemplate>
    <ItemTemplate>
        <tr>
            <td>
```

```
                    <asp:Label ID="EmployeeIDLabel" runat="server"
                        Text='<%# Eval("EmployeeID") %>' />
                </td>
                <td>
                    <asp:Label ID="EmployeeNameLabel" runat="server"
                        Text='<%# Eval("EmployeeName") %>' />
                </td>
                <td>
                    <asp:Label ID="JoiningDateLabel" runat="server"
                        Text='<%# Bind("JoiningDate","{0:d}") %>' />
                </td>
                <td>
                    <asp:Label ID="SalaryLabel" runat="server" Text='<%#
                                   Bind("Salary","{0:c}") %>' />
                </td>
                <td>
                    <asp:Label ID="DepartmentIDLabel" runat="server"
                        Text='<%# Eval("DepartmentID") %>' />
                </td>
            </tr>
    </ItemTemplate>
    </asp:ListView>
```

The following screenshot shows the output on execution of the application:

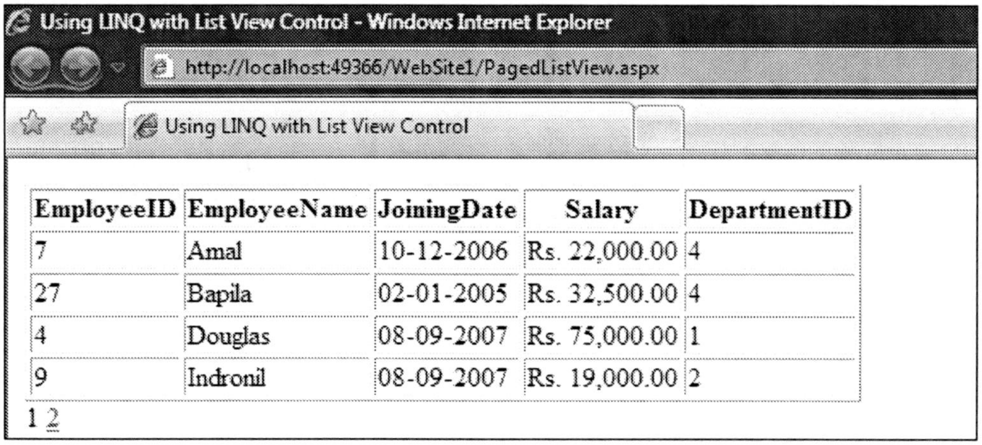

As you can see from the above output, the output is sorted based on the employee names.

Summary

In this final chapter we have had a look at LINQ and how we can use it to bind data to the ASP.NET data controls and the newly introduced ListView control of Orcas. I admit that LINQ is too powerful and extensive to be covered in one single chapter. However, I have thrown light on the most important areas and presented you with, how you can use the awesome power of LINQ in our applications to query and bind data to the data controls. That's the end of our journey! Happy reading!

Index

A

B

C

D

F

G

H

L

Programming Windows Workflow Foundation

ISBN: 978-1-904811-21-3 Paperback: 252 pages

A C# developer's guide to the features and programming interfaces of Windows Workflow Foundation

1. Add event-driven workflow capabilities to your .NET applications.
2. Highlights the libraries, services and internals programmers need to know
3. Builds a practical "bug reporting" workflow solution example app

---

ODP.NET Developer's Guide

ISBN: 978-1-847191-96-0 Paperback: 328 pages

A practical guide for developers working with the Oracle Data Provider for .NET and the Oracle Developer Tools for Visual Studio 2005

1. Application development with ODP.NET
2. Dealing with XML DB using ODP.NET
3. Oracle Developer Tools for Visual Studio .NET

Please check **www.PacktPub.com** for information on our titles

Printed in the United States
152245LV00003B/12/A

9 781847 193957